The Building of
MODERN SWEDEN

The Reign of Gustav V
1907-1950

The Building of
MODERN SWEDEN

The Reign of Gustav V
1907-1950

by

O. FRITIOF ANDER

AUGUSTANA LIBRARY PUBLICATIONS

Number 28

LUCIEN WHITE, *General Editor*

⟦PRINTED IN U·S·A⟧

AUGUSTANA BOOK CONCERN

Printers and Binders

ROCK ISLAND, ILLINOIS

Dedicated in

memory

of

G. Hilmer Lundbeck, Sr.

Preface

THE RESEARCH INVOLVED in the writing of *The Building of Modern Sweden: The Reign of Gustav V* was begun as a result of two successive fellowships from the John Simon Guggenheim Memorial Foundation during 1938-1940, and the author feels deeply indebted to the Guggenheim Foundation for the opportunities which it afforded him to do research work at the Library of the University of Uppsala, the Royal Library, and the Library of the University of Lund.

The first draft covering a period in Swedish history from 1815 to 1938 was submitted to a number of friends in the historical profession for suggestions. Those who kindly consented to read the manuscript included Professors Gunnar Westin of the University of Uppsala, Paul Knaplund of the University of Wisconsin, Clarence A. Berdahl of the University of Illinois, Ralph H. Gabriel of Yale University, and George M. Stephenson of the University of Minnesota. The manuscript would have lent itself better to three or four smaller volumes rather than a large one, and it became necessary to revise it. Footnotes and a bibliography were eliminated to reduce the cost of publication, and later a revised manuscript was prepared, which centered upon Sweden's history between the two world wars.

In its varied stages the author became indebted to Professor Alrik Gustafson of the University of Minnesota and his very close friend and colleague, Professor Traugott Richter. To further reduce the cost of publication of the manuscript, illustrations and charts were removed, and it is now being published in hopes that there is a renewed interest in the democratic processes and that this might be extended to Sweden, where democracy has triumphed in a very significant sense during the last fifty years. Gustav V died only a few years ago, and it seemed appropriate to call the revised manuscript *The Building of Modern Sweden: The Reign of Gustav V.*

Dr. Lucien White, librarian of the Denkmann Memorial Library of Augustana College, is the editor of the Augustana Library Publications, and the author wishes to express a very deep sense of appreciation for the assistance of Dr. White in preparing the manuscript for publication. In spite of careful editing and proofreading, errors will appear, and for these the author is alone responsible.

A debt of gratitude should also be expressed to the Board of Directors of Augustana College for leaves of absence which made the research possible. Last but not least a debt is expressed to my wife, Ruth E. Ander, who has been a co-laborer in all the stages of this work.

Summer, 1958.

O. FRITIOF ANDER
Augustana College

Table of Contents

Introduction

THE BUILDING OF MODERN SWEDEN: *The Reign of Gustav V* is a history of Sweden during the first half of the twentieth century with an emphasis upon the period before and after World War I. The title suggests that Sweden has been transformed into a modern state during the reign of Gustav V, when democracy triumphed. This is essentially true, but many historical forces which were responsible for the transformation of Sweden were not new. Sweden is an old national state, and nationalism was an old sentiment, which played a vital role during the twentieth century in the small Scandinavian country.

William L. Langer in his presidential address before the American Historical Association on December 29th, 1957, suggests that a deeper understanding of the past might be gained through the findings of modern psychology. He has particular reference to psychoanalysis and developments included in "depth psychology." Historians have long been acquainted with psychological explanations not only for individual behavior but for group behavior. Many complex factors determine individual complexes and behavior patterns. These are significantly related to the total experiences of the individual. The historian perhaps does not know how to measure or test rational behavior even though he would recognize that there is an indelible imprint upon the present generation of Americans which is related to the sum total of experiences of Europeans transplanted on the American soil since colonization. But each generation acquires new experiences, and these cause a constant reinterpretation of the past as group experiences are enriched. It would be correct to speak of an individual American from a psychological point of view as well as of an American who represents the feelings and emotions of a group. Similarly, and this is important, there is a Swede who speaks and reacts to changes in the environment as only a Swede could react.

The Swedish people are the product of Western Civilization, but in a very special sense they are a people with a common past over many centuries, a past filled with many deep sorrows, defeats, humiliations, plagues, famines, and with hopes and dreams of greatness which were not achieved. The geographic and climatic factors of the country in which the Swedes lived lengthened the shadows. Melancholy colored the art and music. How significant were these psychological factors in delaying the transformation of Sweden into a modern democratic state? The old order, whether social, political, or economic, rested upon sanctions of past experience. That which was new met resistance.

The historians have long been aware of both the promises and pitfalls of the application of psychology to historical interpretations. Was the man who urged reform and change rational? What is the yardstick of rationality? The reactions of the Swedes to World Wars I and II seem very rational to them, but they might question the rationality of those who engaged in the wars. A long policy of peace and neutralism makes peace seem rational to the Swedes. Perhaps it is an illusion, but they believe that they will be able to continue to pursue this policy of neutrality in the future. The standard of measurement is to be found only in terms of the satisfaction which comes from an illusion of security. It is pragmatism applied on the Swedish soil with different results from those secured when applied to the American soil. The Swedes are, therefore, incapable of understanding fully those who have engaged in the last two great wars even though they have suffered vicariously with them. It is not likely that a Swede could write a great war novel. But the Swedes have produced a Wilhelm Moberg and a Pär Lagerkvist, both of whom have captured the pathos of man.

To start a history of Sweden with the year 1907 seems, therefore, rather unsatisfactory. But wherever it would begin, it would call for an introduction if past experiences are so important in the lives of a people. The folk movements of the nineteenth century, which did so much to transform life and thought in Sweden were intimately associated with expressions of humanism, a political liberalism, a great religious awakening and a significant temperance movement, all of which led to an impatience with conditions as they were. Mass emigration followed. Man's faith in man's ability to create not only new ideals but to fashion old ones into useful instruments in the making of a better society caused misunderstanding and procrastination, as the old did not yield readily to the new. This stemmed in part from the fact that the folk movements were not of Swedish origin. These historical forces were of Anglo-American origin and in some respects were universal. There had perhaps never been a time when barriers could be erected against ideas. Now changes in transportation and communication facilitated the exchange and spread of ideas and ideals. Psychological barriers became less important than before. The American concept of progress and change inherited from the Enlightenment became more meaningful, and men dedicated themselves in a patriotic zeal to build a more prosperous and happy Sweden which would justify loyalty and devotion and discourage emigration.

The transformation of Sweden into a modern democratic nation was not peculiar in one sense of the word. The trend toward democracy was seemingly a significant force throughout all of Western Europe during the nineteenth and the beginning of the twentieth century. The manner in which democracy triumphed and the receptiveness of the Swedes to democratic ideals might have been peculiar and determined by the past experiences of the people. The type of leadership was colored by the environment. Such persons as Karl Staaff, Hjalmar Branting, and Per Albin Hansson were thoroughly Swedish. Even the King, Gustav V, reacted to the historical forces only as a king of Sweden could to retain the loyalty of his people. The total experiences of the Swedish people determined the course of the march of democracy and charted the road toward a welfare state embodying not only a political concept of democracy, but a social and economic one as well. Thus *The Building of Modern Sweden* is more than an outline of a political evolution.

During the nineteenth century man aspired to create a better world by harnessing and channeling the economic forces intimately interwoven with changes in agriculture, commerce, and manufacture. Many modern historians are reluctant to use the term "revolution" when they describe these. But alterations in the realm of the ideal and reality necessitated many painful adjustments. The trend to resist change grew strong, and the century passed in the throes of great pain, leaving the major adjustments to be endured during the first decades of the twentieth century. These were marked by a serious class struggle which led to fears of violence and revolution. A common heritage and growing loyalty to symbols of king and nation caused the people to unite in an effort to resolve their problems. The fear of revolution from within and war from without tempered feelings and created unity of purpose.

Some of these fears were stimulated by two world wars. The fondest dreams of the humanists had not been charted when the first war broke out, and the validity of their dreams had not been ascertained when the second war began. The first one hastened the democratic processes, while the second one called for a temporary halt. Both wars turned man into a Frankenstein. Though Sweden was spared involvement, war surrounded her, and ideals clashed with the basic concept of survival. Sweden became conscious of the fact that her long period of neutrality, dedicated to the maintenance of peace at almost any cost, had not isolated her. She was a part of the great community of nations. Concepts of honor and righteousness outside her borders could not be ignored. Severe conflicts between right and wrong occurred. Concepts of honesty and integrity were weighed on the scale of pragmatism. Expediency tended to become synonymous with honor and righteousness.

Was it because Sweden was a small country that she succeeded in resolving and maintaining a policy of neutrality and remaining aloof from power politics? Other countries smaller than Sweden aspired to the same hope and failed. Fate played a significant role, and it inspired a greater confidence than faith. A form of cynicism developed which was not unlike that which was nursed in countries engaged in the war. Sweden was not self-sufficient. The wars caused serious dislocation, and they resulted in the adoption of a war economy. With the return of peace a period of reconstruction followed in which hardships were suffered. These perhaps were less severe in a neutral country, but the wars greatly influenced thought and ways of life even in Sweden. In some instances they promoted the ideals of humanism; in others they encouraged the growth of naturalism or realism, for which Sweden had long been a fertile soil. The voice of August Strindberg in 1900 seems somehow to be re-echoed in the voice of Pär Lagerkvist in 1958. It seems both historically and psychologically sound that the voice of Strindberg should be more Swedish and influenced less by alien influences than the voice of Lagerkvist, which is one of universal fatalism. Yet Strindberg's world of reality found an echo in Eugene O'Neill, and it seemed fitting that the great American playwright and disciple of Strindberg should will that his play, "Long Day's Journey into Night," should first be staged in Sweden. O'Neill must have believed that he had his most appreciative and understanding audience in the land of Strindberg.

The chapters of this study are arranged in a chronological order, but some overlapping seemed unavoidable. Again and again it proved necessary to turn back to the past and beyond the scope of the title of the book. The chapter on "Emigration and Americanization" proved difficult to confine to a given period, since its scope covers more than a century and its story has just begun to be told. Efforts to provide an historical setting for a great deal of data did not insure objectivity. History is not science.

The author was born in Sweden and in that country he received his first impressions and early education. The atmosphere was a conservative one, and one which was essentially hostile to important alterations in the social, political, and economic structure. He emigrated to America, and his major education was received in a climate which was friendly to democratic changes. It does not therefore seem improper to him that he should applaud the advancement of democratic ideals and the principles of humanism. He is, of course, aware of his own prejudices and his deep sympathy for Sweden, the land of his birth. He has therefore sought to be critical and perhaps has been overly concerned about objectivity. Criticism of any people, past and present, is judged by individual concepts of rectitude and righteousness.

No effort was made at any one form of interpretation. Those of a psychological nature are indirect and implicit without efforts to measure rational or irrational behavior. Perhaps some efforts were made at blueprinting a social interpretation, but the modern man is an economic man. The stress, however, placed upon an economic interpretation was entirely unintentional. Perhaps the author's early training under such scholars as Frederick C. Dietz and L. G. Bogart left an impression of an approach to history.

Paternalism in Sweden was old. Many concepts found in America were alien in Sweden. Liberals during the early part of the nineteenth century objected to the continued "medieval" restrictions upon man's initiative, but Sweden was no fertile soil for a concept of a malevolent state. There was no need for a Carey or a Clay. Henry George was read in Sweden, but his voice too was as strange as that of an Andrew Carnegie, a John Bates Clark, or a William G. Sumner. Only when a voice seemed more universal in its appeal to humanism and when the soil of Sweden had been conditioned for it did it receive a response as did William James' concept of pragmatism. But in reality Sweden remained largely unsophisticated and it continued to be the home of Selma Lagerlöf and a fairy land inhabited by its own fairies. Of course, there were thralls, but they too were Swedish—or were they foreign?

Swedish historians have long looked upon "emigration" as a thrall to be shunned. They have been as profoundly influenced by nationalism as have our American historians. They have turned with relish and joy to the days when Sweden was a great power. But the fact that Sweden lost one-fourth of its population from 1840 to 1924 has not given them a great concern even though they might admit that immigration to America was a most significant factor in the evolution of modern Sweden. The history of emigration from Sweden is related to every aspect of Swedish life since 1840. It represents the impatience of nearly one million people with the gradual changes in the social, political, and economic structure of Sweden. To those inspired by a strong sense of patriotism, the emigrant seemed like a deserter or a traitor. Emigration, it was thought, weakened the national state as it deprived it of an invaluable human asset. Many unkind epithets were hurled at the emigrants. This in part explains the reluctance of Swedish historians to turn to a serious study of emigration. But the "psychological" block which has hindered historians from devoting their serious attention to the study of emigration has now largely been removed.

Emigration stopped almost entirely after 1924. Sweden's precarious international situation made it necessary for it to covet and foster a strong friendship with the United States. American isolationism disappeared, and America, during World War II and since that time, has not appreciated Sweden's continued policy of neutrality and its desire to remain aloof from NATO. Emigration had compelled drastic actions in the transformation of Sweden. It became Americanized. As a result, returning emigrants were greeted like friends and close relatives. America became a bulwark of assurance for Sweden's continued existence. Fears of Russian expansion are old in Sweden, but the Swedes are reluctant to gamble on the outcome of the impending struggle for power between America and Russia, so they would like to believe that they are "neutral."

Much has been said about the rapid Americanization of the Swedish immigrants. Though this may be true, they retained a strong loyalty to the mother country, and with old age the immigrant grew sentimental as he turned to childhood memories. The reasons why he had left Sweden grew dim as he told and retold his grandchildren his impressions of the land of fairies and the midnight sun. These two million sons and daughters of emigrants formerly scorned became an important asset, and their friendship deserved cultivation. Sweden also grew more and more American in habits of thought and taste. A psychological interpretation of emigration and Americanization would be fascinating study in the hands of a psychoanalyst trained in the historical profession.

The stress has been placed on the period prior to 1938. The historian of contemporary affairs does not have the advantage of "hindsight." This history is essentially of contemporary times, but the period since 1938 seemed too contemporary. The democratic processes which had created Sweden into a political democracy before and after World War I were still in a state of flux at the outbreak of World War II. It does seem certain that Sweden has rejected communism as alien to its soil, and that a form of capitalism has been accepted within the framework of a welfare state which might have made a Frank Lester Ward happy, while despairing a William G. Sumner. Has Sweden become a sociocracy? The Swedes would like to think that they have found a satisfactory "middle of road."

A student of contemporary Sweden, though recognizing the psychological significance of the past upon group reactions in shaping convictions and "folkways," might easily conclude that mores are no less influenced by chance or fate. The American concept of the dignity of man undermined social disparities, but faith in man in Sweden, whether an illusion or not, has often become confused with confidence in fate. The rational or irrational belief in destiny is no less significant in Sweden than in America. But it is less associated with God and more with Providence.

The historian is not a scientist, but he should be an artist. Unfortunately the ablest historian has never captured the dimensions of a great artist. He is unable to work on one part of the canvas without destroying the perspective. He might be conscious of dimensions and perspectives, but he cannot share these as the artist is able to do. As the historian concerns himself with his trees, bushes, flowers, and flower beds, and other details of landscape, the major interest of his concern, namely, man, the entire man, seems blurred. Perhaps this is man, and the historian's portrait of man may be more accurate than that of the artist. But certainly the historian is aware of his own prejudices and is ready to recognize his inability to achieve those standards of objectivity which he seeks. His mastery of data and detail must always be questioned. He is the product of his own times. Is there not more than an element of truth in Carl Becker's conclusions that every man is his own historian?

This work has long been in the process of conclusion. If it disturbs some readers and pleases a few, these should be adequate rewards for the labor involved in its preparation. The author harbors no illusions in regard to the significance of his interpretations and conclusions. The sources which he has utilized are the customary secondary and primary sources which are always at the disposal of the historian. They consist of works of Swedish historians, economists, and political scientists, contemporary records such as journals and newspapers, and an abundance of printed reports and records of an official nature. None were free from ethnocentricism, and the least obviously tainted were perhaps the most contaminating ones.

CHAPTER I

THE CONFLICT OF THE OLD AND THE NEW

G USTAV V CAME to the throne of Sweden in 1907 at a critical moment in the history of the small Scandinavian kingdom. It can scarcely be said that a new age had arrived, and yet it seemed as if everything that had been was in a process of dissolution. The liberal political and social trends arising in the late nineteenth century were beginning to produce definite results. Old ideas clashed with new ideas, and old institutions were decaying. Man searched for stability and for an expression of a sense of unity which had disappeared, and it was, therefore, natural that he should look both to the past and to the future to satisfy his needs.

In this age of groping and uncertainty the challenging, volcanic genius of August Strindberg, Sweden's greatest modern literary genius, played an interesting, though largely iconoclastic role. The family, man, woman, society, traditions and customs, morals and religious standards were the objects of his restless and frequently devastating analysis. There was nothing holy which Strindberg did not bring down to earth, though his later years were on the whole somewhat less revolutionary than his early and middle years. Strindberg portrayed man's motives as most frequently being based upon prejudice, fears of censorship on the part of a staid society, or the desire for material award or social acclaim. Representing a concentrated spirit of revolt against conformity, Strindberg did a service by centering his attacks upon those groups which were most deserving of scorn, the upper and middle classes whose sense of values was based upon a social structure which could scarcely be maintained in a changing world.

Despite his genius, Strindberg will perhaps never be widely known outside Sweden, owing in part to the fact that

1

his early, essentially satiric production concerns itself so frequently with the weaknesses of Swedish character and the iconoclastic appraisal of an old, half decrepit civilization. Swedish institutions were being measured by new yardsticks prepared by the forces of liberalism, democracy, economic readjustment, and social change.

All individuals did not react to these impulses as did Strindberg. Many preferred to shut their eyes and not to think at all. To them, life and its problems had not been radically altered by revolutionary changes in agriculture or the growth of the factory system. The fact that they did not enjoy suffrage did not interest them, for they were apathetic in their attitudes toward the great political issues of the day. Others were vocal in their disagreement with Strindberg. They saw in Strindberg the iconoclast of everything fine and noble in an old society built upon holy concepts of morality.

If social, economic, and political reforms had had such an inveterate individualist as Strindberg to depend upon, democracy would indeed have had to wait. As it was, a clear-cut political liberalism had not found a strong voice in Sweden at any time during the nineteenth century. It is doubtful that the French Revolutionary writers of the eighteenth century had greatly influenced the overthrow of Gustav IV in 1809 and the consequent adoption of new constitutional laws. The abolition of the Four Estates upon which the Swedish legislative body, the *Riksdag*, was built, was not accomplished until after 1865. At that time, the Liberals were few and divided, and only a small additional percentage of the population was given the right to vote. The only thing that had really happened was that wealth was substituted for birth as the basis of political privileges. The *Riksdag* continued to represent wealth and vested interests, and up to the time of the reign of Gustav V all efforts of Liberals to alter this situation had run aground. Their ranks and strength were weakened from within and without. The voice of Sven Adolf Hedin, whose political philosophy was based essentially upon French eighteenth century thought, spoke boldly for humanism until it was silenced by death, but by that time liberalism had found other spokesmen. Political parties were in the process of being formed, and issues were sharpened.

Karl Staaff, who had become the leader of the Liberal Coalition party, was greatly impressed by the evolution of the British Parliament during the nineteenth century. He represented a group of Sweden's intelligentsia who were working for a program of universal male suffrage and parliamentary responsibility of the government as the foundation of a new democracy. Staaff had few personal friends, and though he was courageous in his demands for democratic political reforms, he was a politician who sought to strengthen his party's position by courting the votes of the religious dissenters and the nonconformists. But the elements which for decades had been associated with political liberalism were hardly in harmony with Staaff on this point. His concept of parliamentary responsibility of the government seemed foreign to Sweden, where the monarchy had become a sacred institution and the king a symbol of national unity. Staaff believed that the two chambers of the *Riksdag* were not of equal importance. The members of the First Chamber were elected indirectly and in accordance with obsolete principles set down in the Local Government Act of 1862. It represented vested interest, capital, and political privilege. The Second Chamber was, according to Staaff, representative of the people, its members being elected directly for a period of four years compared with a period of nine years for the members of the upper chamber. In direct state elections, each voter was limited to one vote, while in local elections, the Local Government Act provided for a graduated suffrage scale. It was possible in Sweden at the turn of the century for certain individuals to control local election results. Since they were naturally unwilling to sacrifice their privileges, they rallied around the King when Staaff insisted that the King's cabinet should reflect the prevailing political sentiments of the Second Chamber.

Some other person possessing greater tact than Staaff

might have won wider sympathies for these new ideas in Sweden. As it turned out, the issue appeared to many Swedes as one of Staaff versus the King, with the result that the real significance of the political controversy was obscured.

Hjalmar Branting, leader of the Social Democratic party, often called Socialist, shared some of Staaff's ideals. As a young man, Branting had dedicated his life to the cause of labor even though his education, economic status, and social background entitled him to a position of privilege. He, like Staaff, fought for the extension of suffrage, but to him, universal male suffrage was only a means to an end, namely, social, economic, and political equality. He and his followers desired to break entirely with the past through a gradual political evolution which they referred to as a revolution. The group which looked to Branting as leader had grown stronger and stronger as organized labor gained in strength and confidence.

When Gustav V became King, another even more radical element, also often called Socialist, raised its voice, demanding a swift revolution and a violent extermination of those representing privilege. The term "Socialist" was perhaps misleadingly applied to all who sought a social, economic, and political change in which the old established order would have to be either sacrificed or amended. As a rule the Socialist was labeled as hostile to organized Christianity and especially to the Established Church of Sweden.

It was natural in a country like Sweden where customs played such an important role that these new thoughts would disturb many whether they were based upon broad Anglo-American ideals of democracy or upon the philosophy of Karl Marx. Around the beginning of this century, Sweden experienced a national awakening which found expression in a very rich literature. Poets and novelists turned their attention to folklore and the culture of the provinces and rural life in their search for old and stable institutions which represented the historical traditions and achievements of a

4

people. They regretted the dissolution of traditional values and regarded it as a destruction of historical heritage. They lamented materialistic concepts and the passing of an age so rich in harmony, beauty, stability, and friendliness.

The foremost representative of this group of writers was Selma Lagerlöf. Her best work, *Gösta Berlings Saga* (1894), romanticizes the old country estate which combined agriculture and manufacturing under the direction of cultured local gentry. The paternalistic interest of Värmland gentry in their workers was undoubtedly real, but the modern corporation with far greater capital had supplanted an antiquated institution, and no romanticizing by Miss Lagerlöf could revive it. Other writers, like Verner von Heidenstam, went further back into the history of Sweden to satisfy their awakened national consciousness.

The fine arts also sought to express something truly Swedish. In 1906 the Northern Museum in Stockholm was completed. The architect, Isak Gustaf Clason, tried to express a national historical tradition in his work. Some time later, Ragnar Österberg tried to emulate Clason in the construction of Östermalm Secondary School, in which a bold and imaginative design sacrificed the practical aspects of the building. L. I. Wahlman embodied national traditions in Engelbrecht Church, an inspiring edifice which seemed to rise with majestic strength out of the rocks on which it was built.

The painters were represented by such men as Anders Zorn, Karl Larsson, and Bruno Liljefors, who succeeded perhaps better than the architects and the writers in their search for unity and harmony, something which was genuinely Swedish. Among the painters, Zorn portrayed the sturdy peasant girl from Dalarne, full of joy and happiness. He painted her at the fireplace of the old log house in her colorful costume, and he followed her with his easel and brush to the lake shore. Bruno Liljefors captured the scenic beauty of his country and its wild life, while Karl Larsson loved the simplicity of his own home, its bright peasant colors and old furniture, in which dwelt a happy family group. It was the home and the family which he felt expressed the essential soundness of the national tradition. Nationalism was indeed resurgent, and under its powerful impetus the Swedish Home Sloyd Association was founded in 1899, reviving interest in dying national art.

In a sense, it cannot be said that these developments in the arts were entirely beneficial. It was impossible to prevent the coming of a new age by looking back and building upon memories or old institutions or a mode of life which could not continue. Transition was only made the more painful. The reactionaries did not hesitate, furthermore, to capitalize upon a stronger national sentiment and patriotism. These, unlike the Liberals, had been greatly influenced by the cultural and political trends in Germany. It could indeed be said that much unrest in Sweden was the result of the clashing of contrary influences.

The German way of life was advocated by the Conservatives and the Anglo-American way of life by the Liberals. Many economic reforms in Sweden during the nineteenth century could be traced directly to Bentham, Bright, and Cobden, and economic liberalism was far stronger than political liberalism. A definite reaction set in around 1888-1892 when the so-called "new system "was adopted after a bitter struggle. During these years, Sweden launched upon a program of tariff protection and militarism, and reaction and nationalism thrived. Democracy was mocked. The period of compulsory military training was extended, while suffrage demands of the people were denied. Freedom of the press and speech were endangered and prison terms were meted out to radicals. A law was adopted to destroy the power of organized labor.

The dissolution of the union between the kingdoms of Sweden and Norway was hastened. Norway had definitely become influenced by Anglo-American influences. Liberalism and nationalism had merged into a healthy development in Norway, while conservatism, reaction, and militarism characterized Swedish nationalism. A dissolution of the union was, in consequence, inevitable. The Conservatives in Sweden had desired to strengthen the bonds of the union between the two kingdoms, and they would perhaps have been willing to grant Norway greater equality if they could have laid the foundation for a common defense. The Conservatives strengthened the conscript army and navy by longer periods of compulsory training and demanded larger appropriations for fortifications, warships, and materials, and succeeded in arousing fears of Russia, which Norway did not share.

The dissolution of the union in 1905 shocked Sweden. It did not create unity within the kingdom, but inaugurated instead a period of bitter party struggles. After the elections in the fall of 1905, Staaff assumed the duties of prime minister but was unable to carry out his program of suffrage reform and resigned. His uncompromising attitude undermined the confidence of some of the members of the Liberal Coalition party. He had offended the Social Democrats, or "Socialists," as they were called, by a series of measures which were regarded as hostile to organized labor. He had also antagonized the King.

The new prime minister, Arvid Lindman, a former naval officer and industrialist, made the government hum with efficiency. He presented to the *Riksdag* a suffrage proposal with many ingenious devices aimed at checking the influence of labor and thus cushioning the possible effects of the introduction of democracy. The Lindman suffrage proposal removed any doubts as to how little Sweden had been touched by democratic political influences. It would not have been accepted if the liberal forces of Sweden had rallied in opposition to it, but the *Riksdag* had wrangled so long over the suffrage question that Lindman's measure was accepted in 1907 and reapproved again in 1909 as prescribed by the constitution.

The new measure granted suffrage to all male citizens of twenty-four or over who had performed their military service, were not on poor relief, and who had paid their taxes over a period of three years prior to an election, if

7

their incomes warranted such taxes. Conservative influences were also to be safeguarded by provisions for minority representation or proportionalism. The property qualifications of the members of the First Chamber were reduced from 80,000 crowns to 50,000 and their annual income qualifications from 4,000 crowns to 3,000. The Local Government Act was later modified to limit any person to a maximum of forty votes in a local election. This was indeed significant, for it was estimated that prior to 1909 less than seven per cent of the voters controlled local election results. No one could say that democracy had triumphed in Sweden by 1909; it was only beginning to emerge.

The Lindman administration presented two hundred legislative proposals to the *Riksdag* of 1907. Approved, among other things, was an agreement between the government and the giant corporation of Grängesberg Oxelösund by which the state became part owner in the iron fields of the corporation with the right to purchase stocks held by the corporation in 1932 or 1942. In return, the government pledged that it would not place an export duty on iron ore and that it would not resort to methods of taxing the corporation out of existence. The *Riksdag* approved 5,000,000 crowns for the construction of new warships. Large appropriations were granted for state railroad building, the Northern Trunk Line to be continued to the Finnish border while the Inland Line was to provide the city of Östersund and northern provinces with an outlet to the sea at Gothenburg. In order to overcome the abuse of liquor sales by taverns, which enjoyed an ancient privilege as hostelries, the *Riksdag* decided to pension tavern keepers and their widows. The existence of these ancient inns was an obstacle to the temperance movement as expressed in local option, and by this action the local governments were allowed greater freedom in solving the temperance question.

King Gustav was undoubtedly pleased by the efficiency of Lindman and the growth of government paternalism. The people were proud of the King's regal and stately bearing.

The new ruler was an unusually able man. In fact, it may be said that Gustav V was the ablest king that had occupied the Swedish throne for more than two centuries. He had both intelligence and energy, and rather unfortunately, for a modern king, had a will of his own. The fact that he refused the usual ceremony of coronation was motivated not only by thrift, but also by the belief that such a ceremony was unnecessary. He harbored the deepest personal antipathy for Staaff, an antipathy which was to influence the first years of his reign. As King of Sweden, he believed that he represented the people of his kingdom, sometimes more so than the *Riksdag,* and he was not unwilling to appeal directly to the people if a need arose.

The Lindman cabinet enjoyed the confidence of the new King, for it was a conservative militaristic government. The King had definite ideas of his own as to what constituted adequate defense. He felt that he was unusually well informed on international affairs. Labor and liberals did not, therefore, react toward Gustav V with enthusiasm. His greatest asset was his ultranationalism, but age had not yet mellowed him into an able constitutional monarch. In 1907 his position was, as he put it, "above political parties" and he did not wish nor intend "to function without the cooperation of the people." He had the profoundest belief in the responsibility which attended the power of a monarch.

The first *Riksdag* during the reign of Gustav V was calm. Large appropriations were made to encourage the cultivation of new land by drainage projects and to improve communications. Fishermen were provided with state insurance against accidents in their work, and the home ownership movement was encouraged, partly to discourage emigration. The *Riksdag* approved the purchase by the state of the rich Svappavaara iron field in Norrland, and adopted a plan for state-supported tuberculosis sanatoriums.

The election to the Second Chamber in 1908 lacked excitement. The Liberal Coalition party, before the election of 1908, had developed into a national political party. The Conservatives, however, were suffering from disorganization. They stressed the danger of labor unrest and coined the slogan, "A common front against Socialism."

Neither the Liberals nor the Social Democrats could accomplish much without cooperating with one another. The Liberal press maintained that the two parties at the beginning of the *Riksdag* of 1909 should work out a program agreeable to both, and thus pave the way for a Liberal government. In 1907 the great international Socialist, Vandervelde, had visited Sweden, at which time he stated: "Rather a defeat than victory secured through cooperation with the bourgeois parties." Branting and Vandervelde had, however, quite contrary opinions, since the former opposed proportionalism and was not especially interested in either the cooperative movement or temperance as a means of improving the living conditions of labor, while Vandervelde was a strong proponent of the cooperatives and the temperance movement.

Branting realized that a Liberal government might "inaugurate a number of needed bourgeois reforms," but he did not care to pledge himself to a program which would tie the actions of the party he led. Branting wrote that though the Socialists had 33 members in the *Riksdag*, his party was not strong enough to participate in a coalition government. When he refused to outline a program on which he would cooperate with the Liberals, the Liberal press expressed the belief that Branting's position was influenced by the fact that the Liberal Coalition party had withdrawn its opposition to proportionalism in November 1907.

This may have been true in part, for Branting was positive that the cause of labor had been injured by proportionalism. In defending his attitude, however, Branting referred to action taken by the International in 1900 and 1904, stating that the Frenchman Briand lost his membership in the Social Democratic party in France when he participated in the formation of the Clemenceau cabinet. Conservatives, fearing cooperation between the Liberals and Socialists, also considered the possibility of cooperating with the Liberals.

In the end, Staaff was forced to give up all thought of a purely Liberal cabinet, and the Lindman administration remained in power.

The *Riksdag* of 1909 was heated. Branting and Staaff sought to undermine the Lindman cabinet, which, supported by the First Chamber and a strong minority in the Second, weathered fierce attacks. Branting appeared more and more as the leader of the opposition and strongly attacked the government for its infringements on the freedom of the press when two Socialists were imprisoned for ridiculing the government, though he disclaimed sympathy with their nihilistic attitude.

When the *Riksdag* had approved the Lindman suffrage reform, Staaff and Branting wondered if the time had not come for the government to dissolve the *Riksdag* and order a new election to the Second Chamber on the basis of the new franchise. Such an election would strengthen the Liberals and Socialists and further embarrass the Lindman government. The prime minister answered that he could not express himself on the question. Minor matters assumed major importance as the opposition criticized the cabinet. Staaff and Branting failed to demonstrate, however, that the political weight in the *Riksdag* was found in the Second Chamber. The ill will existing between the Conservatives and Socialists was also fanned by a contest between employers and laborers unparalleled in Swedish history. Lockouts and strikes had finally resulted in a general strike, during which time the reactionary Lindman administration showed its true colors as a definitely partisan government.

During 1905 Staaff had considered the need for coordinating the defense program of the army and the navy. It was Lindman, however, who in 1907 appointed a large committee to study the question. The main purpose of the committee was to study the finances of a strong, coordinated defense, but Lindman permitted a number of officers to serve as expert advisors. This was opposed by Staaff, for he believed that the investigation should be undertaken

11

entirely by civilians. At the *Riksdag* of 1911, the Liberals called the work of the committee a complete fiasco. Staaff attacked requested appropriations for the army and the navy. The long period of eight months of compulsory military training involved, he believed, a financial burden which Sweden could not carry.

Fredrik Wilhelm Thorsson, an able Social Democrat, supported by the members of his party and a few Liberals, sought to have military appropriations cut. Staaff, however, accused the Social Democrats of desiring to reduce the defense of the country without a plan to improve it, while he accused the Conservatives of having only one thought, to increase military expenses. He believed that the defense of Sweden should be built on a mathematical estimate of what the country could safely afford to expend.

The Conservatives answered the Liberals that the question, in view of the general European situation, must be based on the risks of a weak defense. Whatever the cost, they argued, Sweden must be strong. The prime minister pointed out that from 1883 to 1903 Sweden had built thirteen warships, but had built none since that date. He requested 4,750,000 crowns for a naval building program to include a warship of the new *F* type. In the joint voting of the two chambers, Lindman carried the requested appropriations in spite of a rather strong opposition group.

Next to the defense question, the Lindman administration was attacked most vigorously for its proposed labor legislation growing out of the general strike of 1909. The government sought to secure legal sanction for collective bargaining which would make the violators of agreements responsible before the law. A special court was recommended to handle such cases, and legislation was also proposed that would have made certain strikes illegal because they threatened the general welfare of the public. With the aid of the Liberals, the Socialists succeeded in defeating this legislation, charging that it was directly aimed at curbing the power of organized labor.

In spite of the stormy sessions of the *Riksdag* of 1910 and 1911, the Conservative government accomplished a great deal. The *Riksdag* approved the renting or leasing of state waterfall property to private corporations for a period of seventy-five years, and large appropriations were granted for the expansion of government activities in railroads, telegraphs, telephone and electrical power stations. Swedish Conservatives did not fear paternalism. Increased taxes on large fortunes, inheritances, and incomes were approved. Higher tariff protection and a new trade treaty with Germany were ratified.

The election campaign of 1911 centered chiefly around the controversial question of national defense. This election tested for the first time the relative strength of the political parties in the *Riksdag* after the suffrage reform. Subsequent to the adoption of the suffrage reform, Branting had stated that the real war against the money lords had begun. Political party leaders, including the prime minister, stumped the country. Lindman assailed the cooperation of the Liberals and the Socialists, insinuating that the former accepted dictation from the latter. To embarrass the Conservatives, the Social Democratic party cooperated with the Liberals in all election districts where they themselves were unable to put up their own candidates. The campaign organization of the Liberal party distributed about 1,300,000 pamphlets, besides circulars, and the Conservatives also expended large sums to "educate" the public. The election gave the Liberals 102 votes in the Second Chamber, and the Social Democrats 64, while the Conservatives were reduced to 64. The Conservatives had made the most of a tense international situation to carry the public for a stronger national defense. The Moroccan crisis had caused all sorts of rumors of war in Europe, and in Sweden credence was given for a while to a rumor that the German and English fleets had exchanged fire in the North Sea. In 1911 the Italian-Turkish war provided the militarists with fuel for their hypernationalistic propaganda, but Lindman was nevertheless compelled to resign.

Gustav V requested, perhaps reluctantly, Staaff to organize a cabinet.

Staaff invited the Social Democrats to join in a coalition government, but they refused. For this, they were severely criticized even among their own party members, but the leaders had decided that the party must bide its time. Staaff was thus permitted to form a Liberal cabinet, which was completed October 7, 1911. His appointments were not surprising, except that of Alfred Petersson of Påboda, an advocate of proportionalism, who was appointed minister of agriculture. Petersson became the first dirt farmer in a Swedish cabinet, his appointment being largely motivated by Staaff's desire to make the cabinet democratic. The Conservatives criticized especially the appointments to the defense posts, since the ministers of the army and navy were both civilians.

One of the first requests Staaff made to the King was for the dissolution of the First Chamber in order to allow the principles of proportionalism to temper the Conservatives' control of this chamber. The King complied, with the result that the Conservative votes in the First Chamber were reduced to 86, while the Liberals secured 51 and the Social Democrats 12 seats.

Staaff also appointed four committees to study the problem of defense. The public was certain that this study would lead to a recommendation for the reduction of military expenditures, and when the prime minister informed the *Riksdag* that the building of the warship of the *F* type must be postponed, this belief gained ground. The *Riksdag* had already appropriated money for this ship, and the King indicated clearly that he did not favor the views of the prime minister, an action for which he was severely criticized by the Liberals and Socialists.

The general elections had destroyed every possible Conservative hope of controlling the joint votes of the two chambers. They had made the two chambers more alike, the First Chamber no longer representing merely the nobles, large land owners, civil servants, and industrialists. Taking the opportunity that the general European unrest offered, the Conservatives and militarists launched a program for voluntary subscriptions for warship construction in order to show Staaff that the public sympathies were in favor of a stronger national defense. They secured the support of Sven Hedin, an internationally recognized scientist and explorer, who resurrected the Russian "boogieman" by the publication of *A Word of Warning* in January 1912, and 850,000 copies of this were distributed throughout Sweden. Hedin was a chauvinist with strong German leanings, and in a patriotic fervor he depicted the lurking danger of Russia if Sweden did not awake to the dangers of a weak defense. August Strindberg had intended to give Hedin's work a reply, but he died before he completed it.

The strong spirit of nationalism awakened by Hedin's writings placed the anti-militarists in an unfavorable light. The public, assuming that the voluntary collection for warship construction was a sign of self-sacrificing patriotism, poured donations into the treasury of a patriotic society which had been organized in the latter part of January 1912. By May this society informed the King that enough money had been collected to build a warship, and that the funds would be turned over to the government as soon as it was assured that the money appropriated by the *Riksdag* of 1911 for the construction of an *F* type warship would be used for that purpose. A hundred and twenty thousand persons stricken by Russophobia demonstrated their patriotism by generous contributions. To what extent the agitation stimulated by Hedin was actually based upon facts is difficult to say, but to Hedin and the Conservatives Russian military preparations in the Baltic, railroad building in Finland, Russofication of Finland, and Russian espionage in Norrland were real signs of danger.

Staaff decided to accept the gift of money raised by voluntary subscriptions. He did not believe, however, that the propaganda of the nationalists was based upon facts; for he thought, like many another statesman in other countries at that time, that civilization had advanced to the point where no statesman would assume the responsibility of involving his nation in war. Staaff, to counteract any possibility of being pictured as unfriendly to adequate national defense, also recommended to the *Riksdag* increased appropriations for naval construction. The funds collected by the nationalists were set aside for the building of the cruiser *Sverige*. The resentment toward the King for his partisanship and sympathy for the awakened spirit of patriotism led to a motion by Carl Lindhagen, a Stockholm radical, to make a complete change in the constitutional laws of Sweden and establish a republic. Branting, however, strenuously opposed Lindhagen's proposal, and the motion received only twelve votes.

During 1912-1913, Staaff was uncertain on the question of defense. He perceived the unrest among the great powers of Europe. He had, however, made a pledge in the election of 1911 that the term of compulsory military training would not be extended, and this pledge he did not wish to violate. He was not unwilling to test the change of public opinion by dissolving the Second Chamber and ordering a general election, but he wished to wait until public opinion had become more rational. Many Swedes believed a Russian spy was hiding in every corner. The Conservatives insisted that the question of defense was so important that Staaff could not afford to wait until it was too late, and naturally they desired to profit from the growing fear of Russia.

Though the question of defense cast its dark shadow over both sessions, the *Riksdag* of both 1912 and 1913 accomplished a great deal. The most important action was the creation of an old age pension system. Under this system the people themselves contributed premium payments to a state fund, and the state and local governments contributed a share for persons with small incomes. The high protection enjoyed by the sugar industry was reduced. Fear over the activities of spies in Sweden caused a new espionage law to be passed. The *Riksdag* also decided that revenues secured from the sale of liquor should be used by the state, which, in return, agreed to appropriate annually to cities, towns, provincial assemblies, and agricultural societies certain annual amounts until 1938. In order to prevent the government from encouraging the sale of liquor and increasing its profits, it was stipulated that the government should be limited in its revenue from the sale of liquor to 41,900,000 crowns, and that the surplus be used for a state fund to combat the use of intoxicating liquor.

In December 1913, Staaff outlined his views on the question of defense, clearly revealing the effects of Conservative militaristic propaganda and the general European unrest upon the prime minister's attitude. He hoped in part to keep his pledge of 1911 by stating that the term of military service in the army would not be increased until after the people had been given an opportunity to express themselves at the election in the fall of 1914. Meanwhile, the term of service would be increased in the cavalry, artillery, and other units. The army and the navy would be strengthened as far as possible and appropriations increased for fortifications. Staaff believed that he had made important concessions to the militarists, but the Conservatives felt he had not gone far enough. In a speech in December 1913, he failed to judge the fervor of nationalism aroused by the militarists' propaganda and consequently prepared his downfall, precipitating a cabinet crisis in which the King played an important role.

Gustav V, either upon the request of the Conservatives or because of his own opinion that the time was ripe for the strengthening of the national defense, requested Staaff to call a new election to the Second Chamber. When Staaff refused, many Liberals grew distrustful of his ability as a leader, and the Conservatives were provided with more fuel in their attacks upon the prime minister.

As the eventful year 1914 approached, the people of Sweden were sadly divided. Thousands of farmers, organizing a demonstration, arrived in Stockholm in February 1914, to express their sympathies for the King's position. Nationalism ran riot, as they marched to the royal castle to assure their ruler that they were ready to assume any added burdens of defense that the safety of Swedish independence required. The King expressed his appreciation for the sentiments of the farmers and said: "You are here with me to make it known to everyone that no demand is too great and no burden too heavy when it concerns the preservation of our ancient liberty and the safeguarding of our future . . . In both good and evil days the ties between the king and the people shall with the help of God never be broken." He assured the people that he would never compromise upon a question which he believed concerned the safety and security of the nation.

This speech of Gustav V had important political repercussions. Staaff, maintaining that the King had no constitutional right to express his political views, sought in vain to have him modify his statements or reinterpret them. When he refused, Staaff resigned. In the *Riksdag*, Branting sharply criticized the effort of the monarch to reintroduce the will of the King over the people. Staaff, as prime minister, he said, represented the *Riksdag* elected by the people. Staaff ably stated the question by asking if it were possible for the advisors of the King to pursue one policy and the King another. The Social Democrats, to show their disapproval of the King's attitude as well as the farmers' demonstration, outdid the farmers in a labor demonstration against the increased burdens of a stronger national defense. They also paid tribute to the prime minister. In the heat of excitement, some of the workers shouted: "Long live the Republic!" and the mayor of Stockholm joined them in their cry.

Thus, on the eve of World War I, Sweden seethed with unrest. The situation in 1914 cannot be fully appreciated, however, without an understanding of the rise of organized labor.

Chapter II

ORGANIZED LABOR AT THE OUTBREAK OF WORLD WAR I

A S THE GREAT EUROPEAN POWERS prepared for war in the years before August 1914, the Swedish problem was more than one of a strong or a weak national defense, more than one concerned with royal prerogatives or parliamentarism, more than a personal combat between the King and Staaff, and much more than a political party struggle with the Liberals and Social Democrats pitted against the Conservatives. It was not, moreover, merely the fear of a coming struggle between the Great Powers in which Sweden might be involved. It arose rather from the delay in suffrage reform and the struggle between organized labor and management which had created hostile camps and made a strong national consciousness impossible among those who suffered from social, economic, and political inequality.

At the close of the first decade of our century, labor represented a powerful organized group which from time to time demonstrated its power. Although the Social Democratic party was organized in 1889, it had not succeeded in electing a member to the *Riksdag* until 1896. As wages improved and laborers qualified for suffrage in the general elections to the Second Chamber, the party increased its strength in the *Riksdag,* until the suffrage reforms of 1909 made it possible for the party to elect 64 members to the Second Chamber in 1911.

The Social Democratic party was closely allied to the National Federation of Trade Unions which had been organized in 1898, giving labor effective means in the struggle for better wages, shorter hours, and the right to organize. From 1863 to 1889, there were more than 200 labor conflicts;

between 1890 and 1900, some 1200; between 1901 and 1905, 657 strikes, 67 lockouts, and 79 conflicts involving both strikes and lockouts. Finally, in 1909, came the general strike, which for four weeks threatened to cripple the whole economic life of Sweden.

The strike of 1909 greatly depleted the treasury of the National Federation of Trade Unions, and the Federation and the Social Democratic party lost many members. The Federation assumed, in consequence, a more cautious policy. But on the first of May red flags and the marching of thousands through cities in an annual labor demonstration reflected the bitterness of the class struggle. Frightened middle-class people, white-collar workers, non-unionized labor, farmers, wealthy industrialists, and business men saw in the army of organized labor a potential revolutionary force ready to overthrow the government and establish a republic. Phrases and words were singled out from the numerous May Day speeches made by the labor and Social Democratic leaders to prove that, under the banner of the red flag, they planned revolution. Such terms as "proletariat," "revolution," "republic," "class war," "solidarity of the proletariat," "Marxism," and "socialism" aroused grim forebodings.

The atheistic concepts of the leading labor leaders and the hostility of the Social Democratic party to the Established Church troubled a nation which, though not a church-attending people, harbored a deep-rooted respect for the Church. To show their contempt for organized Christianity, many Social Democrats were not married by the Church or by any civil authority, but lived with their common-law wives, a practice which to many seemed to indicate scorn for the sanctity of marriage. For more than two decades prior to World War I, a group of young radicals preached violence, sabotage, syndicalism, and anarchy.

The Swedish public in 1914 was confused. It could see little difference in the ideals of Social Democrats, Socialists, Anarchists, or Syndicalists. All had their roots in labor agitation; all advocated a revolution; all were hostile to organized

Christianity; and in the May Day demonstrations all joined in a common cause to impress the nation with the strength of labor. The confusion was not the result of ignorance alone. It was due more to the inability of the leaders of labor to convince the public that the Social Democrats did not advocate a violent revolution, but a gradual change, so gradual that Hjalmar Branting believed that the party could just as well be called a Reform party.

Yet Branting, though opposed to the use of such terms as "proletariat," the "rule of the proletariat," and "revolution," permitted himself from time to time under stress to resort to strong language. Perhaps Branting was, on the whole, inspired more by the zeal of a reformer than by the ideals of Marxian socialism. He had an almost unlimited amount of patience, but when very sorely tried made insinuations that frightened people. He was an opportunist in the sense that he believed that labor must take advantage of everything offered to further its cause, but his final aim was somewhat obscure. As a Marxian, Branting defended his constant adaptation to new conditions by maintaining that Marx did not believe in "an absolute truth," that theory too must change as all things changed.

Thus the very foundation on which Branting built his early ideals of socialism — state ownership of the means of production — could not represent an absolute truth on which the greatest possible state of happiness for the greatest possible number of people could be built. Branting, though pleading the cause of labor, could never suggest reforms that would involve suffering to any other social class. The rights of labor were sacred to him but no more sacred than the rights of every citizen.

To appreciate fully the apprehension in Sweden over the growth of the Social Democratic party and the National Federation of Trade Unions, a brief outline must be given of the development of these organizations prior to 1914. The Social Democratic party was built on local party organizations called "communes," which combined all societies and organizations that worked for the aims of the party. No society could join the party except through membership in the local commune. This was stressed particularly at the congress of the party in 1900 as a means of more effectively organizing each local area for political purposes. The supreme authority of the party was the party congress, which consisted of delegates from all communes who outlined the program of the party. The congress determined when and how often it would meet and elected the party executive committee. This body, in annual meeting, was authorized to elect from among its own members an administrative committee to carry on the administrative work of the party.

When the party was organized in 1889 there were about 250 labor unions in Sweden. These were local trade unions, not more than one-fifth of which joined the Social Democratic party in 1889. At that time there were only about thirty Social Democratic clubs, but they played a very important part in organizing labor unions, and influencing all labor organizations. For nearly a decade after 1889, the Social Democratic party functioned almost as a federation of labor unions. When the number of strikes and lockouts increased, the public associated it with the strikes, and it was frequently labeled the "strike party." Some members believed that this was detrimental to the party's political influence, and advocated that the Social Democrats should dissociate themselves from the labor unions; but Branting and other leaders did not believe such a step desirable, and the Social Democratic party retained its close labor union affiliations. In no other European country were labor unions so closely associated with the Social Democratic party. This was partly because in Sweden no racial and religious differences divided labor. So long as Swedish labor had no franchise, a Social Democratic party could have no political power. The party must therefore unite with labor in an effort to secure suffrage reform. From 1889 to 1909, this was the most important part of the program of the Social Democratic party.

The labor unions and the Social Democratic party were

almost welded into one in 1898, when upon the recommendation of the Social Democratic party a Labor Congress organized the National Federation of Trade Unions. This federation, consisting of both local and national labor unions, made membership in the Social Democratic party compulsory, providing for a party assessment on the members of all unions which was to go into effect three years later. The Social Democrats were given a voice in the Council of the National Federation of Trade Unions. Several trade unions as a result of this action refused to join the Federation, and a few of them that were especially dubious about the program of the Social Democrats organized the Swedish Workingmen's Federation in 1899. This never became an important organization, because the National Federation of Trade Unions decided in 1900 to repeal the most objectionable feature of the relationship of the labor unions to the Social Democratic party, namely, compulsory membership in the party.

The party urged all local unions to cooperate with the communes of the Social Democratic party. Through the communes it was possible for the party to cooperate with unions in making membership in a labor union dependent upon membership in the commune. A few trade unions recognized this fact and were very reluctant to join the Federation, but gradually, through the rise of able leaders in the labor unions closely associated with the Social Democratic party, objections were overcome.

The aim of the Federation was to help member unions in strikes and lockouts by providing financial aid to labor involved in such activities, but in order not to be constantly depleting its treasury, it did not provide any help until at least five per cent of the members were involved. Since the Social Democratic party was an international organization, closely cooperating with the Second International, the Federation also pledged aid to foreign labor organizations.

Conservative labor unions also believed that the existence of the Federation would encourage strikes in certain trades. But as no local union, not even a central committee of local unions, had the right to engage in a strike without the approval of a national trade union in which they were members, the fears proved to be unfounded. In fact, the existence of the Federation discouraged rather than encouraged strikes that were thought to be of doubtful success, but gave to the labor organizations the powerful weapon of sympathy strikes and the threat of a general strike.

The close association of the Social Democrats and the National Federation of Trade Unions made possible the suffrage strike of 1902 and the preceding labor demonstrations. In an orderly labor demonstration on April 20, police had clashed with the demonstrators. Public sympathy for labor was instantaneous. In the ensuing demonstration, college students, professors, and members of the *Riksdag* participated in expressing disapproval of action of the Stockholm police. About 120,000 workers went on a strike for three days to bring pressure to bear on the *Riksdag* for suffrage reform. Nearly one-third of these workers lived in Stockholm. The others made less impressive strikes in Malmö, Gothenburg, and other cities. It was not a general strike in the true sense of the word, but only because the National Federation of Trade Unions was not strong enough to call such a strike.

The strike of 1902 impressed employers with the power of organized labor and encouraged them to organize in order to counteract this power. Before the end of the year, two employers' associations were founded, and a third, established in 1896, was reorganized. They were the General Employers' Association with Malmö as headquarters, the Swedish Employers' Association with Stockholm as headquarters, and the Swedish Manufacturers' Association, which also established its headquarters in Stockholm. At the time, the Swedish Employers' Association experienced the most rapid growth, and by 1905 it had 236 members, who employed 41,000 workers. The Association fixed membership dues on the basis of the number of employees.

With the rise of employers' associations, the modern method of bargaining and collective agreements was introduced between employers and organized labor. The common method of settling labor conflicts became that of agreements between the central agencies representing the two parties involved. It was not a sudden development, for the employers were reluctant to recognize labor unions as representing authoritative bodies in a collective agreement. But times changed, and the employers' associations became eager to include as many trades as possible in a collective agreement.

Collective agreements forced both labor unions and employers' associations to study standardized wages. Labor unions stressed the variation in the cost of living in different parts of Sweden, and the employers stressed the cost of production, which, in part, included a study of the cost of living. The employers also saw a distinct advantage in national collective labor agreements, as they united employers and did away with unfair competition. The labor unions hesitated to accept national agreements that might prevent them from making use of local advantages. However, the Manufacturers' Association succeeded after two general lockouts in 1903 and 1905 in forcing labor unions in the engineering trades into a national collective agreement.

This interesting agreement became the prototype of many collective agreements on a national scale. It consisted of two parts, one dealing with general conditions of work and wages in the trade, and the other providing for regulations for the settlement of future disputes. By 1909 about one-third of all collective agreements were on a national scale. The Social Democrats fought legislation aimed to make labor unions accountable before the law as more than benevolent insurance organizations. Agitation for fixing the legal responsibility of labor unions increased after the general strike of 1909 in which collective agreements were violated. Employers brought suit against labor unions, and the Supreme Court upheld the verdict of the lower court that labor unions were responsible before the law as legal associations which could be sued for breach of contract. It was of great significance that the labor unions failed in their argument that sympathy strikes were not aimed at employers and were thus not violations of legal agreements.

On the eve of the general strike of 1909, the National Federation of Trade Unions had 162,329 members. The president of the Federation, Herman Lindqvist, an unusually able and wise leader, had directed the Federation since 1900. He was cautious, had never been a strong advocate of a general strike, and always opposed one when circumstances indicated that such a strike would fail. But there had been much agitation among the Social Democrats for a political strike more impressive than the one of 1902, and this led to a consideration of a general strike of such proportions as to inaugurate a new social order. Younger members of the Federation, impressed by its growth, wanted the Federation actually to test its strength.

Lindqvist had no sympathy for this type of reasoning, but impatience with the Federation had caused a loss of members during the latter part of 1908. In no country were labor and employers better organized. The Swedish Employers' Association had at the beginning of the strike about 1,258 members employing 153,000 workers; the Swedish Manufacturers' Association had 162 members employing about 35,000 workers; and the General Employers' Association had a membership of about 2,000 employing about 45,000 workers. All in all, the members of the various employers' associations employed about 260,000 workers.

Labor and employer groups were organized along both offensive and defensive lines, capable of using powerful weapons. Labor organizations resorted to strikes, sympathy strikes, blockades, and, less seldom, boycotting. The employers' organizations used the dreaded weapon of lockouts in addition to their power to hire and fire. For a time, labor seemed to have the upper hand because economic conditions were good, but in 1908 an economic depression gave the employers the advantage.

The employers now sought once and for all to settle the question of sympathy strikes, which in their opinion

26

violated collective agreements. In 1908 the three largest employers' associations gave warning of a general lockout if strikes and blockades violating collective agreements did not cease. The government acted, and pressure was brought to bear on the employers not to carry out their threats. Because of the depression, employers sought to reduce wages when collective agreements expired, and the atmosphere was loaded with ill will. The unions in turn wanted recognition in the agreements of the rights of labor to organize as well as to establish closed shops.

In July 1909, the Swedish Employers' Association threatened a general lockout unless labor unions accepted the views of the Association. Leaders of the Federation consulted prominent figures of the Social Democratic party, and on July 27 a general strike manifesto was issued. Five days later the strike began, involving about 285,000 workers. It was the largest strike in the history of labor in any country up to this date, and Sweden received the attention of the entire world in this struggle between capital and labor.

The National Federation of Trade Unions took every precaution possible to avoid violence. It ordered that workers employed in the care of sick and of animals, workers in light and power plants, and in departments of sanitation were not to participate in the strike. The effect of the strike was impressive. There was no smoke coming from factory chimneys, no noisy street cars, and cabs disappeared from the streets. In the harbor, idle workers sat and sunned themselves. It looked as if all Sweden had gone fishing. The public had feared violence, and many persons had stored up huge quantities of food. Not a few had purchased guns and ammunition in case violence should break out. But these fears subsided when the King travelled through the streets of Stockholm without a bodyguard as if nothing had happened.

In order to finance the tremendous cost of the strike, representatives of labor had been sent to the United States, England, France, and Germany in an effort to secure financial aid from labor organizations of these countries. These representatives were rather successful, but the brunt of the burden had to be carried by the National Federation of Trade Unions. The strike could not have come at a more inopportune time. The severe economic depression did not involve as great a hardship on employers as upon labor. The morale of the strikers gradually broke down, and labor finally urged the government to act as a mediator. Many Liberals supported labor in this move; but the government issued a special proclamation in which it reproached labor leaders for trying to inveigle the employees of the state into the strike. This, it was felt, was an action that made the general strike not merely a contest between labor and employers but also a direct attack upon society and the state. The government maintained further that the strike was an open violation of agreements between labor and employers and that, therefore, it was impossible for the state to act as conciliator. This was the first heavy blow dealt the Federation in the general strike.

The second setback came when the Swedish Workingmen's Federation ordered its members to return to work on August 17. This group had been induced by the much larger National Federation to join in the strike, but now it severely criticized the National Federation for its violation of pledges and contracts and urged all non-union workers to return to work. This organization also sharply criticized the National Federation for ordering agricultural workers to strike during a harvest season. Gradually the strike became a contest between the National Federation of Trade Unions and the Swedish Employers' Association. This removed the chief objections of the government, and on September 12 a board of conciliation was appointed. Many members of the Federation had, by this time, however, dropped their membership and returned to work, until on September 24 only about 100,000 men remained on strike. By October 9 a majority of workers employed by the Swedish Employers' Association had returned to work, and the National Federation, fighting a losing battle, decided to limit the strike to iron manufacturing. The employers had at first refused to consider arbitration until all the workers had returned to work, but now they proposed a basis for arbitration by which both parties would consent to negotiations for compulsory arbitration, during which time both lockouts and strikes would be prohibited. The Federation refused, but by December the power of the National Federation of Trade Unions was broken.

It had been difficult to avoid clashes between workers and the police. As the strike continued, the workers had grown impatient and irritable. Many of them were in no mood to obey the police. The National Federation, realizing the danger of possible disorder, had appointed custodians of the public peace, whom the workers more readily obeyed. Since the general strike was notable for the orderly conduct of the strikers, the use of troops by the government was entirely uncalled for, and numerous arrests which followed did not serve to foster patriotism. The hostile attitude of the government also contributed to the creation of two distinct camps, a labor proletariat and a property class. The government must be largely blamed for prolonging the strike, which cost the labor unions 7,000,000 crowns, most of which was raised in Sweden. The strike weakened the National Federation of Trade Unions until its membership dropped below 100,000. Many workingmen became convinced that strikes and other weapons used by the National Federation of Trade Unions were futile and costly to labor, and in 1910 a syndicalistic labor organization started the Central Organization of Swedish Workers which advocated sabotage, violence, and poor work for poor pay. To the Syndicalists, collective agreements were not only undesirable but not binding.

Syndicalism was not something which appeared suddenly after the general strike of 1909, although previously it had little opportunity to express itself in the existing labor unions. Its origins in Sweden can be traced back to a situation within the Social Democratic party prior to 1900. In 1891 Hinke Bergegren began the publication of *Under Röd Flagg* (*Under the Red Flag*). Bergegren was an anarchist who scorned Branting, ridiculed the eight-hour day, the suffrage program of the Social Democrats, and the compromises, which, he said, only allowed "capitalists to steal less from labor." The attack of Bergegren did much to clarify the stand of the Social Democratic party as a peaceful organization opposed to all violence, but at the same time it could not prevent some groups from following the teachings of Bergegren.

This was especially true among the younger members of the party. In 1892 the first youth club was organized to train workers for leadership and to study various economic and social problems. By 1899 there were a large number of these clubs, and they arranged for a national Congress of Socialist Youth. The name, Society of Social Democratic Youth was adopted, and publication of *Brand (Fire)* as its official organ was begun. The extension of the compulsory military training period without a suffrage reform made it more and more difficult for the leaders of the Social Democratic party to combat Bergegren and his followers. The radical program of anti-militarism, anti-parliamentarism, irreligion, and agitation for an immediate violent revolution, expressed in *Brand,* was welcomed by the younger workers.

The leaders of the Social Democratic party hesitated to expel the radicals, hoping that in time youth would grow wise and put aside foolishness. Certain leaders among the younger group, led by Per Albin Hansson, had no desire to follow the anarchists. Hansson tried to secure control of *Brand,* but when his attempt failed an open rift seemed unavoidable among the youth clubs. The youth clubs that were in sympathy with the program of the Social Democratic party organized the Social Democratic Youth Association and its official organ became *Fram (Forward).* Hansson served as editor until 1909, at which time the newspaper had 40,000 subscribers. From the first, efforts were made to heal the schism among the youth groups, but the Social Democratic party could not escape severe criticism as long as Bergegren continued to preach murder, violence, and dynamiting of the Swedish *Riksdag.* Finally in 1906 Bergegren was expelled from the party. The radicals then tried to carry the Social

Democratic party congress of 1908 in order to reprove the party leaders for their action, and when this failed many of of the other anarchists decided to leave the party. Thus the Social Democrats had cleaned house.

It was not too soon, for the Social Democratic party had received a very bad name. Bergegren had defined his own attitude excellently. He wrote: "As for myself, I consider murder on a small scale excellent, and such attacks will fill the governing classes with terror. We shall fill the hearts and minds of the people with the poison of hatred in order to make them ready to commit any kind of violence whatsoever." The leaders of the Social Democrats looked upon this as a teaching that could only have originated in a madhouse.

The dynamiting of the ship *Amalthea* (a receiving ship for British blacklegs during a dockers' strike in Malmö in 1908) was the most infamous illustration of the influence of the anarchists. But the followers of Bergegren embarrassed the Social Democrats in a number of other ways. In 1909, for instance, a Swedish general was murdered, possibly by mistake, for the murderer probably believed him to be a Russian attached to the Russian party during the Czar's visit to Stockholm. The young Socialists were a disturbing element also at the open air meetings, demonstrations, and rallies of the Social Democratic party. They were called "Young Hinks" after their leader, Hinke Bergegren. In 1909 Branting wrote, "We do not have in the young Socialist club radical friends who try to march ahead of the main army, but we must count them among our enemies who seek systematically to tear down what we wish to build . . . ." Inasmuch as the young Socialists provided the reactionaries with ammunition, the Social Democratic party was forced to treat them as enemies.

During 1909 and 1910 the Social Democratic party was somewhat strengthened by the addition of two able Liberals. They were the great humanitarian Carl Lindhagen, an idealist who could not be really happy in any political party, and

Erik Kule Palmstierna, who was a religious dreamer and a pacifist. Both were too fanatical to be as valuable as they might have been to the party, but the fact that they joined at a critical time when prestige was needed proved helpful.

The Social Democratic party continued to have troubles after 1908, when the definite break occurred between the party and the young Socialists. Zeta Höglund and Hjalmar Gustafson, members of the Social Democratic Youth Association, had started a newspaper of their own called *Stormklockan,* and they had many followers who were more in sympathy with the young Socialists than with the Social Democratic party. The party in turn grew more conservative, having decided at the party congress of 1908 not to give offense to the religious convictions of any of its members. The party had also become more friendly to the cause of temperance. In 1905 it had actually expressed itself in favor of prohibition, but decided in 1911 not to take any definite stand. At the party congress of 1911 it was also decided that the extreme doctrinaire program adopted by German Social Democrats at Erfurt two decades earlier was hardly applicable to conditions existing in Sweden. Therefore the program was revised.

As Sweden had a large agricultural population, the Social Democratic party could never hope for much success as long as it advocated that land should be the common property of all citizens, since small farmers of Sweden owned about two-thirds of all the farms. The congress of 1911 proved to be rather exciting, as means of attracting farmer support were considered. Many Social Democrats maintained that they could not and should not depart from any principles of socialism, while others, like Fabian Månsson, a leader who had risen rapidly in popularity on account of his wit and cleverness, said: "We shall not stick blindly to theories, whether Marxian or not; the main thing is food and happiness for the people."

Månsson had risen from the ranks of labor. He had no education beyond that of the public schools, and his language suggested little more than a sharp wit and a rough and dry humor of the backwoods. In reality, he was a serious student and an able writer, who late in life surprised Swedish scholars and delighted people of literary taste with his masterful interpretation of the religious conditions in Sweden in a novel, *Righteousness through Faith.*

At the party congress of 1911 and 1912 there even emerged some evidence of distrust of Branting's leadership. This great leader knew that theory and practice were two entirely different things. It was his task, on the one hand, to retain the confidence of labor, and, on the other hand, to win the confidence of the *Riksdag.* As the leader of the Social Democratic party in the *Riksdag* he refused to make his party responsible to the party congress. He maintained that, as public servants and members of the *Riksdag,* the Social Democrats could not be responsible to a party congress. Many Social Democrats felt that their members in the *Riksdag* were not elected by the party but by the people, and that state secrets could not be divulged to any national party. Of course, a type of responsibility of the members of the party in the *Riksdag* to the national party could not be avoided, and this was realized in 1917. By that time, the Social Democrats had weathered the worst storms, and the difference between the radicals and the followers of Branting were more clearly defined.

In 1912 a committee of five had made a study of the relationship of the Social Democratic party to the labor unions. It was found that few union members objected to the party rule that unions could join it collectively. In 1908 the privilege of remaining outside the party had been granted to individuals, even though their union belonged collectively to the party. It was found that many availed themselves of this privilege, though members of the unions that belonged collectively to the party formed a very considerable majority of the individual members. In 1914 the party had about 50,000 members, and of these only 2,500 were not members of a labor union. Thus the relationship between the Social

Democratic party and labor was a very close one, even though in 1909 the National Federation of Trade Unions had decided to eliminate the provision which provided for close cooperation of labor unions with the communes of the Social Democratic party.

Though the Federation after 1909 made no reference in its regulations to ties with the Social Democratic party, these ties nevertheless existed. The party was allowed representation at the labor congress of the Federation, and the Federation was allowed representation at the party's congress. The action of the Federation was undoubtedly motivated by fears on the part of a few that the Social Democratic party had secured a bad reputation for its long toleration of the Syndicalists. When the radical Socialists were driven out of the Social Democratic party in 1908, it was possible for the Federation and the Social Democrats to continue to work in close cooperation.

The Social Democratic party had also learned by experience that the encouragement of the organization of youth clubs for the purpose of study and training of leaders might be disastrous without proper guidance by older and wiser members.

At the time that the party took its action to oust Bergegren and Schröder in 1906, a "folk high school" was organized at Brunnsvik to train young men in leadership. This school was supported by voluntary gifts among Social Democrats. An effort was made in 1907 to secure a state subsidy for the school, but it failed because the school was looked upon as an agency of the Social Democratic party. The labor unions then decided to come to the rescue, and in 1912 it became the center of a nationwide movement called the Workers' Educational Association, which encouraged the organization of reading circles and received financial aid from the Social Democratic party; the Consumers' Cooperative Society; the National Federation of Trade Unions; the Temperance Society, Verdandi; the Social Democratic Youth Association;

34

and the Association of Typographers. All of these organizations pledged themselves to contribute three *öre* per member to the Workers' Educational Association.

The funds were used in large part for the support of the school at Brunnsvik, for special lectures, for a summer school course, and for the maintenance of circulating libraries. The school acquainted the students with the workings of a labor union, stressing the historical development of the labor movement. Courses dealing with social, economic, and political problems were presented in a scientific and scholarly manner. Thus guidance was given to the youth clubs and an institutional movement was created that provided a bulwark against radicalism.

The full effect of the influence of Brunnsvik and the Workers' Educational Association was not fully realized until after World War I. Though it represented an effort to check radicals, it could not, at the beginning, save the public from fears and apprehensions over the rise of organized labor and the rise of labor as a political power. The mass of the people could not discern the gulf existing between the old line Social Democrats and the young Socialists. To an ignorant and prejudiced public, there was only a step from Branting to Bergegren. It was easy for the general public to confuse the Central Organization of Swedish Workers with the aims of the National Federation of Trade Unions, though no one knew the difference better than the employers. It was easy likewise to confuse the Socialist youth clubs with the Social Democratic youth clubs, a confusion somewhat more justified because the Social Democratic youth often allowed their own enthusiasm to run away with them.

Radical intellectuals like Zeta Höglund and Fredrik Ström were most dangerous when it came to leading labor in the path of Communism. Both of these men were at this time under strong Bolshevistic influences, which Branting tried with all his power to combat. On the eve of World War I, the Social Democrats had tried to rid themselves of all radicals. To the student of history viewing facts impartially, it is doubtful that in cleaning house the Social Democrats did a thorough job. It perhaps mattered little as long as Branting was the leader, for he was a man who did not permit visions to obscure reality.

CHAPTER III

AGRICULTURE AT THE BEGINNING OF WORLD WAR I

THE SWEDISH PEOPLE throughout the nineteenth century had great faith in the benefits of education, which were visible not only in the labor movement but even more noticeable in agriculture. After 1900 the fruits of the work done by the Royal Academy of Agriculture, the provincial agricultural societies, numerous garden societies, agricultural schools, and dairy schools were so apparent that the radical changes in Swedish agriculture effected in the generation before the outbreak of World War I might be entirely attributed to education.

The influence of higher educational institutions and parish libraries, as well as that of the public schools, would probably have been less effective if agriculture had not shared, with industry, a stability that was in no small measure due to the tariff policy adopted between 1888 and 1892. The effect of education is plainly evidenced by the fact that in 1880 Sweden was one of the most backward agricultural countries in Europe, while in 1914 she was surpassed only by Belgium, Holland, Germany, and Denmark in the relative productivity of her soil. The natural fertility of the soil of these countries was so much greater compared to that of Swedish soil that the rise in Swedish agricultural production was, to say the least, revolutionary.

The tariff policy adopted in Sweden was not prohibitive to foreign competition, but it gave Swedish farmers a chance to compete on even terms with foreign competitors in the home market. It was, however, more than a tariff for revenue, and after 1895 there was a tendency to revise the tariff scale slightly upward on only a very few products, such as pork

37

and corn. More important revisions in the Swedish tariff policy were not considered necessary until after the adoption of a new tariff by Germany in 1902.

The new German tariff was largely intended to force Sweden to join the German commercial system to which Austria, Belgium, Italy, Russia, and Switzerland were soon to belong. The German tariff caused much anxiety in Sweden, for it was feared that exports to Germany would suffer while German exports to Sweden might increase. In 1906 Sweden entered into the system temporarily, and in 1911 a new trade treaty with Germany and a new tariff were approved by the *Riksdag*. By this tariff there was a general upward revision in order that Sweden might secure bargaining advantages in her trade treaties. This did not mark a radical departure in Sweden's tariff policy, for these revisions were in some instances sacrificed in the German trade treaty. Germany's chief interest in a trade treaty with Sweden was to prevent Sweden from levying an export duty on iron ore.

Under the protection of a stable tariff system, agriculture flourished. In 1890 the functions of the Royal Academy of Agriculture were limited by the creation of the Bureau of Agriculture. This bureau assumed the supervision of the agricultural schools, dairy schools, homecrafts, seed control stations, agricultural chemical laboratories, and agricultural research fellowships. Its aim was to stimulate the development of scientific and intensive farming, and it worked in close cooperation with the twenty-six provincial or local agricultural societies, which in 1890 had about 26,000 members. The societies were not dependent upon membership fees for their work, but secured subsidies from the various provincial assemblies. The increased financial resources of these provincial societies made their district conventions potent educational institutions, and from 1880 to 1914 they developed a very progressive and realistic educational program on soil productivity, horticulture, and animal husbandry.

One of the main reasons for the greater productivity of

Swedish soil in 1914 as compared with 1880 must be attributed to a greater use of both natural and scientific fertilizing material. The old barns were dark and unsanitary, providing no means for the proper use of animal refuse, which was believed to be so valuable a fertilizing agent that it increased the productivity of the farm each year the equivalent of one hundred and fifty gallons of milk per cow. After 1890 the agricultural societies stressed the importance of properly built barns, a program which prior to 1890 had been essentially limited to larger farms. The use of artificial fertilizer was also developed, and the provincial agricultural societies cooperated closely with the chemical laboratory stations, which by 1900 had been increased to nine, in analyzing the soil as well as the fertilizing material sold by numerous manufacturers. Between 1896 and 1900, Sweden imported artificial fertilizers valued at nearly $11,000,000 besides manufacturing for its own use chemical fertilizers valued at $6,000,000. Much attention was also paid to proper seed for planting. By 1900 twenty seed control stations were supported by the agricultural societies.

Recognizing the importance of a proper underground drainage system to replace the wasteful open ditch system, the agricultural societies in 1900 employed thirty-eight drainage experts, whose services were available to farmers at a nominal fee. The great expense of piping made the cost of such a system prohibitive except to owners of fairly large farms until tile provided a cheaper material. This system of drainage was at first introduced in Skåne in the south of Sweden.

Prior to 1914 the government had given financial aid principally toward the development of agriculture in northern Sweden, and a credit of 5,000,000 crowns had been established in 1883 to encourage the cultivation of new land. After 1900 this fund was increased to allow loans up to 1,000,000 crowns annually, and annual appropriations were made to aid in scientific draining of land.

The agricultural societies had stimulated interest in horticulture as early as 1840. But the earliest efforts of the Royal Academy of Agriculture had placed the stress on gardening from the esthetic rather than the commercial point of view. Increased market possibilities offered by railroad transportation and the growth of cities and towns as a result of industrialization made it possible to promote gardening also as a commercial enterprise. The agricultural societies encouraged and provided financial aid for the organization of garden societies, of which there were about twenty by 1900. The garden schools of the Royal Academy of Agriculture, the Academy of Science, and the Alnarp and Ultuna schools trained master gardeners, who travelled from farm to farm giving instruction in the planting of trees, shrubbery, vegetables and flowers, and in the general care of gardens. From the experimental fields of the garden societies and the agricultural societies, it was possible for farmers to purchase at a nominal price or even to secure free of charge not only seeds for plants but also smaller trees and shrubbery. In one province, from 1886 to 1890, one society distributed 14,000 fruit trees. Ten per cent of this number were outright gifts to 349 poor crofters, who also secured, free of charge, about 1,400 bushes.

The agricultural societies also encouraged landscape gardening around railroad stations. These landscaped grounds, which in reality became small parks, made a deep impression upon the people and during the eighties they were the only spots illustrating the skill and art of the landscape gardener. They soon had competition in the grounds around the public schools, which the agricultural societies tried, not without some success, to turn into miniature garden schools. To stimulate further an interest in gardening, the societies offered annual prizes in horticulture. They also combined their program with a constantly growing interest in bee culture and the production of poultry.

Before 1880 Swedish farmers had neglected poultry as

a source of income. After this date, however, agricultural societies enthusiastically encouraged the raising of geese and chickens, trying in this way to create for the farmer additional income through the development of a small poultry business.

The development of by-products on the farms was particularly significant because the old home crafts had been given a death blow by the growth of the factory system. State and provincial officials joined with the leaders of the Royal Academy of Agriculture and provincial societies in expressing regrets, not so much over the loss of revenue for the farmers as for the loss of an art so closely identified with the Swedish peasantry. The decline of the home craft industry had been very gradual over several decades. The government and the agricultural societies had spent lavishly but in vain to preserve a "dying culture." The only measure of success they achieved was the preservation of the old peasant art in schools and as an "art of home craft" rather than a peasant craft.

The main contributions of the Royal Academy of Agriculture and the provincial societies in educational work were in the field of scientific farming, more extensive use of farm machinery, rotation of crops, development of the dairy industry, and improved grain production. This work of the agricultural educational agencies was very helpful and timely because emigration to America and the shift of rural labor into Swedish towns and cities created a shortage of help and increased wages, making the farmer more conscious of labor-saving devices and more appreciative of the value of gardens and methods of improving production.

In 1878 Sweden imported 4,279 farm machines including 539 threshing machines, 709 field rakes, and 28 steam engines. Before 1890 the use of farm machinery had been limited for the most part to southern and central parts of Sweden, but after 1900 modern farm implements had reached the northern provinces. Most of the implements used in Sweden had been imported from America, but when it was discovered that American implements were constructed for American use and were not well adapted to the nature of European farming, the growth of Sweden's own farm implement industry developed on a larger scale. Swedish industries, instead of inventing entirely new machines, confined themselves to the improvement and adaptation of the American models to Swedish conditions. American plows made by John Deere, Oliver, and others could be used in Sweden only to a limited extent. American harvesting machines offered greater difficulties. They could be used successfully in America where little value was placed on straw, but would be ruinous to the Swedish farmer who could not waste anything. The heavy cost of more complicated types of farm machinery presented another problem which was in part solved by the organization of cooperative purchasing societies among the farmers. By 1914 expensive farm machinery was, through these cooperatives, available even to many small farmers.

Dairy farming began gradually in the last half of the nineteenth century to crowd grain production. Ever since 1840 the Royal Academy of Agriculture had encouraged dairy farming, and the government had granted special concessions to large estates engaged in livestock breeding. Special dairy schools were founded, and the government fostered the establishment of creameries, using teachers from Denmark where dairy farming had made more rapid strides than in Sweden. Progress was, however, very slow. This was partly because the large livestock estates stressed pure breeds, and the study of the adaptability of breeds imported from England, Holland, and elsewhere, required much time. It was crossbreeding that eventually provided a breed suitable for greater milk production in Sweden.

Livestock breeding depended upon sufficient feed for cattle, and the feed supply could be increased only by scientific care of the farm, rotation of crops, and more careful attention to hay production, pasturage, barns, and fertilizer. A change could not take place in a decade or even in a couple of decades. The farmers had to be convinced that the maintenance of twenty cows on a farm of 100 acres might be impractical without rotation of crops and scientific fertilizing. The tendency was to keep too many cows and to starve them when feed was scarce and costly during the winter, with the result that milk production was kept at a minimum. Gustav de Laval's invention of the cream separator in 1877 was perhaps of considerable importance in finally bringing about a broad intensification of dairy farming.

Though agricultural colleges and other schools stimulated an interest in scientific farming, their influence for a long time was evident principally on the larger farms, while it was the small farm owner who needed help most. In order to reach the small farm owner, the agricultural societies used a novel method. Industrious young owners of small farms who showed an interest in scientific farming were singled out from time to time and offered an opportunity to study scientific farming with expenses paid by the agricultural societies. Some of these young men were sent to Denmark to study dairy farming.

The development of the dairy industry in its broad, inclusive phases is an interesting chapter in Swedish history. It involves the controversial problem of the relative virtues of dairy farming and grain farming in the light of growing market possibilities for milk, butter, cheese and by-products of dairy farming. The problem is international in its ramifications, involving questions of export and import and national self-sufficiency. It is closely related to war and connected problems. The government, the Royal Academy of Agriculture, and the provincial agricultural societies placed continually greater stress upon dairy farming. If tariff protection had not modified and tempered this program, it might have been disastrous for Sweden during World War I, for Sweden had built its agricultural program on a peace economy.

The increased tariff protection for grain producers modified this peace economy, and created a stability which was wholesome in reacting against the propaganda for dairy farming. After 1890 agricultural educational agencies deplored the tariff protection since it encouraged a slovenly and careless use of the soil. This was true in part, but what appealed most to these agencies was the production of articles for export. These articles the dairy farms could provide in butter, pork, and beef, while the grain farmers needed artificial protection even to maintain a share of the domestic market. Many students of the problem thought that Sweden should import cheap grain and cheap feed, thus giving cheap bread to the entire population, including the farmers, while reaping the profits of an ever-growing export demand for dairy products. Corn could be imported for the feeding of pigs, cheap oats for the cattle, and grain for the people. Hay and alfalfa and fat cattle would enrich both the soil and the farmers of Sweden, the principal profit deriving from export of dairy products. Such a farm economy program, already characteristic of Denmark, was, however, entirely dependent upon peacetime conditions.

The results of vigorous propaganda by dairy farming can best be seen not in the increase in the number of cows, but in increased production of fodder. If hay and other fodder are taken as the index to the change which took place in Sweden, it appears that the trend toward dairy production from 1885 to 1905 was twice as rapid as from 1865 to 1885. Furthermore, beef production nearly doubled between 1870 and 1913 to reach 136,000 tons, pork production tripled to exceed 107,000 tons, and milk production doubled to exceed 3,320,000 tons. In 1913 Sweden was able to supply most of its own fodder needs, importing only ten per cent of its total consumption. Butter was exported to the extent of 41,000,000 crowns. The export of pork exceeded Sweden's import of pork by 5,500,000 crowns.

After 1900 the private creameries began to notice the effect of the hand separator as well as competition from the cooperative creameries in their business. Hand separators enabled farmers to make their own butter, eliminating the middleman's profit. Middleman profits were reduced further by the growth of cooperatives which sprang up rapidly as a result of the shortsighted policies of private creamery owners, who frequently gave the farmer short weight and made unfair deductions. By 1914 cooperative creameries were rapidly beginning to displace the private ones.

The growth of the dairy industry required measures for sanitation control, and in 1898 the first milk control station was founded. The chief aim of milk control stations was to improve the quality of milk rather than the quantity, and records were kept in order to advise the farmer which cows should be used for breeding purposes. In 1897 state inspection of livestock was inaugurated to check the spread of tuberculosis and the hoof and mouth disease among cattle. In 1898, after the adoption of the pure food laws, inspection was extended to slaughterhouses. The emphasis on cleanliness and quality could not help influencing the owners of private creameries in their stress on sanitation, an attitude which the farmers did not always appreciate.

Agricultural societies stressed the manufacturing of both cheese and butter, but the risks involved in the manufacturing of cheese were discouraging, and butter became by far the leading dairy product. Dairy farming might have progressed more rapidly if the farmers had not discovered that the dairy products were just as sensitive to world market conditions as grain. During the nineties there were numerous sharp fluctuations in the market value of dairy products. Furthermore, private creameries were dependent upon wholesale dealers for distribution of their goods, and both of these agencies were fighting a losing battle against the cooperative creameries. This was bound to have an adverse effect on the dairy industry.

The impressive export of butter was, therefore, not a true index of a stable growth of the dairy industry in Sweden. The farmers who made their own butter or sold milk to a private creamery, or belonged to a cooperative creamery association were not convinced that the agricultural societies had led them into a safer economy. Oleomargarine, which could be manufactured more cheaply than butter, was preferred by the laboring classes, and their use of margarine to a large extent made it possible for Sweden to export great quantities of butter.

Thus, certain natural forces had checked a change in Swedish agriculture and preserved Sweden as chiefly a grain-producing country instead of a dairy country. By 1900 rotation of crops had greatly reduced the wasteful method of letting fields lie fallow. Hay and fodder crops were allowed to rotate with grain and root crops. The rutabaga was important as feed for the cattle, and the planting of rutabagas, potatoes, or hay gave the soil a rest for grain production. Progress in grain farming owed as much to the cooperative movement as did the dairy industry. It was the organization of farmers' cooperative associations after 1895 that made possible the greater use of farm machinery by small farmers, as well as the collective purchase of artificial fertilizing material at lower prices.

Some scholars maintain that the increase in the amount of cultivated land is significant in explaining the increased productivity in the decades prior to 1914, and that the actual results of scientific farming are not very evident. They ignore the fact that the cultivation of new land was encouraged in less productive areas and that there was an actual substantial increase in the fertility of the soil.

One of the most important crops in Swedish agricultural economy is the sugar beet. Its cultivation was encouraged by the educational propaganda of agricultural societies, and in 1869 the government decided to encourage this industry by tariff protection. But in order to remove objections to the special favor granted, the government decided that after the benefits of protection had aided the industry for a few years, a special tax would be levied on sugar production. This tax went into effect in 1873 and amounted to one-fifth of the tariff duty. It was later changed in 1876 to two-fifths and in 1891 to one-half of the tariff duty. This protection stimulated the growth of a sugar trust in the most southern province of Sweden and caused a growing sentiment that the government must alter its sugar policy.

The arguments for such a change gained ground after a convention in Brussels in which Sweden participated. Sugar-producing countries agreed at this convention not to encourage unsound bounties for the export of sugar, and thus Sweden had no reason to protect the sugar industry from foreign competition benefiting from bounties. Sweden, reluctant to reduce the duty on sugar, which amounted to 17 öre per kilogram for refined sugar and 11.75 öre per kilogram for raw sugar, decided instead to tax both imported and domestic sugar at the rate of 13 öre per kilogram. This involved increased taxation on domestic sugar; but it increased home production, for it placed foreign competition at a great disadvantage. The Swedish Sugar Corporation grew wealthy and the public began to complain. In 1908 the government decided to reduce the tariff and increase the tax. The small competitors of the Sugar Corporation suffered and again the large corporation owners profited because they not only were refiners but also producers of raw sugar. In 1913 the government again reduced the tariff duty to 11 öre per kilogram on refined sugar and to 8 öre per kilogram on raw sugar. The refined sugar of the Swedish Sugar Corporation was taxed at 16 öre per kilogram while the competitors of this corporation were taxed only at 12 öre per kilogram. This unique piece of legislation is one of the most striking illustrations of a government's power to create and destroy. It proved to be an important step toward government control of the Swedish Sugar Corporation.

The growth of the Swedish Sugar Corporation represented another interesting development in Swedish agriculture, the acquisition of farms by corporations. This development was most serious however, in northern Sweden, where

47

the huge lumber corporations threatened the economic well-being of independent farmers and discouraged scientific farming. These corporations were not interested in farming, but rented out farms to tenants whose primary value was in providing cheap labor and in protecting the forests from fire. These tenants were not encouraged to exert themselves in improving the land, and their tenure was precarious. The danger of these corporations to agricultural development had long been realized, but it was not until 1906 that the purchase of land in the northern provinces by corporations was restricted by law.

In spite of these developments, Swedish agriculture continued to be dominated by a class of small farm proprietors. In 1880 about 80 per cent of the farms were owned by farmers cultivating no more than 60 acres each. This situation has remained almost unchanged. At the beginning of World War I, there were not more than 106,000 persons who could call themselves country squires or country gentlemen out of an agricultural population of about 2,300,000. On the other hand, there were 1,400,000 who belonged to the class of small farm owners, 283,000 tenants, and 369,000 agricultural laborers. The fact that the percentage of independent farmers did not decline with the growth of corporation ownership of land can only be explained by the government policy of encouraging the cultivation of new land and by the breaking up of the large ancestral estates. By 1907 one authority stated that only a few of the old country estates belonged to the original family owners. The nonentailed estates owned by the nobles had been largely sacrificed in a number of agricultural crises in the nineteenth century. In some instances these estates were divided and sold to farmers. In other cases they were bought by newly-rich merchants, who sold parts of the estate or rented out all or part of it to tenants, while they themselves retained the old mansions or manor houses for summer homes.

According to law, the nobles were privileged to dispose

of their entailed estates if they could prove that the transfer of the entailment to other property and other investments did not endanger the value of the estate. Entailment could thus be transferred from one estate to another in the country, from land or rural property to city property, and to other forms of investments. Before World War I many of the nobles had transferred their entailment rights from large country estates to other forms of investment, especially to city properties. The rural estates were thus freed and could be disposed of the same as any other large country estates.

Sweden's rural life changed greatly in a century. Improvements in farming had often placed the farmer in debt. How serious these debts were cannot be determined, but in 1895 the value of mortgages on rural property was estimated to be nearly 40 per cent of the actual tax-assessed value of the property. This was considerably less than the mortgage burdens resting on city properties, which exceeded 54 per cent. The value of mortgages was based on taxation value which was usually very conservative. A more accurate estimate would be to reduce the percentages by anywhere from 10 to 30 per cent. This would make the mortgages seem very conservative, and, as indebtedness rested chiefly on the large farms, would indicate the sound financial position of the small farm owner. But when mortgage values increased from 1,288,654,659 crowns in 1902 to 2,191,727,003 crowns in 1912 such a statement must be modified. The value of rural property could not in 1912 have exceeded much over 6,000,000,000 crowns. In 1908 the value of the agricultural production was placed at 800,700,000 crowns. In spite of the fact that farming represented the largest investment of any industry, its annual production was less than that represented by mining and manufacturing, which in 1908 was estimated at 1,655,900,000 crowns.

CHAPTER IV

SWEDISH INDUSTRY ON THE EVE OF WORLD WAR I

A T THE OUTBREAK of World War I, Swedish industry had largely assumed its modern characteristics. For three decades industrialization had proceeded rapidly. Sweden's export trade doubled within a period of 13 years before the war, and the value of her manufactured goods increased twentyfold between 1870 and 1914. In 1873 Swedish mines and factories employed only about 82,000 workers, while in 1914 they employed nearly 350,000. In 1870 Sweden had a population of 4,169,000, of which 3,629,000 were classified as rural. The capital city at that time had a population of only 169,000, and Gothenburg was proud of the fact that its population of 76,000 entitled it to claim that it was nearly twice as large as Sweden's third city, Malmö. Forty years later all three cities had doubled in population.

Yet many of the factors which determine the location of industries, such as access to raw materials, transportation facilities, and skilled labor, had caused Sweden's industrialization to be essentially rural rather than urban. The introduction of steam and, much later, of electricity made it possible for industries to free themselves of their dependence upon waterpower, and made possible a wider choice in the selection of factory sites. Cheap labor and lower taxes encouraged the location of industries in rural sections. Around these factories centers of population soon grew into villages and towns more urban than rural in character, though still classified in official statistics as rural.

In spite of the fact that Swedish industries were more decentralized than industries in countries possessing coal, there was nevertheless some centralization in certain industries. The match industry was largely confined to Jönköping

51

and Tidaholm; the textiles to Norrköping, Gothenburg, Borås and Alingsås; gin manufacturing to the province of Kristianstad; sugar refineries to Malmöhuslän; machine shops to Stockholm and Eskilstuna, the last also famed for its cutlery; electrical appliances to Västerås and Stockholm; iron works and foundries to Stockholm and the provinces of Södermanland and Gävleborg; paper and wood pulp to the province of Värmland: sawmills to the coast of Bothnia with Sundsvall as the center; iron mining to Norrbotten and Kopparberg; tobacco manufacturing to Stockholm, Gothenburg, and Malmö; the glass industry to Kronoberg, Värmland, and Älvsborg counties; cement making to Gotland, Öland, and the eastern shore of Lake Vänern; shoe factories to Stockholm, Örebro, Vännersborg, and Malmö; and fishing to the county of Gothenburg and Bohuslän.

In 1908 Sweden exported goods valued at 482,000,000 crowns and imported goods valued at 608,900,000 crowns. In 1913 imports and exports had increased to 817,300,000 crowns and 846,500,000 crowns respectively. Between 1861 and 1910 exports exceeded imports only during two years, 1865 and 1870. Great Britain was Sweden's best customer, with Germany a close second, these two nations buying more from Sweden than Denmark, France, Norway, Russia, and the United States together. Great Britain took most of the Swedish pig iron and steel, wood pulp and paper, butter, pork, glass, matches, and bought more lumber from Sweden than did Germany and France together. Germany took nearly all of the export of iron ore, cream, and berries. Norway took most of Swedish livestock, beef, and machines.

Sweden, in turn, purchased most of its goods from Germany, which provided her with machines, grain, fertilizing material, and hides. Great Britain provided Sweden with coal, iron rails, and ships. The United States supplied corn, cotton, fruit, tobacco and oil. Denmark sent eggs; Norway, fish; and Brazil, coffee; while France and Russia provided Sweden with the important product, oil cake, a cattle feed.

Swedish industry and agriculture were very dependent upon peacetime conditions. Interference with the imports of coal, oil, and cotton would play havoc with Swedish manufacturing and transportation, while grain imports were also essential. Only about half of Sweden's grain requirements was domestically produced, and the Swedish dairy industry was dependent upon the importation of cattle feed, especially of oil cake.

In 1914 Swedish industries could be classified into five groups, the most important being that of the production of food. Specialization had reached a high degree, flour mills and the sugar industry being responsible for half of the value of the production of food-related industries.

Second in importance was lumber. This branch of industry was even more specialized than the food-related industries, the sawmills producing more than half of the estimated value of lumber production. The sawmills also provided more employment than any other industry. Wood pulp and matches were also important in the lumber industry. The manufacture of paper was included in the "chemical industries," which, though important by 1911, was not counted among the five major industries.

Third and fourth in importance were the textile industry and the iron and metal industry. The fifth largest division was formed by the machine industry and such related industries as the manufacture of tools, implements, weapons, and shipbuilding. The growth of this industry flourished especially because of tariff protection granted it during 1888 and 1892. Within it thrived numerous large manufacturing corporations which had developed substantial exports, though the industry aimed essentially to supply the domestic market.

The growth of Swedish industries may be attributed in general to a worldwide economic prosperity, checked only by minor depressions, over a period of more than two decades prior to the outbreak of World War I. The more immediate factors which contributed to industrial prosperity in Sweden were improved means of transportation, sound banking and credit institutions, economies achieved through mergers of corporations, the organization of cartels, great natural resources of lumber and iron, and a financially sound government unencumbered by war debts.

Sweden's industrial development during this period was accompanied by corresponding advances in the field of transportation, communication, and banking. In 1891, the farmers were relieved of their responsibility for road improvement which had rested unfairly upon them as a class, and the kingdom was divided into road districts. The construction and maintenance of roads was placed on a modern tax-supported basis. Many of the county and major parish roads were converted into highways, in which the state shared the cost with local governments. This reorganization was necessary as a result of greater use of roads leading into cities, to railroad stations, and to harbors. Heavier traffic necessitated more substantial construction, stone being used to a considerable extent after 1890.

The competition between state and private telephone companies appeared at first to be on an even basis, but the state soon began to absorb private competitors. In 1885 the total mileage of telephone lines was only 2,173 kilometers, while in 1900 it had reached 111,986, of which the state owned more than half. After 1895 the state entered on an extensive program of purchasing private companies' properties as well as greatly expanding its already existing service, and, by the outbreak of World War I, the state had a virtual monopoly of the telephone system, as it did of the telegraph system, which had developed along with the railroads.

In 1880 not even the southern and central provinces of Sweden were provided with adequate railroad facilities. At that time the total railroad mileage amounted to 5,876 kilometers, of which 1,956 were state owned. In 1910 the total mileage had increased to 13,829 kilometers, of which the state owned 4,418 kilometers. The increase of state railroad mileage was largely due to the construction of the main trunk line in the northern part of Sweden and the purchase of financially embarrassed private roads.

The most interesting venture in state railroad building was the decision of the government to construct a railroad connecting the iron fields of Loussavaara and Kirunavaara with the Baltic port city of Luleå on one side, and the Norwegian border on the other, i.e. to Riksgränsen, from which point a railroad would be constructed in Norway to the harbor city of Narvik. By 1896 the government was securing a substantial revenue from the Gällivare-Luleå railroad. The cost of construction of a road beyond Gällivare to the richer iron fields and finally to the boundary seemed prohibitive, and the government hesitated. The corporation which owned the iron fields of Loussavaara and Kirunavaara sought to secure a concession for the construction of a private line, offering in return for this privilege to donate 2,000,000 crowns toward the fortification of Norrland. The question was finally solved by an agreement between the state and the private mining corporation that the state would construct the railroad on the condition that the corporation guarantee the government a minimum amount of freight annually to allow the state an interest of at least 3.8 per cent on its investment. The state was thus saved from any possible loss and forced the corporation in addition to guarantee a net income of 4 per cent on the state investment of the older Gällivare-Luleå railroad. This was to prevent the export of iron ore entirely from Narvik, Norway, which was closer to the iron fields than Luleå.

The most significant railroad projects in the years prior to World War I were the construction of the Inland Railroad Line connecting Gällivare with Östersund and Gothenburg, the connecting of the Northern Trunk Line with the Finnish railroad system, the connecting of the Swedish system with the German railroads through the Trälleborg-Sassnitz ferry service, and the electrification of 130 kilometers of the railroad line from Kiruna to Riksgränsen. Transportation facilities were also improved by providing double tracks on lines most heavily engaged in traffic and the use of heavier railroad rails.

Improvements in ocean and inland waterway transportation were no less significant. From 1900 to 1914 the merchant marine was modernized. In 1870 the merchant marine of Sweden had a tonnage of 346,000, comprised largely of sailing vessels. In 1908 the tonnage of the merchant ships had been increased to 770,000 tons, of which sailing vessels accounted for only a small percentage. In 1903 the government established a credit fund for the encouragement of shipbuilding, which soon entered into a healthy period of aggressive expansion. In 1904 the Trans-Atlantic Steamship Company and the Nordstjernan Steamship Company were organized. Three years later the Swedish-East Asiatic Line was founded, and in 1914 and 1915 the Swedish-American-Mexico Line and the Swedish-North American Steamship Company began operations.

The banking system received a severe test in the fall of 1907, when a worldwide depression hit Sweden. During the last part of 1907 and the first months of 1908, a number of business failures revealed scandalous irregularities, manipulations, and outright thefts in many business enterprises. There was no panic or rush on the banks, but the crisis revealed certain shortcomings in the banking system. Not having developed as rapidly as Swedish industries, it was inadequate for the expansion required by industrial growth. The National Bank had been too conservative in issuing paper money. The private banks had heavy obligations abroad, and gold left the country until an actual money shortage existed.

As the National Bank had become a central bank, or a bank of banks, by the law of 1897, it was found necessary that it should come to the rescue of private banking institutions hard pressed for payments on obligations from abroad. Hence, in 1907 the *Riksdag* authorized the National Bank to secure a foreign loan of 50,000,000 crowns. By 1908 the National Bank was able to loan to private banks, and the crisis passed. Two private banks that had been too liberal with credit were reorganized, and their difficulties caused other banks to consider seriously some means by which they would be able more adequately to serve the needs of industries. A large number resorted to merger as a solution, while Stockholm's Enskilda Bank decided in favor of increased capitalization.

These developments in banking are best illustrated by some statistics. In 1900 there were twenty-six private banks with a capital of 91,912,600 crowns and reserve funds valued at 38,084,000 crowns. Fourteen years later the number of private banks had been reduced to fourteen and capitalization increased to 105,250,000 crowns, while the reserve funds had nearly doubled. The number of commercial banks or corporation banks increased rapidly until they numbered sixty-one in 1913 with a capital of 289,002,723 crowns and reserve funds valued at 160,594,178 crowns. On the eve of World War I the private banks had reduced the amount of their debts abroad to 9,700,000 crowns, a 50,000,000 crown reduction from the 1908 figure. The National Bank, on the other hand, had assets abroad valued at 79,500,000 crowns. All the banks were in a strong liquid financial position in spite of their increased volume of business and the extension to industry of long-term credit.

As the banks experienced growth and established themselves in a stronger financial position through increased capitalization and mergers, industrial corporations achieved important economies and increased efficiency through the growth of "big business." Though the Corporation Law of 1895 greatly encouraged the organization of corporations, some of the industrial giants of 1913 had been in existence more than twenty-five years. The giant corporations, with a capital of over 5,000,000 crowns, were: Bofors Gullspång (founded in 1896), Fagersta Bruk (1873), Bofors (1880), Ljusne Waxna (1881), Luossavaara Kirunavaara (1890), Sandviken Iron Works (1896), Stora Kopparbergs Bergslag (1888), Trafikaktiebolaget Grängesberg Oxelösund (1896),

Uddeholm (1870), and Wargön (1888). Several of these corporations had in 1913 a capitalization of from 7,000,000 crowns to 15,000,000 crowns. The largest of them were Trafikaktiebolaget Grängesberg Oxelösund and Luossavaara Kurunavaara, with capitalizations respectively of 99,792,000 crowns and 80,000,000 crowns.

In 1905 corporations owned 15.4 per cent of all properties in rural and urban districts. The largest property owners were Stora Kopparbergs Bergslag Corporation, with properties valued at 22,750,000 crowns, and Korsnäs Sawmill Corporation, with properties valued at 13,500,000 crowns. In 1900 only 53 corporations owned properties valued at over 2,000,000 crowns, but five years later this was true of 88 corporations. Another very interesting development was the control through stock ownership of one corporation over several others. Thus the Trafikaktiebolaget Grängesberg Oxelösund owned 39,996 of the 80,000 outstanding shares in the Luossavaara Kirunavaara, 5,996 of 6,000 outstanding shares in Gällivare Mining Corporation, and 556 out of the total of 560 shares in the Grängesberg Mining Corporation. A similar development of a holding company controlling numerous related industries occurred also with the Uddeholm Corporation.

Integration of Swedish industries was further stimulated by the close-working relationships of the major industries. Iron works were dependent upon mines, but they were also in need of charcoal. Sawmills and wood pulp industries did not at first compete with one another, as wood pulp industries used material unsuitable for sawmills. They did, however, use material that was important in the production of charcoal. The possibility of waste by the sawmill corporation of material that could be used for both wood pulp and charcoal was always present, while the competition of the iron works and wood pulp industry tended to make the cost of the raw material needed by the iron works and the wood pulp industry high. It was, therefore, natural for an iron works corporation to purchase large forests, develop a sawmill industry,

58

a wood pulp industry, and a charcoal industry. Competition would be eliminated and every possible use could be made of the forests. By purchasing the mines and the forests, the iron works safeguarded itself against the rise in the price of raw material and also achieved diversification. The iron and lumber industries were much more sensitive to world economic conditions than the wood pulp and paper industries. Thus, by 1914 the tendency in Sweden was toward consolidation of sawmill, wood pulp, paper, and charcoal under the management of a giant corporation, which might also be successfully extended toward control of transportation.

Another form of merger was that which involved vertical combination, most common in the machine, match, and electrical industries. Vertical combinations aimed at control of partially fabricated goods needed by these industries. A third form of combination, called horizontal, combined corporations producing the same goods. This form of combination reduced employment through reduction in the number of plants. The most striking example of this form of combination prior to the World War were the larger trusts such as the Swedish Match Corporation, Grängesberg Corporation, Höganäs Corporation, the Swedish Roller Bearing Corporation, the Sugar Corporation, the United Canning Corporation, Stockholm Breweries, and United Knitting Mills. Sometimes one corporation, such as Holmen's Bruk, exemplified all three forms of combinations.

The government encouraged rather than discouraged the formation of cartels, in order to make possible more efficient and economical operation. Technical research aimed at increased production for export was also encouraged by the state. It was for this purpose that the government as early as 1747 founded the Iron Bureau. In 1914 this association had a fund of 10,000,000 crowns for the encouragement of research aimed at greater efficiency in the mining and iron industries. In 1887 the government backed the founding of the Swedish Export Association, which received subsidies

from the state. Two years later the Swedish Iron Works Commercial Association was founded.

Although the original purpose of the last two organizations was greater efficiency, they formed a type of organization which might be called a cartel. The elimination of competition became the chief aim of such cartels as the Swedish Wood Products Export Association, the Swedish Cotton Mills Association, the Swedish Cotton Spinning Association, the Swedish Manufacturers' Association and numerous others. The Swedish Manufacturers' Association, then as now, encouraged legislation to promote the growth of industries. To it the government submitted all proposed legislation affecting industry, and the Association in turn suggested legislation to the government. The work of the Association was divided into highly specialized units with experts in charge of each bureau.

The first electrical rolling mill in the world was established in Sweden in 1874. Less than seven years later, Jonas Wenström was able to construct a dynamo for direct current; and in 1890 he patented his three-phase motor and power transmission. Among the foremost pioneers in the telephone industry were Lars Magnus Ericsson and Henrik Tore Cedergren. As early as 1894 Sweden began to export electrical apparatus, and by the outbreak of World War I, the electrical industry had assumed an important place. By 1915, 59,577 horsepower electrically driven motors were used in mining and 78,192 horsepower motors in iron works and iron manufacture. This reduced the number of water turbines, water wheels and steam engines and increased the horsepower. The inability to provide electrical power immediately to all industries handicapped what would otherwise have been a much more rapid change toward a greater use of electricity. Only the larger, favorably situated corporations could build their own power stations. Small industries made greater use of oil and gas motors. Though the Swedish electrical appliance industry was constantly growing it was unable to satisfy the domestic demand.

The more extensive use of electricity again depended upon action by the government. In 1885 the Swedish city of Härnösand became the first city in Europe to introduce a system of electrical lighting. In 1896 twenty Swedish cities enjoyed this convenience and the demand throughout Sweden was for more power stations. This demand could not be met except by the government, which took the initiative and established large power stations at Trollhättan in 1906 and at Älvkarleby and Porjus in 1915.

Technical improvements were soon noticeable in all Swedish industries, and competition increased, especially in the world lumber market. Although the United States and Germany had led in experimenting in chemical preparation of wood pulp, it was a Swede, Carl Daniel Ekman, who achieved the most important success in this field. His discovery of the sulphite method laid the foundation for an ever-increasing export of wood pulp from Sweden.

This industry developed, in Sweden as elsewhere, along two lines, the mechanical and the chemical. More vigorous government control of the natural resources through the preservation of forests stimulated labor-saving devices and less waste. The preservation methods adopted by the state were essentially of two types, extension of state-owned forests and control of private forests. By 1911 the so-called Crown Parks included 4,636,779 hectares. Other types of state and public forests included nearly as many hectares. In 1896 a committee was appointed by the government to study the possibilities of state control of the forests because exploitation of the forest resources by the sawmill industry was proceeding at an alarming rate. The committee made a thorough investigation, requiring nearly four years, and after the government had carefully considered the recommendation of the committee, it recommended a series of laws, which the *Riksdag* approved.

These laws, effective in 1905, provided for state inspection of private forests, and exploitation which endangered growth of young trees was forbidden, except when forest land was turned into productive agricultural fields or building lots. Private owners were forbidden to rent their forest land to corporations for a period longer than five years. A Board of Forest Control was created for each province to report violations of the law and to stimulate an interest in better care of private forests. The expense connected with the work of the boards was to be secured from fees levied on lumber and wood pulp export.

As the forests owned by cities were usually poorly cared for, the laws of 1903 placed all city-owned forests under the direct supervision of the Bureau of Forestry, and the government gave warning to the cities that this might be a direct step toward state assumption of ownership if the cities did not take better care of them. Inasmuch as the laws covered all provinces not included in earlier legislation, all the forests of Sweden were thus placed under state protection.

Gradually the reckless exploitation of forests subsided. Corporations became convinced that the government would never be ready by 1905 to enforce the laws, and that the period of grace would be extended. However, the forest master and his assistants worked feverishly, and the period of grace was not extended, though in 1909 some of the shortcomings of the laws of 1903 were removed. Sawmills and wood pulp industries painted in the provincial press a dark picture of industrial stagnation and great unemployment, in which starvation would replace plenty. However, government paternalism had gradually silenced the voice of the extreme individualist.

Though Sweden produced in 1890 only 1.6 per cent of the total world production of iron ore, she mined 7,554,026 tons of iron ore in 1913, amounting to 4.5 per cent of total world production. This was particularly remarkable because the United States, Germany, France, England, Russia and Spain had during the same years developed their iron resources extensively. However, Swedish iron ore production differed from that of the United States, England, France, and Germany in that since 1882 the mining of iron ore in Sweden was for export purposes. This was due chiefly to the fact that the discovery of the Thomas-Gilchrist process made it possible for all countries to develop low-quality ore.

Swedish foundries also adjusted themselves to new methods. The introduction of the Bessemer and Martin processes as well as the Thomas-Gilchrist method eliminated smaller foundries, which were unable to meet the heavy cost of adaptation. Successful experiments were made with electrical furnaces in the production of pig iron and bar iron. Between 1902 and 1914 about a half dozen important electrical foundries had been set up. In 1902 a blast furnace was successfully constructed for the smelting of slag of a low iron percentage. By 1913 this method was perfected to such a degree that great savings were achieved in fuel consumption. Meanwhile, the number of blast furnaces decreased sharply, while production increased. Between 1891 and 1895 about 150 blast furnaces were in operation, while in 1914 there were only 116. In 1840 the capacity of production of a blast furnace was about 400 to 500 tons and in 1914 around 6,000 tons. Yet Sweden had not kept pace with the other iron-producing countries as a producer of pig and bar iron. Whatever advantages Sweden had in the bar and pig iron production in 1914 was in the greater purity of the Swedish product.

In the manufacturing industries, however, such inventors as Gustav de Laval, Gustav Dalén, and Sven Winqvist provided Sweden with such important articles of export as the separator, the pilot light, and roller bearings, while L. M. Ericsson's genius provided Sweden with telephone apparatus for export.

The Swedish government's financial soundness was also an important factor in the growth of her industry. The total national debt at the end of 1913 was only 648,300,000 crowns, all of which was invested in productive enterprises. Taxes could not be called heavy, and whatever evils the encouragement of trusts and cartels by the government might have produced were already being checked by 1914 through the growth of the cooperative movement.

Though the early attitude of labor unions in general toward cooperatives was, to say the least, equivocal, it was the labor unions which successfully launched the modern cooperative movement. Encouraged by a period of prosperity and by the Corporation Law of 1895, which more clearly defined associations, prominent labor leaders took the initiative which in 1899 led to a Congress of Cooperative Societies. The Congress resulted in the organization of the Consumers' Cooperative Association.

The man who was largely responsible for the calling of the Congress and the successful organization of a national association was Axel Rylander of Stockholm. Though he was prominent in Social Democratic circles, the cooperative movement and the Social Democratic party had little in common at this time. In 1908 at the Congress of the Consumers' Cooperative Association the membership fee was fixed at 50 crowns, which represented one share in the cooperative society and entitled the holder to one vote. The profit of the cooperatives was to be used as follows: 10 per cent for inventories, 15 per cent for a reserve fund, 2½ per cent for propaganda, 5 per cent to be distributed among members, and the rest to be distributed on the basis of purchases. The aim of the consumers' cooperatives was to reduce the prices of food and other necessities.

Another form of cooperative, encouraged by the agricultural societies, had the opposite aim, namely, to increase producer's profits. At first, the tendency among the farmers' cooperatives was to organize into provincial associations, but in 1905, upon the initiative of the governor of Gefleborg, a National Association of Farmers was organized. The societies forming this national association were not all producers' cooperatives, but they were more important than the purchasing cooperatives. It is, however, dangerous to overemphasize the importance of the cooperative movement prior to World War I.

Chapter V

SOCIAL CONDITIONS IN 1914

In contrast with the interest that the Swedish government showed in the advancement of agriculture and industry, social legislation, in the years preceding World War I, was permitted to lag. In 1914 Sweden was far behind Germany and England in this area. Whatever concessions labor had secured had been achieved through the sheer strength of their organization and popular fear of socialism. The Factory Inspection Law of 1889 provided for only three state inspectors, and was limited to such industries as endangered the life of the worker. The Accident Insurance Law of 1901 did not compel employers to insure their employees in either the State Insurance Institute created in 1902 or in private insurance companies. Many employers refused to insure their workers, and for workers to collect damages through the courts was exceedingly difficult as it had to be proved without doubt that the accidents were caused by the direct negligence of the employer.

As the public school system improved and public school officials were able to enforce the Compulsory Education Act of 1842, the child labor legislation of 1881 became reasonably effective. A law of 1909 forbade night work by women in certain industries. The most progressive piece of labor legislation, however, was that which in 1906 provided for state subsidization and control of employment agencies. The government, under this law, assumed expenses connected with finding employment for the unemployed. As industrialization proceeded, it was discovered that modern industries were more or less seasonal, and through the government-controlled employment agencies it became possible to provide unemployed workers in one district with employment in another where there was a scarcity of labor. The government's subsidized agencies made no charge for their services. In this respect, the law of 1906 was "humane," but when employment implied the severance, if only temporarily, of family ties, the charity toward labor seemed less significant, and one might justly wonder if the employers were not better served by the government's policy than were the employees.

Labor unrest was in no small degree stimulated by the Åkarp Law of 1899, which in an ingenious way supplemented the shortcomings of an infamous gag law in 1889. The Åkarp Law overshadowed all labor legislation prior to 1912. It provided penal servitude up to two years for anyone attempting, by violence or threat of violence, to force workers to participate in strikes or to prevent workers from accepting employment.

The government finally decided in 1912 that something must be done to soothe the wounds of labor. A Social Board was created, providing for cooperation of industrialists and workers, as well as the supervision of labor legislation and its enforcement. The Social Board was to assume responsibility in factory inspection, supervise the work of the employment agencies to make them more effective, and enforce the Accident Compensation Law of 1901. The Board had nothing to do with arbitration in the strictest sense, because an earlier law providing for conciliators in labor disputes was not compulsory. Though in 1912 labor distrusted the Social Board, the possibilities of the Social Board as an agency in creating a better understanding between labor and employers was present.

A program of old age and invalid pensions was not adopted until 1913, almost three decades after Sven Adolf Hedin had suggested such a program for workers. Hedin had been greatly interested in a state accident and old-age pension system similar to that provided in Germany. As finally adopted to go into effect at the beginning of 1914, the program differed greatly from the original one proposed by Hedin in 1884. Hedin had aimed merely at the extension of insurance to the laboring class. The Old Age Pension System

66

of 1913 provided for a national insurance or "folk" pension for poor and rich alike. This shift to a more inclusive insurance program seemed necessitated by the fact that it would be exceedingly difficult to define labor, and many citizens who were not technically "employees" had smaller financial resources than skilled workers. National insurance against permanent disability and old age had to rest entirely upon individual fees and government contributions. Since this created an injustice for those unable to pay their fees, local governments were made responsible for the payments of such dues.

The Old Age Pension Law was in this respect an extension of local poor relief obligations. As such it provided the communities with a form of insurance against mounting costs of poor relief, for the contributions of local communities to the pension fund were matched by contributions by the state. The advantages of government contributions to increase the value of each individual's payment toward the fund made it necessary for the government to limit the amount of not only the minimum but the maximum that each person was allowed to pay. Pension fees paid depended upon the amount that each individual had contributed and on the cost of living in the locality in which he lived. No matter how much the pensions varied, however, they were entirely inadequate.

Yet many people believed in 1913 that the government in removing the fear of destitution in old age had taken a step which would definitely discourage thrift. Remove the shame of charity and the fear of poverty, these people argued, and no one will save. Instead everyone will look to the state for a living. There is little doubt but that the pension law greatly stimulated improved care of the poor by communities. It was surely high time for these improvements, for a more haphazard system of poor relief institutions than that existing in Sweden could only be found in the more backward countries.

The idea of thrift, which must underlie any system of self-help, was encouraged also by the temperance movement.

It should not for a moment be thought that the interest of the Swedish government in temperance was based purely upon a form of idealism aimed at keeping the nation sober. The government encouraged sobriety in order to stimulate thrift.

Before 1900 the modern Swedish temperance movement had taken firm root, receiving its impulses largely from the United States. In 1887 the "Malinites" and the "Hickmanites" merged into a national organization, the International Order of Good Templars, with a membership of about sixty thousand. The merger was not a complete success, a group leaving this organization in 1888 to found the National Order of the Good Templars. Another group called just plain "Good Templars," received its inspiration from Swedish emigrants in America. In the early eighties the first Blue Ribbon Club was founded, also inspired by American influences. Prior to 1890 women had organized the White Ribbon or the Swedish Women's Temperance Society (W.C.T.U.). The growth of these organizations in the decade before the turn of the century was remarkable. The total membership of all temperance societies in 1895 was estimated at 201,564 or about 5 per cent of the entire population of Sweden. The growth was in no small part due to efforts by parents to interest their children in temperance, and to the spending by the government of small sums to spread temperance propaganda. The temperance movement created a temperance press of weekly and bimonthly publications.

All was not well, however. On the one hand, many objected to the indifference of the temperance societies toward religion. The old temperance movement in Sweden under the direction of Peter Wieselgren had had its roots in a religious revival. The various temperance organizations organized after 1880 had no message except that of temperance. Deeply religious people objected especially to the sponsoring of dances by temperance societies. Some believed, too, that the temperance societies should take an active part in politics, while others opposed any discussion of politics at temperance meetings. The questions of the relative values of temperance and abstinence and what constituted intoxicating drinks tended to spread disunity in the national organizations. The revival of the old Swedish Temperance Society (Moderation Society) made this question more real. It was politics on the other hand that caused the organization of the Temperance Order of Verdandi in 1896, a society with a dominant Social Democratic element.

In 1905 the government received 23,000,000 crowns in revenues from distillery taxes, 1 per cent of which was set aside for the cause of temperance. In addition to this direct tax on distilleries, the *Riksdag* in 1903 approved a special tax in the form of a sales tax on the producer, which must be paid prior to distribution. The state had also taken measures to prevent the sale of intoxicants to minors, had checked the abuse of sale of liquor through pharmacies, and had regulated the sale of liquor on ships sailing under the Swedish flag in Swedish waters. In 1904 the use of the postal service for the sale and distribution of liquor was forbidden. In 1905 the government decided to restrict the sale of liquor over the bar, reduced the number of hours for sale, lowered the content of alcohol to 35 per cent for distilled liquor, and limited the quantity that a person could purchase at one time for home consumption. The Gothenburg System, which permitted the distribution of liquor only among specially licensed companies, whose profits were limited and whose surplus earnings went to charity or education, had been introduced in a very large number of cities and communities. In 1905 this system was made compulsory throughout Sweden. In 1913 the state took complete charge of the sale of liquor, reimbursing cities, communities, and provinces for their losses. At this time, the *Riksdag* limited the amount of earnings that the state would secure through the sale of liquor to 41,900,000 crowns and decided that revenues beyond this amount should be used to combat drunkenness.

The continued financial support of the government was thus permanently assured the temperance movement. The temperance societies had, however, after 1895 developed considerable sentiment for total abstinence and for political action aimed at prohibition on a national scale. The Social Democrats, noticing that the prohibition program caused division within their party, finally discarded party leanings toward prohibition and expressed merely a rather vague sympathy for the cause of temperance.

The opposite was true of the Liberal Coalition party. It was a party based on social class, and the class it depended upon included civil servants, the white-collar group, and professional men. General political trends were such that the party would be swallowed up by either the Conservatives or the Social Democrats unless it found a firmer basis of support in society. Under the leadership of Staaff the party developed more and more into a temperance party in order to appeal to the strong free-church and temperance movements. This alliance of bureaucrats and professional men with temperance advocates and dissenters aroused considerable unrest within the party. In 1914 Staaff sought to secure the *Riksdag's* approval of local option, but resentment toward Staaff in the First Chamber more than objection to local option caused the effort to fail.

Since temperance and thrift are closely related to health, it might be said that it was the Board of Health which, at least in part, was responsible for the government's interest in the temperance movement. By 1914 the government had made great progress in checking the spread of contagious diseases. Hospital service, chiefly communal and provincial, had been brought within the reach of every citizen, and great improvement was made in the care of maternal cases and children. After 1885 the duties of the Board of Health were extended to include investigation of sanitation in food establishments, where conditions were found to be deplorable. Many restaurants, milk stations, bakeries, and slaughter houses were condemned as unfit for the distribution of food. Vigorous action to eliminate these conditions was not possible, however, until after the approval of the pure food laws by the *Riksdag* in 1898.

The work of the Board of Health was of necessity largely confined to cities prior to World War I. The greatest danger in the past had been the inability of the authorities to segregate victims of infectious diseases. By 1890 twenty smaller cities had built special infirmaries or hospitals, and in 1890 Stockholm began to build a hospital. By 1914 hospitals were to be found throughout Sweden.

In building resistance to disease, it was recognized that the proper care of children during adolescence was very important. The long, sunless winters and the crowded, unsanitary home conditions in the cities were detrimental to the health of thousands of children. Between 1890 and 1914, under the supervision of local school authorities, summer colonies were established to provide undernourished children an opportunity to enjoy the fresh country air, absorb sunshine, secure proper diet, and play. The summer colonies charged no fees, but the privilege to spend a summer at a colony was usually limited to those children whose poor health or stunted growth indicated improper care at home.

The maintenance of sanitation in cities had, prior to 1895, been turned over to private entrepreneurs. In 1895 the city of Malmö organized a Department of Sanitation, the city assuming complete charge of all matters dealing with sanitation. A sewage system and water pipes were laid, which overcame some of the worst problems. By 1914 nearly all cities had made great progress in improving their sanitary systems, assuming, as in Malmö, the direct charge of the problem.

Improvement in sanitation, better medical care, improved home conditions, and a better diet caused a sharp drop in the death rate. From 1871 to 1880 the death rate per 1,000 inhabitants was 18.27, while in the first decade of the twentieth century, it had dropped to 14.89. Though medicine and surgery usually get a lion's share of the credit for this remarkable improvement, the rise in living standards was also a vital factor.

Between 1880 and 1914 the old straw roofs on the homes of farmers began to disappear, until by 1914 such homes were rarely seen outside of the province of Skåne. Shingle and tile roofs went hand in hand with the introduction of iron stoves for heating and cooking purposes. The iron stove had found its way to almost every church by 1880, and it was no longer necessary for people to worship in entirely unheated buildings. In Skåne clay houses were supplanted by homes built with brick, and all new homes were made larger and airier. By 1914 many rural homes were painted a bright red color with white window frames. One of the reasons that red was used was because it was believed to be most practical and durable. Barns and sheds were painted to match the dwelling house. Attention was also given to landscaping, and where there had once been rocks and a few juniper bushes in the yards of farmhouses, there now were often shrubbery and flowers.

In cities improvements were probably even more noticeable. The problem of housing, which had been a serious one throughout the nineteenth century, became even greater with the influx of rural population to the cities in the last quarter of the century. This stimulated a building boom, but, as the demand for apartments increased faster than the supply, rents continued to rise.

In the late seventies and in the eighties, a group of civil servants and clerks with limited salaries decided to solve their own immediate problem of finding cheaper and better housing accommodations by organizing cooperative housing associations. These associations by 1885 owned sixty-four buildings in Stockholm, having a taxable value of 9,933,000 crowns. Similar organizations in Gothenburg owned thirty-nine homes or buildings valued at 725,100 crowns. The profits from home ownership, however, tempted many of these associations to deviate from their original purpose, and these became profit-making organizations. By 1890 this was true of all except one of thirty-five associations in Gothenburg, and also of a majority of the fifty-seven associations in Stockholm. The fact that the Workers' Building Association in Gothenburg had remained faithful to its original aim may in part be attributed to the fact that it was more truly an association of labor, securing funds for building purposes from the Gothenburg Savings Bank. This bank had set aside a special fund for the building of homes for workingmen, which the Workers' Building Association could avail itself of on condition that the bank would be guaranteed a return of four per cent on its fund. By 1891 this fund had existed for twenty years and had made possible the construction of fourteen buildings.

The close relationship between the Gothenburg Savings Bank and the Workers' Building Association was a development entirely independent of influences by such foreign cities as Marseilles, Lyons, and Strasbourg. But it was the Paris Fair of 1889 that called attention to both the progress and the need for better homes for the families of workers. In conjunction with the fair a World Housing Congress was held expressing hope that savings banks and insurance companies would cooperate in making possible cooperative workingmen's building associations.

Sweden was sensitive to new impressions. Dr. Elis Heyman, founder of the Health Society in Stockholm, had since 1885 been deeply impressed by the relationship between sanitary living conditions and health. Unfortunately, Heyman died in 1890 and six years elapsed before the city of Stockholm decided to investigate living conditions. Society was shocked at the findings, and the city adopted a program for the erection of improved homes for workingmen. A number of houses actually were built. However, the obligation of the city was limited mainly to supervision, as the cooperative housing associations increased in numbers.

The most popular of these were the so-called "Own Home Society." It was organized in 1892 and by 1905 had 141 locals or chapters in 13 provinces with 5,398 members. Most of its activity was confined to smaller towns and cities and it was especially successful in the province of Östergöt-

73

land. The popularity of this movement and the interest shown in it by provincial governors greatly influenced the government in establishing the Public Home Ownership Fund in 1904, which was intended to provide loans at a low rate of interest for the building of rural homes. By this measure a credit fund of 10,000,000 crowns for home building was established.

Life changed more radically in matters pertaining to food, clothing, and amusements. The greatest change in food was in the greater consumption of meat, butter, sugar, wheat, bread, coffee, and fruit. With regard to clothing, by 1914 men were rarely seen wearing homespun, even in such weaving centers as Vesterbotten and Dalarna. National costumes were to be found chiefly in the museums, and both men and women wore ready-to-wear clothes. Hats were replacing caps, and ladies and maidservants began to rival one another in imitating Parisian styles. Only the elderly women wore kerchiefs to church, and then most often black to denote mourning. Younger peasant girls and maids still used bright kerchiefs while working in the fields, but on Sundays they wore hats. Men in 1914, including both gentlemen and servants, often had two overcoats, one for winter and one for summer, something which had been almost unheard of a quarter of a century earlier. The farmers went to funerals, dinners, weddings and similar events in silk hats and formal dress.

Amusements changed as radically as clothes and food. The reading of newspapers and illustrated journals caused a decline of the old parish libraries after 1880. The public was not satisfied with the devotional literature of the old libraries, and to satisfy the desire for more challenging literature the younger generation formed reading circles. The government encouraged the foundation of public libraries, and circulating libraries became popular. The older generation had been happy to attend a country fair, but the chief interests of the younger generation became dancing and membership in societies sponsoring dances. Amusements became organized, membership in some society being almost essential for a happy social life. These groups sponsored picnics, and the young drank coffee and ate coffee bread, rusks, and fancy cookies in far greater quantities than their parents had done.

The bicycle revolutionized rural and city life. People ventured miles beyond their homes in search of social adventure. In 1885 the Swedish Tourist Association was founded to encourage travel by train. Interest in athletics increased, and by 1893 there were 340 societies devoted to the promotion of athletics and sports, such as bicycling, track, gymnastics, swimming, football, rowing, skating, hunting, and sailing. Nearly all were local societies, but by 1903 a number of mergers of smaller national associations had taken place and the Swedish National Gymnastic and Athletic Association was formed. Temperance and labor organizations as well as the government encouraged this interest in athletics. The climax of the great national interest in athletics was the Olympic Games in Stockholm in 1912, when the world for the first time became acquainted with the great advancement made in athletics in Sweden.

Few people realized the real significance of the work of the athletic associations. In 1914 they were a most important organization in the process of leveling social classes. On the sidelines industrialists, bankers, bureaucrats, clerks, professional men, and workers cheered for the same men, jeered the same men, and conversed with each other about prospects of victories. In the arena there was no class distinction, and even on the sidelines class lines were less definitely drawn. But a keen observer in 1914 would have noticed that as the Swedish flag was hoisted, it was primarily the people in the grandstands who were thrilled, while a certain rumbling could be heard from the galleries where the working classes found themselves. When the national anthem was sung, the grandstand received only a weak echo from the galleries. The cleavage in the social structure may not have been wide, but it was deep, distinct, and very real.

Chapter VI

THE OUTBREAK OF WORLD WAR I
AND
THE FOUNDATIONS OF NEUTRALITY

SWEDEN FACED an extremely difficult problem in trying to remain neutral during World War I. Like many other European countries, she was dependent upon importation of both food and raw materials. Few countries had, however, developed an economic system which was more dependent upon the free flow of goods than Sweden, which imported annually about 400,000 tons of grain and feed and over 200,000 tons of oils and fats, and was dependent upon England for coal, upon the United States for rubber, copper and cotton, and upon Germany for chemicals, dyes, and medicinal supplies.

A study of a map of Sweden reveals how completely hemmed in she was by the nations at war. The waters along her east coast, the Gulf of Bothnia and the Baltic, provided both Russia and Germany with their most important outlets to the sea. To the west, from the northern part of Skåne to the northern shore of Bohuslän, an arm of the North Sea provided Sweden with a western outlet. The large British navy, even though challenged by German submarines, was largely able to control Swedish trade through the North Sea, while Germany controlled the Baltic.

Sweden has a coastline of 4,738 miles, and violations of Swedish neutrality within the three-mile limits of her territorial waters could hardly be avoided. Policing of these waters was more than a Herculean task for a nation of 6,000,000 people. The fact that Sweden was a small country made her protests against violations of the rights of a neutral ineffective, and no neutral country was ever subjected to as effective an economic blockade as was Sweden.

The problem was further complicated by the fact that Sweden in 1914 was seething with internal social and political unrest. Gustav V in his speech before the demonstrating farmers on February 6, 1914, had definitely sided with the militaristic group. Furthermore, he had urged Staaff, the prime minister, to recommend a dissolution of the Second Chamber. Such a measure the King believed would deal a blow to the Staaff administration and make possible the adoption of a program by the *Riksdag* more in accord with his views on national defense. The prime minister was forced to resign.

The day after his resignation, Staaff addressed the Second Chamber, defended his position, and maintained that basic constitutional principles had been threatened by the King's attitude. The Social Democrats were even more critical. What made the situation worse, was the fact that the King had allowed his actions to be dictated by his own personal dislike for Staaff.

When the other political parties interpreted the conflict between Staaff and the King as a constitutional question, it was impossible for the leaders of the Conservative party to assume the leadership in forming a new cabinet. They suggested to the King that, in view of public sentiment, it would be wise to request some Liberal to form a new cabinet. This move, they said, would eliminate any possibility of associating the cabinet crisis with any ill will toward the Liberal party. Thus, King Gustav, in order to avoid being stamped as a partisan, requested Louis De Geer, Jr., to form a cabinet, but De Geer failed to find support among the members of his party.

The sovereign then approached Hjalmar Hammarskjöld, who accepted the challenge. He represented the essence of reactionary forces within the Conservative party. He had been on two previous occasions a member of the cabinet, but he was not known as a political leader. He had an international reputation as a scholar and an authority on international law. The members of Hammarskjöld's cabinet were all able men, although not one had been intimately connected with party politics.

The circumstances under which the Hammarskjöld cabinet was organized were most unfortunate. Branting wrote in *Social-Demokraten* that though both power and intelligence could be found in the new cabinet, it really looked as if the government had become the legal department of Enskilda Banken (the Wallenberg Bank). Hammarskjöld made clear to the *Riksdag* that the primary aims of the administration was a speedy solution of the problems of national defense and ordered the dissolution of the Second Chamber and a public election. Thus, on March 5, 1914, the people were thrown into a heated political campaign. The Hammarskjöld administration enjoyed the advantage of royal support, many believing that to cast a vote for the Conservatives was to express sympathy for the views of King Gustav on the question of national defense.

The Liberal party split, numerous Liberals leaving the party to join the Conservatives. Pamphlets were published by hundreds of thousands, and party leaders toured the country. Local party organizations and local so-called "patriotic societies" were formed to support the Hammarskjöld cabinet, regardless of former party connections of their members. Staaff stressed in his speeches the principles of a constitutional government. He was, however, painted by the Conservatives as a traitor. In fact, a professor lecturing before his students accused Staaff of treason, an incident which reflects the intensity of the political feelings at the time. The Social Democratic party demanded a reduction in the period of compulsory military service to six months and a general reduction in military expenses.

The total vote cast in 1914 was 763,423, whereas only 607,483 had voted three years earlier. For once, each vote expressed a definite view. Staaff suffered a great loss at the polls, his following in the Second Chamber being reduced from 102 to 71. The Conservatives and the Liberals, who advocated a strong defense, increased their members from

64 to 86. The Social Democrats, on the other hand, increased their representation from 64 to 73. On May 18, the new *Riksdag* convened, and when neither Branting nor Staaff seemed willing to yield on the question of national defense, a deadlock seemed inevitable in the joint committee of the *Riksdag* over which Staaff presided as chairman.

As the European situation grew more tense, Staaff manifested a willingness to compromise, but it was the outbreak of World War I which made a solution possible. Immediately upon the news of the outbreak of the war, Branting, who was absent from Stockholm, sent Hammarskjöld a telegram in which he assured the prime minister of his cooperation in a policy aimed at the preservation of Sweden's neutrality. On August 8, Staaff informed Hammarskjöld that his party was ready to accept the national defense proposal of the administration. The proposal adopted provided for an extension of the period of compulsory military training to 340 days in the infantry, 365 days in the cavalry, and in other branches of the armed services from 240 days to a full year. Service in the navy was increased to 360 days, and military service for college students was extended to 485 days. A special national defense tax to provide revenue of 75,000,000 crowns was approved. The *Riksdag* approved a five-year naval building program to include the construction of destroyers, cruisers, and a number of submarines, to which was added an appropriation of 13,700,000 crowns for the strengthening of fortifications.

Sweden had first become fully aware of the crisis in Europe in the very last days of July, when Poincaré visited Stockholm on his way from Russia. He was cordially received by the King, and he assured Sweden that he had been authorized to extend a greeting from the Russian Czar and that there was nothing to fear from Russia. Poincaré had also planned to visit Copenhagen, but instead he hurried home to France. On July 31 the Swedish government issued its declaration of neutrality in the war that had broken out between Austria-Hungary and Serbia. On August 1 the government forbade the export of coal, grain, and war materials. On Sunday, August 2, the newspapers carried the headlines of the outbreak of World War I.

The government ordered partial mobilization, and the church bells tolled for hours. There was great excitement, and the sound of cannon was reported along the coast. Tourists and refugees fled to their respective countries, Germans hurrying out of Russia, Russians out of Germany. The people who were spending the summer in summer homes scurried to the cities. In villages, towns, and cities, the public gathered to discuss the news. Outside newspaper offices citizens gathered by the hundreds in efforts to verify wild rumors. People talked and thought nothing but war.

Some said conflict had been expected for a decade or more and that it was unavoidable, but to the mass of people the news of August 2 came as a violent shock. They had looked upon a war at the very doors of Sweden as unthinkable, preferring to believe that some way would be found to disperse the clouds that had hovered over Europe since the murder of the Archduke of Austria-Hungary. On Monday thoughtful mothers, fearing a food shortage, hurried to the stores and made large purchases. It seemed as if the slogan was "everyone for himself and the devil take the hindmost."

Prices rose immediately. In contrast to the pushing crowds in the stores the harbors were silent. There was no shrill sound of whistles, and no smoke poured from the stacks of the large ships. Shipowners prepared to place their ships in dry docks and discharge the sailors. Mobilization, it was believed, would affect all industries. During the first two days of the war, everything seemed to have stopped except the clock, and even it seemed to run slowly. Industries refused to grant credit. Orders abroad as well as at home were cancelled. The Stockholm Exchange was closed on August 3. People rushed to banks for withdrawals, forcing the banks to close their doors for three days.

Although no nation was prepared for the war, Sweden

was fortunate in having the *Riksdag* in session. On August 2 the cabinet worked feverishly to prepare legislation necessitated by the war, and by August 17 the foundation had been laid for a policy of war economy. On August 3 the prohibition of the export of certain goods was declared. Two days later a moratorium was issued, and on August 8 the National Bank was freed from its obligation to redeem paper money. During August 10 to 17 the State Industrial Commission, the State Unemployment Commission, the State Food Commission, and the State War Insurance Commission were created, giving the state unlimited powers in regulating industry and controlling foods and other necessities. Again the wheels of industry were set in motion, and with the government assuming part of the insurance risk involved in the shipping industry, steamships again plied their customary sea routes.

The action taken by the government tended to minimize the dangers of involvement in the war, but the real problems had been far from solved. The German minister to Stockholm informed Berlin that Sweden was ready to join the Central Powers. Russia was positive that it was only a matter of days before even Sweden would enter the war, a view shared also by Copenhagen, and it was generally believed that Sweden had a secret treaty with Germany. Russia prepared to attack Sweden before Sweden could attack Russia. The Russian fleet in the Baltic had received instructions to attack Fårösund and Gotland, when suddenly the order was cancelled. Did Sweden have a secret treaty with Germany? What might have been the causes for the various rumors of the definite pro-German sentiments of Sweden?

An answer to those questions cannot be made without a brief review of the foreign policy of Sweden since 1905. When Staaff selected the ministers of his first cabinet, he selected Eric Trolle as minister of foreign affairs upon the suggestion of the crown prince, who two years later became Gustav V. Trolle was a career diplomat of noble birth and wealthy family. He was on intimate and friendly terms with the crown prince, who was known to be pro-German. Trolle was well informed as to conditions abroad and prepared to reorient Sweden's foreign policy.

This reorientation was motivated not by a desire on the part of Sweden to leave its policy of isolation but rather by fear that Norway might venture into a dangerous foreign policy which would involve Scandinavia in the quarrels of the Great Powers. Trolle's time, however, was chiefly occupied with improving the efficiency of the diplomatic and consular service. In 1909 the minister of foreign affairs was given greater freedom from the control exerted over him by the prime minister and other members of the cabinet, and it was now possible for him to devote himself to a highly specialized task in a distinct department, while the prime minister could devote more time to domestic problems.

This might have been a dangerous change, especially in a country like Sweden where the *Riksdag* treated matters pertaining to foreign affairs with little interest. Debates on foreign policy were so rare in the *Riksdag* as to baffle the foreign observer. Norway's foreign policy, on the other hand, was directed toward safeguarding Norwegian integrity and independence. In 1907 Norway succeeded in securing such a guarantee from the Great Powers. Trolle did not favor such a guarantee for Sweden because he believed it would weaken Swedish independence, and when Norway refused to accept the Swedish guarantee of her integrity, Trolle exerted himself to prevent England, Russia, France and Germany from signing. When Gustav became King, he showed immediately that he was eager to remove any possible distrust among the Scandinavian countries toward one another. The Swedish King was certain that the international situation was very serious, and he was far from pleased with the understanding reached by France, Russia, and England in the Triple Entente.

The fortification of the Åland Islands had been prohibited in the Treaty of Paris of 1856, but Gustav V now feared that it was no longer in the interest of France and England to prevent such fortification by Russia. The islands are strategically situated to command the trade in the Gulf of Bothnia, and were too close to Stockholm for comfort. Because of technical developments in modern warfare, it was of the utmost importance to Sweden that Russia should be prevented from fortifying these islands. The Russian minister of foreign affairs, Izvolski, was negotiating with France and England to abrogate the clause of the Treaty of Paris which dealt with the Åland Islands, but Sweden successfully prevented such abrogation. In 1908 Germany, Russia, Sweden, and Denmark agreed to the *status quo* in the Baltic; and Germany, Great Britain, France, the Netherlands, Sweden, and Denmark agreed to observe the *status quo* in the North Sea.

In April 1908 Edward VII visited Stockholm, and the following month the Czar of Russia attended the wedding of Prince Wilhelm of Sweden and the Grand Duchess Maria Pavlovna. On this occasion every effort was made to assure the Czar of Sweden's friendship, but Russia seemed indifferent. In fact, she maintained that the Baltic Sea Treaty had removed any restrictions on her right to fortify the Åland Islands.

King Gustav V, deciding to do some travelling himself, called at Berlin and Copenhagen. Rumors circulated in Paris that Sweden had placed herself under the protection of Germany, and the President of France packed his suitcase and journeyed to Stockholm. The Swedish King was offered the opportunity to discredit the French rumors. However, only a few days after the French president Fallières had left Stockholm, the German Kaiser called. During the months of November and December, the Swedish King visited London, Paris, Karlsruhe, and Vienna. The visits by heads of European governments to Sweden were more than mere courtesies returned by the Swedish King. Europe was nervous. The annexation of Bosnia and Herzogovina by Austria-Hungary had brought the Great Powers to the verge of another war.

It was not so much the military power of Sweden which made it the object of the attention of Great Britain, Russia,

Germany, and France as her strategic position in the Baltic. Any great power in control of Sweden would be able to dominate the Baltic. Sweden was by necessity forced to play a cautious game. Inasmuch as Sweden's chief interest in the diplomatic game was to prevent Russia from fortifying the Åland Islands, it was unwise to play her only trump card by definitely allying herself with Germany. It was realized that France, and especially Great Britain, had greater influence over the Russian government than Germany had and might be able to prevent the proposed fortification. If Great Britain permitted Russia to carry out her plan, Sweden would have been thrown into the arms of Germany.

The Russification of Finland was also a reason for alarm. By 1910 Finnish autonomy was a mere illusion, and Russia connected the railroads of Finland with the Russian railroad system. The Russian fleet in the Baltic was strengthened, and a new naval base was built at Reval. Tension mounted, and numerous persons were arrested in Sweden in the belief that they were Russian spies. In July 1912 the Russian Czar and the Swedish King each accompanied by their ministers of foreign affairs, met somewhere off the coast of Finland and the strained relationship between Russia and Sweden was eased for the time being.

Unrest was brewing, however, in the Balkans, and in December the Scandinavian countries cooperated in issuing identical declarations of neutrality. At this time rumors circulated that the three Scandinavian countries had formed a defensive alliance. These rumors were unfounded, but the King had succeeded in overcoming Norway's doubts as to the good intentions of Sweden. This had been made possible through the arbitration of the boundary dispute and of the dispute over the rights of pasturage of the herds of reindeer owned by the Lapps of the two nations.

Inasmuch as fear existed among certain political leaders that Sweden might venture into dangerous foreign entanglements, the idea was advanced that Sweden must attempt to secure from the various powers of Europe the same guarantee for her independence and integrity as had Belgium. The chief spokesman for this policy was the pacifist Eric Palm- stierna, but he found no strong support in the *Riksdag*. The Balkan War, which had closed only one chapter in the Bal- kan unrest with the Treaty of Bucharest, made it clear that Sweden must exert herself to remain free from any alliances. When World War I broke out, the hands of Sweden were free, even though it can be said that its policy had been pro-German. The reorganization of the foreign department by Trolle was now a real danger, especially as the cabinet was headed by Hammarskjöld. His pro-German views were not only shared by Gustav V but by the Conservative party as well.

Fortunately, the Conservatives believed that Germany would score a smashing victory, and Sweden was especially looking forward to a complete humiliation of Russia. The distrust of Russia permeated every social group, while the cultural and economic ties between Germany and Sweden were very close. The entire school system of Sweden was largely built on the German model. No education was com- plete without study in Germany. Most university professors were strongly pro-German and their influence was felt throughout the secondary schools. The Swedish army was an imitation of the German army, and its officers had the un- pleasant, overbearing attitude of Prussian army officers.

But German culture in Sweden was an upper-class culture. The Social Democratic party and the Liberal party, which represented the greatest number of Swedish citizens, looked toward England and France as the standard-bearers of democracy. All Swedish parties united, however, in re- garding Russia as not only the natural enemy of Sweden but as the real enemy of democracy. Thus, it might be said that Sweden as a nation hoped for the defeat of Russia, but that the war as a conflict between Germany on one side and France and England on the other found the people of Sweden divided, a division based largely on old social prejudices.

Being representative of the upper class, the Hammarskjöld cabinet was inclined to endanger Sweden's neutrality by a pro-German policy, but the fall election of 1914 strengthened labor representation in the Second Chamber and made it impossible for the Hammarskjöld government to pursue a too obviously pro-German policy. In order to be able to function at all as prime minister, Hammarskjöld recommended the appointment by the *Riksdag* of a secret committee composed of representatives of all the political parties. This committee, rather than the minister of foreign affairs, was to direct Sweden's foreign policy. The danger that Sweden would thus be thrown into the war was greatly reduced. In fairness to Hammarskjöld, it must be said that neutrality became the foundation of his policy. He had, however, no other course to pursue. Any tendency on Hammarskjöld's part to falter in his neutrality policy would have implied that the reactionary government had failed. The King would then have been forced to turn to the Social Democrats for advice. Thus the Conservatives, torn by the desire to help Germany on one hand and remain in political power on the other, decided in favor of the latter for many believed that a Social Democratic government would be disastrous to Sweden.

The Allies knew that the Swedish government was pro-German, and the anti-Russian sentiment of Sweden was no secret. What aroused fear and suspicion on the part of the Allies was a heated campaign by nationalists and interventionists for actual participation of Sweden on the side of Germany. The interventionists were especially busy during the first two years of the war, and they were by no means all Conservatives. Three members of the Social Democratic party were even read out of the party for their activities in behalf of Germany. In sharp contrast to these were the ultra pacificists, who in 1915 held a Peace Congress in Varberg and urged the preservation of neutrality at almost any cost. Hammarskjöld rebuked both the interventionists and the pacifists in 1915 by making the following public statement: "Lately much has been said about the danger of advocating war as something desirable. This is a real danger if through this the concept is created that Sweden desires war. But it is similarly harmful if in certain quarters it is believed that Sweden desires peace under all circumstances and can therefore be dealt with just any way at all . . . A special danger, which might accompany both war and peace agitation, consists of the possibility of one stimulating the other to new heights of intensity. Through this agitation the unity of the people might be lost sight of or completely disappear, a unity which, I believe, exists among the people and is more essential now than ever."

The problems of a neutral Sweden centered around the necessity of supplying the country with raw materials, keeping industries functioning, and providing the people with food from the outside world. The rights of neutrals and restrictions of belligerents had been defined by the Paris Declaration of 1856, the Hague Agreement of 1907, and the London Declaration of 1909. Though the British Parliament had not formally approved the London Declaration, it seemed at first as if the belligerents were ready to observe a definite international code. According to this code of "ethics," a neutral country remained neutral as long as she did not give armed assistance to a belligerent or supply a nation at war with articles which might be used directly to wage war. The best interest of Sweden seemed to lie in retaining at all costs a standing of neutrality.

CHAPTER VII

THE TRIALS OF A NEUTRAL SWEDEN

WHEN IT BECAME CLEAR that Sweden was in no immi-
nent danger, many were tempted to look upon the
European war as a great drama in which Sweden was only
an interested spectator. Most Swedes did not realize what was
actually happening. As long as the country suffered no real
need, the people attended soccer games, discussed the possibilities of the outcome of the war, and took more or less
definite sides. The danger of becoming involved in the war
was greatly reduced when, upon the initiative of the Swedish
King, a conference of the three Scandinavian rulers was
arranged in Malmö in December 1914.

This conference and subsequent ones drafted plans for
cooperation between the three Scandinavian countries, and
the prime ministers and ministers of foreign affairs of the
three countries were brought into closer cooperation. This
was a healthy development, especially for Sweden, because
Danish and Norwegian pro-British sympathies dampened
Swedish pro-German sentiments. The Danish influences were
especially significant, for in that country the Conservatives
and Liberals were as pro-British as the Conservatives in
Sweden were pro-German, while the Danish Social Democrats were as pro-German as the Swedish Social Democrats
were pro-British.

The meetings gave the people of Sweden a sense of
confidence, as it was believed in some quarters that the
Scandinavian countries had formed a Northern Entente. Few
people realized the grave problems faced by the Hammarskjöld administration in keeping Sweden out of danger. From
the very beginning of the war Sweden forbade the granting
of export licenses for war material, and in January 1915 she
prohibited the transit of war material through Sweden.

Russia was already suffering an acute crisis from the lack of war material and was shut off from her allies by the German control of the Baltic and Turkey's control of the inlet to the Black Sea. In order to come to the rescue of Russia, Great Britain proposed that Norway and Sweden should allow England to transport war material to Russia via northern Scandinavia. When Sweden resisted British and Russian pressure war clouds gathered, and for a while the situation was threatening.

Great Britain, however, after consulting Russia and France, decided to reach Russia by way of the Dardanelles. It was Admiral Lord J. Fisher in England, who, together with Winston Churchill, had recommended the northern routes, and most military authorities in Great Britain favored this plan rather than the attack on the Dardanelles. Russia, however, feared that pressing for the northern route would throw Sweden into the conflict on the side of the Central Powers, in which case Russia felt Germany would definitely have the advantage. Russia also felt none too certain at the time about her position in Finland, and the fortification of the Åland Islands made possible by the war had not yet been completed.

Sweden's neutrality was not endangered by the Allies alone. Germany offered Sweden an alliance against Russia, which included actual aid in case Russia attacked Sweden. This "generous" offer was presented to Sweden by Prince Max of Baden, a cousin of the Swedish queen. Hammarskjöld pretended to look upon the German offer favorably in order to use it as a threat against the Allies and thus secure greater consideration from them. Wallenberg, the minister of foreign affairs, apparently realized more clearly the danger of this policy, which might ultimately lead to an alliance with Germany, and Germany's offer was refused. In 1916 Prince Max repeated the offer of a German alliance, in return for which Sweden was to be permitted to annex Finland. An alliance with Germany was tempting at this time, but Sweden again decided to remain aloof. Germany had been by 1915 very successful in the war, and unfounded rumors circulated that Russia was considering a separate peace agreement, which, if concluded, might lay the foundation for Russo-German cooperation highly inimical to Sweden's interest.

In the summer and autumn of 1916, the shortage of raw material and food became acute. The Conservative leaders, instead of breaking away from the interventionists, became more outspoken in their pro-German sympathies. The Social Democrats criticized Hammarskjöld's shortsighted policy of insisting upon the observance of international law, when such a policy was threatening to bring Sweden into war with the Allies. In the election to the provincial assemblies, the Social Democrats called the Conservative party the war party and succeeded in increasing its number of representatives in the First Chamber by two seats.

The increasingly intensive opposition to the Hammarskjöld administration by both Liberals and Social Democrats gave Hammarskjöld only a short reprieve in December when the Scandinavian countries joined in Wilson's peace note. The Allies were, however, not ready to conclude a peace with Germany, and the advantage of the small neutrals in dealing with the belligerents was soon lost. As long as the United States remained neutral, the protest of small neutrals against the violation of their rights could not be entirely ignored.

The fact that the United States was on the verge of declaring war on Germany in February 1917 completely undermined an already weak Hammarskjöld cabinet. At the opening of the *Riksdag* of 1917, Branting, Värner Rydén and Eric Palmstierna launched a violent attack on the government. It was claimed that the government had failed to check inflation, failed to prevent a shortage of food, failed to reach a satisfactory trade agreement with England, and, worst of all, that it was pro-German and interventionist. The Liberals, led by Professor Nils Edén, joined in the attack, claiming that Great Britain was justified in criticizing Swedish export to Germany of goods not exported to Germany prior to the war. Edén asserted that the rights of a neutral's trade should be based on its trade in times of peace. He argued that a scientific study should be made of the actual needs of Sweden and that England would not protest against the importation of goods that would not be re-exported.

The resignation of Hammarskjöld was demanded by a number of newspapers in 1916. On January 15, 1917, the rationing of bread began, and Hammarskjöld was criticized for not having broken diplomatic relations with Germany upon the request of the United States in February. At the Social Democratic party congress in the same month, "Down with the Hunger Administration" became the slogan. Hammarskjöld was misgovernment personified to Liberals and Social Democrats alike. On March 5 he resigned.

He had served a purpose, but the type of neutrality which he had advocated was no longer possible. The problems of a small neutral during 1914-1916 were difficult enough, but in 1917 neutrality, in the strictest sense, was an impossibility. In February, Germany began unrestricted submarine warfare, and Great Britain notified Sweden that no Swedish ships would be allowed to leave English ports before the arrival of an equal amount of Swedish shipping tonnage. Two weeks later, all neutral ships were ordered into English ports for search.

Sweden had no severe laws dealing with espionage, and as one of the few neutral countries in Europe, she was a paradise for spies seeking information from the legations of the nations at war. Spies mingled with the diplomats and found their way to the functions at court. The hotels were crowded with people who provided information for pay to any nation, often being employed by both the Allies and the Central Powers. Next to the Swedish, American passports were most easily forged and, therefore, most frequently used by spies throughout Europe.

The most natural thing would have been for the King to turn to the Social Democrats and the Liberals with a request that they form a new government, but revolution had broken out in Russia, and there was much labor unrest in Sweden. The King decided, therefore, that it would be unwise to make a radical change in the government and requested Carl Swartz, a Conservative, to form a new cabinet. The selection of Arvid Lindman, a pro-German, as minister of foreign affairs was greeted, however, by distrust from the Social Democrats and the Liberals. Sweden was closer to a civil war and complete breakdown of law and order in the spring of 1917 than she had been since 1809, even though the Swartz administration promised to cooperate more closely with the views expressed in the Second Chamber than the Hammarskjöld cabinet had done and in May actually succeeded in reaching a trade agreement with Great Britain.

The Social Democrats were jubilant over the March Revolution in Russia. Branting and Värner Rydén visited Petrograd and were enthusiastic over the victory, as they thought, of democracy. Fabian Månsson said: "We have seen raw and horrible crimes committed in our neighboring country to the east. It looked as if the people were animals, but the Revolution has swept aside the provocation, the police, and now we are able to see a loyal and peaceful people."

There was real want in Sweden at this time, with shortages of bread, butter, sugar, meat, eggs, milk, and many essential raw materials for industry. On April 17 a hunger revolt spread from one end of Sweden to the other. Stores were stormed for food, and mobs clashed with the police. As May 1 approached, the government was uneasy, for then the customary labor demonstrations would take place. The sale of liquor was prohibited. In Stockholm a group of citizens formed an auxiliary to aid the police in maintaining order. Edén criticized the authorities for accepting the volunteers as unpardonable foolishness. Branting's sharp tongue lashed Swartz, and Månsson accused the government of protecting the interventionists, who were allowed to organize themselves as "comorras" under the protection of the police to

93

safeguard the "league of Rasputin." Many citizens bought special locks for the doors on their homes and took other precautions against possible vandalism. The government was not sure that troops could be used with safety in suppressing lawlessness. On the eve of May 1, the Swartz administration was powerless, showered with the abuse people had stored up against the Hammarskjöld cabinet.

The Swedes were tired of the regulatory measures taken by the Hammarskjöld government, which in the various commissions had created a state within a state with almost autocratic powers. These had been organized at the outbreak of the war, and had become more and more regulatory as the Hammarskjöld foreign policy stimulated stricter allied control of Swedish imports.

Swedish industry underwent three rather distinct phases of development during World War I. The first phase was chiefly characterized by a great industrial expansion encouraged by a growing home market and favorable foreign trade. The government during this period, which lasted to the summer of 1916, tried primarily to protect home needs by export prohibitions and to secure favorable concessions from abroad on goods that Sweden needed. The second phase was characterized by a great shortage of raw materials caused by a more vigorous economic blockade of the trade of neutrals by the belligerents. The extension of the list of contraband goods required strong government controls over industry, with the height of regulation being reached in the summer of 1918. The third period, beginning with the Armistice in November 1918, and extending through 1921, was characterized by the liquidation of wartime regulation and the end of wartime prosperity.

At the outbreak of the war, Great Britain maintained a very liberal trade policy. The "black list" originated with the Trading with the Enemy Act of December 23, 1915. This policy was adopted by France, Italy, Germany, Austria-Hungary, and Australia. Though the United States had protested more vigorously against the black list than any other neutral, the United States outdid all the other nations after it entered the war in trying to prevent trade of American merchants with the firms of neutral countries which might be suspected of trading with the enemy.

As Sweden was suspected of being engaged in extensive trade with Germany, an effort was made by Great Britain to control Swedish trade through a huge trade association. Swedish exporters were thus placed under a double control. This trade association not only tried to prevent the re-export of goods imported to Sweden from the Allies, but added to its black list exporters of goods of Swedish origin placed by the Allies on the contraband list. The belligerent contraband lists at first adhered to the London Declaration of 1909, but on September 26, 1914, Sweden was notified that Great Britain had included iron ore as contraband and the export of iron ore from Narvik was temporarily stopped. When Sweden protested, Great Britain revised its list of contraband to omit magnetic iron, and Swedish export of iron ore from Narvik was resumed. However, at the same time, Great Britain extended the contraband list, stipulating that neutrals must be able to prove that the final destination of goods im-, ported to neutral countries on the contraband list was not an enemy country. Germany, less than a month later, on November 24, included all types of lumber on its contra-band list.

Early in September an American ship ran into a mine off the English coast, and before the end of the year neutrals had been impressed by the danger of mines to trade. The English admiralty declared the North Sea to be a military zone, and insisted that neutral ships follow a certain route from Norway to Scotland along the east coast of England and through the channel. This involved a tremendous risk compared with the northern route south of Iceland. The Scandinavian countries protested, but the admiralty stated that its action had been motivated by hopes of safeguarding neutral trade. Sweden, however, ignored the admiralty. Its ships continued to ply the northern route, and no effort was made by Great Britain to prevent the neutrals from using this route. On February 4, 1917, Germany began its submarine warfare declaring the waters around England, Scotland, and Ireland to be a war zone, and warning that after February 18 every neutral ship ran the danger of being mistaken for an enemy ship.

The situation was the more alarming as the British admiralty ordered all British ships to hoist a neutral flag to avoid danger from German warships and submarines. The use of mines by the belligerents increased, and the Swedish War Insurance Commission was forced to raise the premiums on ship insurance. The three Scandinavian countries joined in a protest to Great Britain against the use of neutral flags by British merchant ships, and the use of convoys was discussed, but the proposal had to be dropped when Great Britain refused to allow neutral convoys to proceed to and from her ports.

On March 11, 1915, Great Britain issued an Order in Council which aimed at preventing German export and import and became the basis of a new policy in the economic war. Again the Scandinavian countries protested. A number of Swedish ships were sunk by German submarines, and shipping lines hesitated to send out their ships. But trade did not cease. The blue and gold colors of the Swedish flag were painted on the ships, and captains were instructed to avoid danger zones and take other precautions. After March 11, Great Britain confiscated large amounts of goods headed for Sweden such as copper, cotton, machines, fats, foods, oil, rubber, and hides. When goods were not confiscated they were held up for a long period of time.

Other obstacles to trade arose also. On April 18, 1915, Germany included coal on its list of contraband. On May 6, by an Order in Council, Great Britain prohibited the export of coal except under issue of export licenses. The amount of red tape involved in securing export licenses forced Sweden to turn from England to Germany for its coal in order to prevent an immediate shortage. Espionage by Great Britain increased, and ships headed to and from America were forced into Kirkwall, where they were subjected to weeklong searches and detention. Some mail was confiscated. While Great Britain irritated Swedish authorities, Germany agreed that Swedish ships passing through the Öresund would not be brought to Swinemünde for search, if they carried goods properly licensed for export by the Swedish government.

Measures taken by the belligerents by the end of 1915 in preventing the free flow of goods speeded the neutrals' adoption of a policy of controlling their exports through prohibitions. By means of export licenses, the governments were able not only to control the export but to bargain with other nations for goods. As long as Russia was engaged in the war, Sweden had a means of somewhat tempering the economic restrictions of Great Britain by refusing to grant licenses for the transportation of civilian goods from Great Britain to Russia on Swedish railroads. Violations of Swedish neutrality by Germany, England, and Russia increased in frequency throughout 1915. During the last six months of that year 31 Swedish ships were sunk and 60 persons lost their lives. Some ships were lost by running into mines, some ran aground, others collided or were torpedoed. Germany forced 120 ships into German ports for search and confiscated goods worth 376,000 crowns, while England forced 40 ships into English ports for search and confiscated goods worth 12,500,000 crowns. Between August of 1914 and December of 1915, England and Germany had confiscated goods headed for Sweden valued at 34,120,000 crowns. The greatest value was represented by cotton confiscated by Great Britain.

The economic blockade by Great Britain in retaliation for Sweden's unwillingness to allow the transport of war material for Russia through Sweden reached unbelievable, even ludicrous proportions. Sweden had to assure Great Britain that certain books written in French would not be sent to the enemy, and that paintings exhibited by Bruno Liljefors in San Francisco on their way home to Sweden would not fall into the hands of the enemies of the Allies.

The British courts were overloaded with work, and ships were forced to wait their turns before clearance papers were issued. Perishable goods spoiled, and other goods were sold at sacrifice prices because of lack of storage space at the ports, and compensation for losses was very unsatisfactory. The constant violations of Sweden's territorial waters caused Sweden in July of 1916 to close the channel called Kogrundrännan, making it impossible for Allied ships to engage in trade along the Baltic coast and leave the Baltic, unless they desired to challenge fate by running into German warships and submarines in the Baltic.

The Allies protested, and in the autumn of 1916, Russia mined the waters around the Åland Islands and the Gulf of Bothnia. On August 18 Great Britain forbade the export of nearly all goods sent to Sweden except upon the condition that the importer sign a written agreement that the goods he imported or products manufactured from the goods would not be re-exported by Sweden, a guarantee which must be approved by the Swedish State Trade Commission. Though the Commission refused to recognize England's right to dictate to Swedish shop owners, the latter were forced to permit their ships to carry trade for the Allies in order to secure coal. On September 20 Great Britain issued a complete export ban on goods to Sweden without modifying it by "licenses or facilities."

Great Britain also extended its control of Swedish import to Denmark. In Copenhagen large quantities of goods headed for Sweden were stored, awaiting decision from Great Britain before they could be freed for export to Sweden. The English courts refused to concern themselves with the goods stored in Copenhagen, while the Danish shippers were excused from more vigorous search and detention in Great Britain on condition that the goods that they carried for Sweden would be stored in Copenhagen. The scarcity of raw materials in Sweden began to cause grave concern.

Trade with Germany became difficult too, owing to a shortage of labor in Germany, the inability of the German railroad system to carry the strain placed on it by the war, and the sharp rise in prices. Though the German contraband list was less inclusive as far as Swedish trade was concerned, the German courts interpreted German contraband very broadly to include almost any kind of export of important goods from Sweden.

It was apparent that it was impossible for Sweden to carry on trade with both belligerent groups. Great Britain had become increasingly suspicious; the entrance of Germany into unrestricted submarine warfare in February of 1917 and the United States' entrance into the war in April made transatlantic trade almost impossible. Great Britain's answer to Germany's submarine warfare was the Order in Council of February 16, which demanded that all neutral ships must voluntarily call at English ports for search or else both ship and freight would be confiscated on the presumption that the ship carried contraband.

Many shipowners ordered their ships to neutral ports, and for a time there was almost complete stagnation in trade. Insurance premiums were boosted. Swedish ships were retained in Allied ports unless they consented to carry trade for the Allies. Between February 10 and June 30, twenty Swedish ships were torpedoed. At the end of June, goods destined for Sweden valued at 70,837,452 crown were tied up in England.

Contraband now included almost every kind of goods. Foreign merchants wanted credit. Especially hard hit were the German merchants. Trade with Russia came to a standstill with the outbreak of the Revolution. Germany declared that neutral ships in the service of the Allies would be treated as enemy ships. Fantastic stories were spread in the United States press of war profiteering in Sweden and of Swedish export of food to the Central Powers. These stories caused the United States and Great Britain to insist that the Scandinavian countries break off all their trade relations with Germany.

The United States, which had been the most outspoken

defender of international law, now completely disregarded it. On June 15, 1917, the United States placed an embargo upon nearly every mentionable item. Export was permitted only after assurance that goods would not reach the Central Powers. In November, upon the initiative of the United States, the Allies decided to cut off all trade with neutrals until satisfactory agreements had been reached in regard to their trade with the Central Powers. The aim was not only to cut off Scandinavian export of goods imported from the Allies but all Scandinavian trade with Germany.

Thus, Sweden was forced in December of 1917 to enter upon negotiations with the United States, Great Britain, France, Italy, and Japan. The United States and Great Britain insisted that Sweden must turn over a specified amount of its tonnage of ships for the use of the Allies, and on March 1 Sweden consented to place at the disposal of the Allies Swedish ships to the amount of 100,000 tons for service in European waters, in return for which Sweden was allowed to import fixed amounts of grain, feed, oil, and coffee. A special agreement was forced upon Sweden by the United States by which Sweden was allowed to import a limited amount of goods from the United States on condition that Swedish ships carry goods from the United States to South America.

Germany could no longer supply Sweden with coal, and the fuel problem had become acute in Sweden. German inflation made trade with Germany nearly impossible. Sweden was thus no longer in a position to insist upon any "rights," and on June 18 the foreign department announced that Sweden had reached an agreement by which it had been assured grain, feed, coal, oil, rubber, cotton, wool, hides, coffee, copper, sulphur, tobacco, and other goods. In return Sweden placed at the disposal of the Allies 400,000 tons, of which half could be used by the Allies in traffic in the war zones. Sweden was also forced to assure the Allies a fixed amount of iron ore on credit terms and was compelled to promise not to export certain goods to Germany.

By March 1 Sweden had thus practically abandoned her neutrality and was engaged in active aid of the Allies. Such an agreement would undoubtedly have been possible at a much earlier stage, thus avoiding much suffering. Had the Conservative government been replaced earlier than in the fall of 1917 by a Liberal and Social Democratic government, the Allies would have been able to coerce Sweden into trade agreements which (though violating international law) would have prevented the economic blockade of Sweden.

It is very doubtful that Germany, in retaliation, would have declared war on Sweden. Denmark was pro-British, and there was little secrecy about her sympathies, and yet the Danish people during World War I hardly knew any want, nor did Germany occupy Denmark. The Swedish policy, therefore, was dictated by a shortsighted pro-German policy exceedingly harmful to the economic and physical well-being of the Swedish people.

Hammarskjöld had maintained that after the war was over the Great Powers would appreciate the services Sweden had rendered in preserving at least a remnant of international law. In Sweden, however, his name is associated more with hunger than with international law, and he gave the Allies, including the United States, the impression that Sweden was pro-German.

This impression was strengthened by the fact that the only press bureau in Sweden, the Swedish Telegraph Bureau, was controlled by a pro-German. In June 1918 a rival news agency was founded in Sweden, but there was already, unfortunately, a scarcity of printer's ink. In September 1917 the American newspaper made the most of a scandal associated with the negligence of the Swedish foreign department. They carried the story of the "sink without a trace" message of the German minister at Buenos Aires, a message sent through the Swedish Foreign Department.

Walter Hines Page writes in his *Memoirs*: "The extent to which Swedish diplomatic agents were transmitting German messages constituted one of the gravest scandals of the war." The American press maintained that the Swedish court was pro-German and that the Swedish department of foreign affairs was an integral part of the German foreign department and that German messages were sent constantly in Swedish cipher through the regular channels of the Swedish department of foreign affairs. German ministers merely called on their Swedish colleagues in a foreign country, and Swedish envoys then sent telegrams to the department of foreign affairs in Stockholm, and it in turn relayed the message to another envoy representing Sweden, which, as an errand boy, delivered the message to the proper German authorities.

The carelessness of the Swedish envoy at Buenos Aires in permitting himself to transmit a German message which he did not make himself acquainted with was unpardonable. Equally to blame was the department of foreign affairs in Stockholm for its failure to check on messages transmitted by or to it. Arvid Lindman, the minister of foreign affairs, was known as a pro-German, but he could hardly have been so foolish or stupid as not to know that the British Naval Intelligence Service controlled the air, and that both the United States and England were able to read the Swedish cipher.

The foreign affairs department in Stockholm had no intelligent excuse to offer to the Allies. It asserted that it had been stupid and explained that it could not imagine that any nation would take advantage of a courtesy which Sweden extended to a belligerent. Sweden protested to Germany for having taken advantage of a privilege. The Swedish envoy at Buenos Aires was recalled, and in the fall election to the Second Chamber the Liberals and the Social Democrats profited by the embarrassment of the Conservatives. The "new system," reaction and militarism had come to an end, and the Prussification of Sweden had reached its closing chapter.

CHAPTER VIII

UNREST DURING THE LAST PHASE OF WORLD WAR I

B Y AUTUMN of 1917 the foreign policy of the Hammarsjöld and Swartz administrations had been reversed. Many factors had contributed to this reversal. The Allied blockade of Swedish trade had caused great unrest, which expressed itself in hunger demonstrations, riots, and at the polls. The functions of the various war commissions were broadened, and new commissions were created. The government failed to coordinate these regulatory agencies, and when it endeavored to make their work more effective, conditions became chaotic.

The intentions of the government were good, but the measures adopted often had exactly the opposite result. The creation of a kind of "capitalistic Bolshevism" must be primarily attributed to the failure of the state to maintain a stable currency and, secondly, to the failure to check an export of goods, especially food, to Germany during the first two years of the war, thus creating an actual scarcity. By a series of maximum price laws, the government encouraged the withholding of goods and extensive black market activity. The imports of goods to Sweden in 1915 and 1916 were such that, with the proper regulation of export and the prevention of smuggling of goods out of Sweden to Germany, there should have been no great scarcity. The government hesitated to confiscate goods until it was too late, and virtually every grocer and farmer, and thousands of private jobbers in the cities were engaged in illegal trade practices.

Though these conditions reflect seriously upon the work of one of the most important war commissions, the Food Commission, its work was made more difficult by the failure of the War Trade Commission to function properly in prevent-

103

ing export of goods, a failure which caused the whole structure of war economy to crumble. The War Trade Commission, in turn, could not have had any knowledge of the trade developments in 1916-1918, and its work was made difficult by the government neutrality policy.

It was against the Food Commission, however, that the public stormed. In 1915 even the work of this Commission seemed simple, being confined to safeguarding the import of food necessities and to regulating food prices. Farmers were urged to increase their grain production, cultivate more carrots, rutabagas, and potatoes. Experiments in baking bread which combined mixtures of potato flour and corn with rye were encouraged. The Social Democrats had been alarmed over the increased cost of bread and had recommended that the government take drastic measures to check it. But in spite of the Commission's price-fixing measures prices rose, and the farmers resented government meddling.

A poor sugar beet crop brought on the rationing of sugar in October 1916, and the following month witnessed the beginning of the regulation of grain consumption, which in January 1917 led to state confiscation of all grain and flour. Bread and flour ration cards were distributed, with special coupons being issued for those engaged in hard physical work. Considerable war profiteering in the export of pork had been permitted by the government on the pretext that lack of feed necessitated slaughter of hogs, but in June 1917 the Food Commission extended its control and price fixing to pork. When price fixing was applied to the dairy industry in 1916, the production of creamery butter and cheese dropped sharply. Farmers found it more profitable to make their own butter and sell it to the highest bidder. On February 16, 1917, the state confiscated coffee supplies above five kilograms per household. Three days later, the sale of coffee was rationed. The Food Commission made extensive searches of farmers' cellars for food, but the whole system tended to break down. Butter went into hiding, and by the end of 1917 it was not possible in many parts of Sweden to secure as much as one kilogram of butter per person a week.

Most groceries were unable to supply the coffee to which the customers were entitled. The supply of bread was inadequate, and the people mixed all kinds of substitutes with flour. Dandelion roots, peas, and various other substitutes were roasted and used for coffee. Potatoes became very scarce, and the people subsisted largely on rutabagas. Only sugar rationing proved at all satisfactory. Maximum prices had to be changed from time to time, usually sharply upward. By the end of 1917, creamery products had increased 137 per cent in price in less than three years; bread, flour, and related goods rose 61 per cent, meat 112 per cent, fish 151 per cent and other foods 121 per cent.

The grain crop of 1917 was one of the poorest on record since 1867, and the rations of bread and flour had to be cut drastically. Pork disappeared almost entirely from the market. Farmers made sudden trips into cities on business, disposing of their products through illegal channels. Black marketeers demanded 25 crowns per kilo, and often more, for butter, and coffee was sold by jobbers for more than 35 crowns per kilo. Prices varied from community to community throughout Sweden.

The newly rich included every social class, and they splurged their wealth and unpleasant personalities upon a sick nation. Not only did they corrupt public officials through bribery, but their activities in a sense were stimulated by government actions. The Food Commission and other agencies had been slow to act. The Industrial Commission did not resort to necessary confiscation until 1916. The Fuel Commission was not created until 1917, when the shortage of coal was acute, threatening to cripple industries and railroad transportation. Any significant coordination of the war commissions was not achieved until 1917.

The war barons invaded almost every industry and business. More corporations were organized during World War I in Sweden than during any other period of its history, most of them created to profit from the peculiar economic conditions created by the war. The government, by placing special war taxes on individuals and corporations engaged in business especially favored by war, thus actually recognized the legitimacy of the war-created industries and even in a sense encouraged the parasites to organize corporations and expand their business. Loans were granted liberally to industries and to banks to stimulate industrial expansion. The national debt rose from 648,200,000 crowns in 1913 to 1,656,200,000 crowns during the war. Corporation, inheritance, and income taxes were increased, and the government commissions expanded into numerous bureaus. The war was as much the golden age of bureaucrats as of war barons.

It is true that the poor had more money, for wages were higher. But their money bought less goods, and government rationing did not permit them to buy necessary food and clothes. The clothing problem became as acute as the food problem in 1917. The government was too slow also in its attempts to solve the housing problem. An examination of the work of the various commissions would indicate that the government agencies nearly always acted too late. Bread lines and unprecedentedly large numbers of strikes, demonstrations, and riots were the fruits of capitalistic Bolshevism.

The World War divided the Socialists throughout the world into three distinct camps. One group maintained that the real cause of the war was imperialism, regardless of its national origin. The second group believed that labor could expect the greatest prospects of success only where industrialization had made the greatest strides. This group believed that labor had little chance in Russia and desired to see Germany defeat her. The third group believed that Germany was the cause of the World War, and that the choice of the Socialists was between German militarism and Western democracy.

Branting belonged to the third group. He had admired the somewhat unorthodox Marxism represented by Jaurès of France. The German violation of Belgian neutrality made

106

Branting strongly pro-British. However, he had the deepest respect for the actions and motives of others, and in spite of his lack of sympathy for Germany, he did not speak harshly of German Socialists, who were swept off their feet by nationalism. He maintained as far as possible the friendliest relations with these men. He admired Karl Liebknecht for his stand in the German *Reichstag* on December 2, 1914, even though Liebknecht violated party discipline.

Branting had no sympathy for the Zimmerwald German and Russian radicals, who he believed were dividing labor. He was jubilant over the March Revolution of 1917 in Russia, but he hated Bolshevism. Branting's great sense of justice was deeply touched by Wilson's Fourteen Points, and he reacted strongly against efforts by the Allies to humiliate Germany. Sweden was indeed fortunate in having this great labor leader during a period of great unrest. The unrest severely tested his ability as a leader, and when the storm reached the proportions of a tempest, Branting's voice was at times silenced by the roar of the mob. Then he would grow less sympathetic, less tolerant, and did not hesitate to rid his party of dissenters.

In spite of the purge of 1908, all was far from well within the Social Democratic party. In 1915, the Social Democratic party decided that its members in the *Riksdag* were bound to support any measures which the party in a special session decided by a majority vote to support. In 1916, as mentioned before, three members were read out of the party for interventionist propaganda. It looked as if the Social Democrats in the *Riksdag* were trying to dictate to the national party. The Socialist Youth Clubs, which had a tendency to sympathize with Bergegren and Schröder, remained officially under the protection of the Social Democratic party after the purge in 1908. Their membership was really very nominal, but through such newspapers as *Brand, Stormklockan,* and *Folkviljan* the gap between the party and the youth clubs widened. A real rupture sooner or later was inevitable, and was precipitated by Zeta Höglund and Fredrik

Ström who wanted to go their own way, and now looked for an opportunity to win followers. They called a Congress of Social Democratic Youth in March of 1916 where a general strike was advocated as the best means of preventing mobilization for war. Branting believed that Höglund had definitely injured the cause of labor, yet he criticized the severity of the prison sentences given Höglund and two others when they were charged with treason. He also succeeded in having the Second Chamber declare that the seat occupied by Höglund in the *Riksdag* was not vacant while Höglund served his prison sentence.

At the regular party congress of the Social Democrats it was decided that the youth organization must withdraw accusations made against the party for having deserted its program and discontinue the practice of pursuing an independent course at elections, and, finally, must accept a united program for all Social Democratic youth clubs in accordance with decisions made by the Social Democratic party. The congress of the Society of Social Democratic Youth refused to accept the three points specified, preparing the way for the organization of the Left-Wing Social Democratic party in 1917.

This party was prepared to work for a complete extermination of capitalism and looked forward to a millenium with no religion, no law, and no prisons. The firm stand of the Social Democratic party against the young leftist wing weakened its representation in the *Riksdag*, but the purge was nevertheless a profitable one. To show that this party was equally unsympathetic with flirtations in the opposite direction, a member was read out of the party for having in a public address expressed sympathy with the Hammarskjöld government.

Meanwhile Branting led his party in demanding suffrage reform aimed at universal suffrage and the abolition of the graduated suffrage scale of 1 to 40 votes in communal elections. On April 27, 1917, he made a telling speech in the *Riksdag* on the question of suffrage reform, calling attention to the March Revolution in Russia and the general unrest at home.

When the *Riksdag* and the government grew fearful of what might happen on the first of May, Palmstierna said in the Second Chamber: "It is hunger, yes, real hunger, the like of which the Swedish people have not suffered for decades that is driving the workers, women, families to place their demands before the government, their just demands . . ." City workers paraded threateningly along the rural highways to demonstrate their ire over farmers who profiteered in foodstuffs. They tried to frighten even innocent farmers into selling their goods, and in the long breadlines women joined men in cursing the government.

The helpless Swartz administration shrewdly called on Branting for advice. Branting told the authorities that he could not answer for what might happen if the government sought to make use of force to frighten the demonstrators, but that in case the government decided to permit labor to demonstrate without any show of fear he would give his word of honor that the first of May demonstrations would be peaceful and orderly. The government decided to place its confidence in Branting's word of honor rather than in troops. The ensuing demonstrations were peaceful and orderly.

Later events might have had serious results. Branting had demanded an answer from the government on the question of suffrage reform. Labor was dissatisfied with the low wages and high cost of living, and sentiment in favor of a general strike gained in consequence of the prime minister's answer to Branting's demand for reform. On June 5, Swartz stated that he was unwilling to advise the King on the question of a suffrage reform in view of the approaching general election at which the people would have the opportunity to express themselves. At the same time the prime minister stated that the government could not compel employers to raise wages nor adopt an eight-hour day.

Branting, regretting that the answer of the prime minister could not have been different, stated: "The Age of

Democracy has begun and it cannot be checked." A radical by the name of Ivar Vennerström proposed that the time had come to liquidate the monarchy. In early summer a large gathering of workers collected on Gustav Adolf Square. While they waited for a word from Branting, a few stones were hurled at the police, who then charged the mob with drawn swords. The violence could be observed from the windows of the *Riksdag*. Branting hurried out. A sad and at the same time stern Branting marched among mounted police charging on the people. His voice probably could not be heard for the shouting, but, as the tall, powerfully built man walked swiftly across the square to the *Folkets Hus* (Labor Temple) the people followed him. Few more commendable and impressive sights had been witnessed in Swedish history. Höglund, just out of prison, rose in the assembly of the Second Chamber to shout: "Long live the parliament of the street." Though small bands of terrorists sought to embarrass the police during the following days, all danger of a severe clash between workers and the police had been avoided.

During the campaign for the election to the Second Chamber, Branting launched a severe attack against the foreign office as a result of the Buenos Aires "Sink without a trace" message. The discovery in Oslo of a German plot to smuggle explosives onto English ships caused Branting to wonder if the department of foreign affairs in Sweden had completely white hands, for investigation had revealed that the plot to dynamite the English ships had seemingly originated among Germans through the German legations in both Oslo and Stockholm. One thing was sure. The legations had made possible the smuggling of the dynamite into Norway from Sweden. The Oslo police discovered the plot before any damage was done, and the people were infuriated at the revelation.

Branting had no evidence that the Swedish department of foreign affairs was in any way involved, but the police in Sweden had discovered a curious expedition in northern Sweden headed by a lieutenant in the Swedish army. The

110

group carried explosives in their baggage and food containing poison, but what the mission of the group might have been was not clear except that it was operating in the interest of Germany. The press, both Liberal and Conservative, severely criticized Branting for associating the foreign department with the plots, and Branting made a public apology.

Liberals, like the Social Democrats, desired revenge for their setback in 1914, when the Conservative party took control, and they waged a vigorous campaign against reaction and bungling. The Conservative party tried to whitewash itself, placing the blame for lack of food and raw materials on Hammarskjöld rather than upon the party. However, the party lost twenty-seven seats in the Second Chamber, the Liberals gained five seats, the Social Democrats gained fourteen seats, and the Left-Wing Social Democrats lost eleven seats. The Farmers' Association secured nine seats and the Farmers' National Association three seats; these were new political parties.

On October 2, 1917, the Swartz cabinet resigned. The King was still reluctant to turn the government over to the victor and called upon the representatives of all three major political parties with a request that they cooperate in the formation of a coalition government, setting aside party considerations in favor of the general welfare. The Liberals were willing to cooperate if the parties could agree on necessary reforms. The Social Democrats stated that they were willing to cooperate only on the basis of a complete and thorough constitutional reform. As the Conservatives did not desire such reform, a coalition government on the basis outlined by the King was impossible.

The King should have turned for advice to the Social Democratic party as the strongest single party in the Second Chamber, but he was afraid to do so. Instead he asked Professor Nils Edén, leader of the Liberal party to form a cabinet. Edén secured the cooperation of Branting, and a two-party coalition government was created in which the Liberals laid claim to six positions, including that of prime minister, while the Social Democrats received four positions. Branting assumed the portfolio of minister of finance, but ill health soon forced him to resign, and the Social Democrat Fredrik Wilhelm Thorsson succeeded him.

Thorsson was an ordinary working man who proved himself to be one of the ablest men to fill a difficult office during a crisis. With the single exception of Edén, it might be said that the Social Democrats furnished the brains in the new government with such able men as Palmstierna, Värner Rydén, and Professor Östen Undén.

The first aim of the new government was to reorient Sweden's foreign policy toward a better understanding with the Allies in order to alleviate the food scarcity. Germany had approached the Swartz government before its resignation, assuring it that Sweden would no longer have to starve, for the "bread basket" of Central Europe was now open to Sweden. Though the outcome of the war was not certain in October 1917, the Edén government prepared to supply Sweden with its necessities from the Allies, even if this implied that Sweden would have to give the Allies active aid in supplying them with needed shipping tonnage. The new government made possible a closer cooperation between the Scandinavian countries, and Denmark's and Norway's fear of Swedish pro-German sentiments was removed. While the negotiations were carried on with results described in the previous chapter, the attention of Sweden turned toward Russia and Finland.

Finland took advantage of the November Revolution in Russia to proclaim its independence on December 6. The proclamation of independence, however, stirred up a volcano, since among the Finnish workers there was a strong sympathy for the November Revolution, and Red as well as White Guards had been organized in Finland during November. For a week Finland was in the grip of a bloody general strike, suffering want almost beyond description.

Sweden, jubilant over Finland's independence, for the time being forgot its own suffering, and in spite of the great

112

lack of food in Sweden her people heroically sacrificed to help the Finns. The Social Democrats were not so sure that what had happened in Finland could be approved before Russia's attitude had been clarified, and efforts to have Sweden immediately recognize Finland as independent failed. The King also hesitated, for no one knew but what Germany might annex Finland. As soon as it was clear that this was not the intention of Germany, Sweden recognized the independence of Finland on January 4, 1918.

The action of Sweden was undoubtedly too hasty, for the real war for Finland's independence had not begun. The Communists tried to embarrass the new Finnish government, establishing, on June 29, a dictatorship of the proletariat. General Gustaf Mannerheim gathered a group of men around him and began a campaign to drive the Reds out of Finland. Meanwhile the question of the disposition of the Åland Islands had assumed importance to Sweden. The islands were inhabited by Swedes, who sent delegates to Stockholm asking that the Åland Islands be annexed.

Mannerheim pleaded for arms and ammunition to defeat the Red government established in Helsinki. Undoubtedly most of the Swedish people favored immediate aid, but Edén was in a dilemma. The Social Democrats were not in sympathy with the work of Mannerheim. To them it was a class war in which it was impossible for the Swedish workers to side with their natural enemy. Furthermore, Edén was sure that Germany would come to the aid of Mannerheim. Finnish volunteers in the German army who had fought Russia were permitted to return home and join the Mannerheim forces. Thus, if Sweden acted in accordance with its strong sympathies and aided Finland, very soon the Swedish army might be fighting side by side with the German army in Finland, and Sweden would thus be at war with the Allies.

Edén was sure that if Sweden actively helped the White government at Vasa, the Finnish government would in return gladly grant the wishes of the people of the Åland Islands. Johannes Hellner, the minister of foreign affairs, believed

113

that Sweden had no choice and must take the risk involved in active aid to Mannerheim. Branting judged severely the crime committed by the Reds in violation of the principles of democracy, but Thorsson and Herman Lindqvist opposed aid in any form. The labor unrest in Sweden tended to lessen the influence of Branting, whose views were stamped as old and pedantic. If Hellner had succeeded in giving aid to Mannerheim, the Social Democrats would immediately have left the Edén cabinet, and the government would have been crippled.

The government, however, could not ignore the pleas of the people of the Åland Islands, who had presented a horrible picture of their suppression by Russian troops. The press and the public were greatly excited. Sweden's stand on Finland provided the main issue of the *Riksdag* of 1918, even relegating suffrage reform to a relatively unimportant place. A group of citizens decided to act independently of the government and prepared an expedition to the Åland Islands to "drive out the Russians." This forced the government to act, and an official expedition was organized which left for the islands on February 13, 1918. The aim of the expedition was "to be humanitarian," and its use of arms was to be limited to cases of necessity in protecting the civilian population.

By the time the expedition arrived, however, its problem had become much more serious. The islanders had organized themselves into an armed band to rid themselves of the Russians. To make the situation worse, a small group of Red Russians had arrived as well as a group of White Finns from Nystad. The mission of the Swedish troops, as things turned out, was to arbitrate between the people of the island, the Kerensky Russians, the Communist Russians, and the Finnish anti-Communists. Strangely enough the Swedes were successful. The Reds consented to being sent to Åbo, the Finns to being sent to Sweden, while the fate of the Russians was left in the hands of the Swedish government. The Russians consented to the evacuation of Russian state property on the islands, which was placed under the guard of the Swedish troops.

To make this effective the Swedish government sent a battalion of machine gunners to the islands. The "humanitarian expedition" had thus become a step toward military occupation. The anti-Communistic government of Finland protested, and to make the situation worse Russia was now giving active military help to the Reds in Finland. Sweden had offered to arbitrate between the Vasa and the Helsinki governments, but such hopes were now entirely out of the question. Thousands of young Swedes joined Mannerheim's army to fight the Reds. The government proceeded to grant export licenses for arms and ammunition to aid the Vasa government, but in March, only four days after signing the Brest-Litovsk Treaty with the Russian Soviet government, Germany concluded an alliance with Finland. Germany demanded that Russian Red troops in Finland be withdrawn.

The relationship between Sweden and Germany was strained because Sweden refused to join Germany in driving the Russians out of Finland. Two days before the offensive alliance between Germany and Finland was signed, a German escadrille arrived at the Åland Islands. The Swedish government had not decided what should be done with the Russian troops on the islands, but the Germans took immediate possession. Sweden protested and retained its troops on the islands until May 16, after which date Germany had agreed to destroy the fortifications on the islands. Meanwhile, with the aid of the Germans, of whom there were about 12,000 in Finland, Mannerheim was able to restore peace, and his government established itself in Helsinki.

When Sweden withdrew from the Åland Islands, the Swedish government notified the Finnish government that it had by no means prejudiced its position in regard to the ultimate settlement of the deposition of the islands. In the Treaty of Brest-Litovsk Germany and Russia had agreed that the future of the islands should be determined by Germany, Russia, Finland, Sweden, and possibly other nations. The

Conservative party criticized the Liberals and the Social Democrats for having alienated Finland from Sweden by their policy of refusing aid to Mannerheim. They believed that Sweden could easily have granted aid to Finland without becoming involved in the war. Instead Sweden had by its inactivity made Finland a German dependency. On April 29 Mannerheim captured Viborg and cut off Russian help for the Finnish Reds, and in October a German prince was proclaimed as the King of Finland.

The general situation now changed rapidly. The German Empire crumbled, the Finnish King resigned, and Mannerheim took over the reins of Finland as chancellor and succeeded in winning the confidence of the Allies. Sweden had meanwhile improved its relations with the Allies. Not only had a trade treaty been signed with Great Britain, but in June and July Branting had visited London and Paris, at which time he made numerous public statements expressing his sympathy with the Allied war aims. The lack of food remained a severe problem in Sweden throughout 1918, reaching its peak in midsummer, though in the autumn things improved rapidly. Branting had centered his activities largely on two problems during 1917-1918, suffrage reform and international peace.

Again the shortsightedness of the Conservative party was demonstrated. The Edén cabinet had hardly been formed in October 1917 before it requested the three major parties to cooperate in drafting a suffrage reform proposal. The Conservatives refused, believing that the question of reform should be left until after the restoration of peace in Europe. The real reason, of course, was that the Conservatives in the First Chamber refused to be dictated to by the Second Chamber, and the party knew that a radical suffrage reform would be disastrous to its interests. Furthermore, the party refused to support the Eight-Hour Labor Bill introduced by the government. This bill was defeated in the First Chamber and was not approved by the *Riksdag* until 1919, when fear

116

for the possible consequences of refusal to approve the bill by the First Chamber modified opposition.

Labor organizations had become stronger than ever, the National Federation of Trade Unions having more than doubled its membership during the war. Labor conflicts increased. David Bergström, the radical Liberal reformer, had as early as 1915 stated that the era of democracy had come to Europe and that both Denmark and Norway had a more democratic form of government than Sweden. He advocated the abolition of the graduated suffrage scale and franchise rights for corporations in communal elections. But in the regular session of the *Riksdag* of 1918, the efforts made by the Edén government to abolish the gradual suffrage scale in communal elections failed because of opposition in the First Chamber.

While the *Riksdag* was in an extra session in November, the news of the Armistice reached Sweden. It was also reported that Germany and Austria-Hungary were in the midst of a revolution. Five days before the Armistice Branting wrote in *Social-Demokraten* that the people of Sweden would be unable to escape impulses from abroad and that the course of events in Sweden would largely be determined by what happened abroad. On November 11 the Left-Wing Social Democrats decided by means of frequent meetings, demonstrations, strikes, and threats of a general strike to frighten the First Chamber into submission. They threatened to call a new *Riksdag* which would raise the wages of the workers, establish the eight-hour day, order complete demilitarization, and establish a republic. The property of corporations and of the state, and of owners of large estates would be turned over to society and controlled by the crofters, cotters, hired men, sons of farmers, and lumberjacks. The same day, Zeta Höglund addressed a large crowd at the Auditorium in Stockholm to celebrate the Revolution in Russia. He spoke of the dictatorship of the proletariat and lashed Branting.

The Social Democrats were not slow to make use of the unrest, and Edén was urged to place the question of communal suffrage reform before an extra session of the *Riksdag*. On November 1, Edén announced that he would take measures to request the repeal of the graduated suffrage scale. The announcement was perfectly timed to coincide with the appearance of Branting before the Stockholm Labor Commune, where the action of the government was approved. In spite of the seriousness of the situation, many Conservative newspapers stated that the Social Democrats were merely trying to frighten the people, and that the Conservatives should not allow themselves to be coerced.

Swartz was sure, however, that the time had come for the Conservative party to yield, but the other leaders of the party made cooperation impossible. On November 15, the Social Democratic party issued a joint manifesto with the National Federation of Trade Unions in which the Left-Wing Social Democrats and the Conservatives were criticized as extremists. The able Gustav Möller in a speech on November 14 had warned Swedish labor that in case workers rose in a revolution, Sweden would not have a revolution like that in Germany, but a civil war of life and death as in Finland. The manifesto maintained that the question of the establishment of a republic could first be decided after the adoption of the suffrage reform followed by a new election to the *Riksdag*, when also the fate of the First Chamber should be decided.

On November 22, 1918, the Edén government claimed that it would be disastrous to wait until the next *Riksdag* to solve the urgent question of constitutional reform and communal election reform. Branting as chairman of the Constitutional Committee succeeded, even if forced to make some concessions, in securing the cooperation of the Conservative party. The committee drafted a program of reform based upon universal suffrage extending to woman suffrage at the general elections of the Second Chamber and equal suffrage in communal elections, and abolishing the graduated scale and the franchise rights of corporations. The concessions made to the Conservatives pertained to the age and tax requirements. Branting, realizing the importance of the reforms to the political strength of his party, stated: "We shall strain our efforts to represent those larger social divisions in our society which up to the present time have been neglected, but in such a manner that through this action we shall not create an injustice for those who have previously monopolized power."

The reforms were carried in accordance with the program adopted by the *Riksdag* in December 1918. Those pertaining to communal franchise were put into immediate effect in 1919, while those involving constitutional reform were approved by the *Riksdag* of 1919 and, in accordance with the Constitution, again in 1921. This was necessary because only a regularly called *Riksdag* could approve any constitutional changes, which in turn had to be reapproved by a regular *Riksdag* after a general election.

Branting had thus succeeded in laying the foundations for a truly democratic form of government, even if his methods in attaining his goal were open to severe criticism. He had brought pressure to bear on the Edén government and had made use of the general unrest in Sweden to frighten the Conservatives. After the end of the session of the extra *Riksdag* of 1918, the Liberals and Social Democrats joined in paying tribute to the heroes of democracy, Hedin and Staaff, whose services in the hour of triumph were not forgotten. Short addresses and the placing of wreaths on the graves of Hedin and Staaff closed a chapter in Swedish history. Thus, within a month a bloodless revolution had been achieved. Democracy was triumphant.

The victory was purely a national one, and the failure of Branting in his efforts to establish a new order of international justice was destined to be catastrophic. He hoped to revive the Second International and bring pressure to bear on the Peace Conference at Paris for a just peace free from any desire of revenge. The fact that Branting represented only a small country, a neutral one at that, overshadowed his own abilities. Little could and should be expected from

119

a man like Branting, representing a small country like Sweden, when Woodrow Wilson, representing a large victorious nation like the United States, failed to check revengeful feelings. Branting's efforts at international peace, even though they failed, add luster to his brilliant career and do not detract from the importance of his work. In the eyes of some, he, like Wilson, might be branded as a dreamer, who, though having probably not the slightest hope of success, nevertheless did what he could.

Shortly before the war, Branting had been recognized more and more by the Second International as a great leader. In 1910 he had presided at the Congress of the International at Copenhagen, and for several years he served as a member of the executive committee of the International. The Second International was made impotent during the war, and two rival bureaus sought to function as its representatives. The bureaus were the result of the split between the followers of Lenin and Emile Vandervelde. The fact that French and English labor looked with suspicion upon the International strengthened the left wing, the bureau at Berne. In 1916, the bureau at The Hague appeared doomed and so did the entire International, unless an international labor congress could be called to revive it. In April 1917 the delegation in the Netherlands representing the bureau at The Hague decided to move to Stockholm and cooperate with the Swedish Social Democrats in calling an International Labor Congress. A Dutch-Scandinavian Committee, organized with Branting as chairman, proceeded to make plans for the meeting.

At first, success seemed probable. The Russian March Revolution had awakened an international interest of labor in such a congress, but at the same time the European nations at war felt an unrest which reached every workshop and every mine. Hope was revived that the International would be able to end the mass murder. The belligerents would not, however, have a party conference dictate to their respective countries. The congress, which was to have been held in

120

Stockholm on August 15, further suffered by being confused with the congress called on the same date and place by the Zimmerwaldian Berne Commission, which refused to cooperate with the Dutch and Scandinavians. The governments of the Allies denounced the Stockholm Congress as a German trap. The name of Branting carried great prestige, however, and the executive committee of the French Socialist party decided only by a slim vote of thirteen to eleven not to participate in the congress. Branting's fame, plus the refusal of the Lenin extremists to cooperate in the Stockholm Congress, caused the government of Great Britain to hesitate. Arthur Henderson, who had visited Russia and seen the effects of the March Revolution, was enthusiastic over the Stockholm Congress. He urged the War Cabinet not to take any action before the Labor party had a chance to express itself on the invitation from Stockholm. Before the Conference of the Labor party, Henderson embarrassed the British War Cabinet by stating that the participation of English labor in the Stockholm Congress would greatly please Kerensky. By a three to one vote the party decided to accept the invitation.

The War Cabinet, however, forbade participation, being strengthened by the decision of Britain's allies. Labor unrest in Great Britain largely contributed to this decision, while the Cabinet, upon Henderson's resignation, consoled itself with a report from France made by M. Albert Thomas that Kerensky did not desire to see the Stockholm Congress held. The belligerent powers, to be sure that there would be no congress, forbade the issuing of passports to persons who desired to attend it.

Woodrow Wilson's Fourteen Points made a deep impression upon the people of Sweden as a serious effort to prevent international chaos and repetition of the events of 1914 through the establishment of a League of Nations. Many firmly believed that a repetition of the World War could be prevented if an institution existed which sought to maintain international law. Sweden, among other neutrals, took seriously the invitation of Colonel House to send representatives to the Peace Conference to aid in outlining the organization of the League of Nations and its aims. The neutrals were invited to an unofficial session of the Commission on the League of Nations. Sweden requested a postponement in order to prepare herself for the session and outline a program, but the request was denied. She was able to send only one representative, and Branting was unable to attend.

Sweden, however, tried to unite the neutrals on a program in order to strengthen their influence in determining the nature of the League. A preliminary meeting for this purpose was held by delegates from Sweden, Denmark, Norway, the Netherlands, and Switzerland. All three Scandinavian countries had hoped to cooperate in working out a program of international law and disarmament, which they believed they could successfully present at the Peace Conference, but they were sadly disappointed. The matter of the creation of the League was treated entirely as an affair of the victors. In fact, the organization of the League was planned in such a manner as adequately to safeguard the interest of the Great Powers. It was the work of conquerors, and the defeated were excluded from membership. After the organization of the League had been determined without consulting with the neutrals, they were invited to join the League as charter members.

The Armistice had also revived the hope of Social Democrats that the International might again become an effective international agency of organized labor. It was of great importance that it should be revived in order to contribute to the solution of peace questions. An International Labor Congress was, therefore, summoned at Berne on February 3-9, 1919, at which Branting presided. The leftists as well as American and Belgian labor refused to cooperate in the conference, and it seemed that the conference was about to turn into a complete fiasco as the representatives of the belligerent countries debated on war guilt. Branting's program, which was to form the basis for the work of the revived International, was finally, however, adopted. This program condemned revolutionary methods and approved of peaceful parliamentary methods of labor in securing political power.

The congress elected an executive committee of three members, consisting of Branting, Henderson, and Huysmans. These three men were instructed to make efforts to influence the Peace Conference at Paris. But the situation in Europe after 1919 testified to how completely Branting failed in his effort "to make it impossible for the Peace Conference to forget Wilson's program of rebuilding the world." Proudly Branting had spoken at Berne: "Here we are also going to draft our ideas of a League of Nations. But we are not going to do as they do in Paris, allow five great nations to dictate. We are going to build on the solid foundation of the cooperation of all." The Second International did not contribute anything of great value at the Peace Conference, except that its strong support of the League of Nations was a strong factor in saving Woodrow Wilson from being forced to sacrifice all of the Fourteen Points.

The Second International was revived, but the war had played such havoc among the ranks of labor that it proved to be a withering flower. In March 1919 the Third International was organized, but the wounds of divided labor could not be healed. Branting could not fight successfully the emotions of narrow nationalism on the one hand and Communism on the other. In regard to the Peace of Paris, he wrote: "The whole peace will thus become an armistice with new secret treaties constantly threatening peace. The only tiny seed of hope remaining from the Paris negotiations is the League of Nations."

123

CHAPTER IX

LIQUIDATION OF A WAR ECONOMY

$\mathbf{S}$ WEDEN WAS ONE of the first countries in Europe to recuperate from the economic chaos created by the World War. Almost immediately upon the Armistice in November 1918, the government decided to liquidate the very unpopular system of war economy. The task which the government faced might be underestimated, in view of Sweden's neutrality, unless the reader is reminded that few of the nations at war had a more involved system of war economy than Sweden and that no country was so self-sufficient as to be immune from the economic crisis which followed in the wake of the war. Moreover, the fact that the war had encouraged a higher degree of self-sufficiency throughout the world, and not least in Sweden, made the return to normal international trade relations a very rough road.

Many bureaucrats favored the retention of the war commissions, or at least a delay in their dissolution, because they provided effective means of controlling economic developments. The Liberals and the Social Democrats, believing otherwise, however, decided to cooperate in an attempt to return the country as much as possible to the economic circumstances which had existed prior to the outbreak of the war. In January 1919 the Edén government eased the rationing of food and this most unpopular of all the wartime restrictions ended during the summer of 1919. The golden days of speculators in foods was over. Strangely enough, almost as if by magic, there was no longer a scarcity, as goods stored for speculative purposes were released. Perhaps much of the regulation never had been necessary. Most of the price laws, however, could not be repealed until 1921 because of inflationary conditions.

The War Trade Commission showed a small profit when

it ceased to function in October 1919. The War Insurance Commission, with an excellent financial record, was able virtually to close its business in July 1919, except for protection granted fishing vessels. By that time the greatest dangers to shipping had been removed. The government had proceeded immediately in 1919 to remove all possible danger from mines along the coast of Sweden. The excellent financial record of the War Insurance Commission indicated that Swedish shipping losses during the war were not as great as had been expected. At the end of 1922 the special insurance protection granted the fisherman was no longer necessary, and the War Insurance Commission was dissolved.

The War Industrial Commission, though one of the more efficient units, was unable to present a record of profits. By the end of the spring of 1919 all restrictions on the sale of gasoline, metals, kerosene, wool, cotton, fats, and other goods had been removed, and by 1921 the regulation of industries had ceased. The work of the Housing, Fuel, and Unemployment Commissions could not be as readily liquidated because in the first years after the war the cost of living and housing increased, and the housing problem could not therefore readily be solved without government aid. The government had done little prior to 1917 to check the owners of apartments and landlords in general from reaping benefits from the lack of adequate housing facilities. When the war broke out, building ceased in spite of the fact that housing conditions were far from satisfactory. Rents rose sharply. The government then decided to encourage the building trade by granting special freight rates for building material. Loans were granted on favorable terms to contractors, but the government policy was far from satisfactory. The complaints of tenants over various practices of the landlords finally caused the Housing Commission to encourage the establishment of Tenant-Landlord Arbitration Boards throughout the larger cities. The War Housing Commission could not be dissolved entirely until 1924, at which time war housing legislation was repealed. The saddest commentary on waste was offered by the Fuel Commission, which could not be dissolved until the *Riksdag* appropriated 121,800,000 crowns over the period 1921-1923 to cover the indebtedness of this commission. The speed with which the government eliminated the work of the war commissions in general is illustrated by the fact that in 1918 the five largest war commissions employed about 5000 people, while on April 1, 1920, they employed only 239 persons.

The rapid dissolution of the war commissions was due not only to public resentment against the work of the commissions but also the general feeling that the May 1918 trade treaties of Sweden with Great Britain, France, Italy, and the United States, as well as closer economic cooperation of the three Scandinavian countries would largely solve the immediate economic problems of food and raw materials. The sharp drop in prices which was expected did not occur, however, except on special war goods or substitutes. The immediate advantages of a neutral became apparent. While the nations which had been at war were engaged in the tremendous task of demobilization and closing down munition works, Sweden witnessed a boom. Peace restored to Sweden a market that it had lost during the war. The seas were free, and Swedish trade broke all records during 1919-1920.

The state finances seemed sound even though the national debt had been increased by about 1,000,000,000 crowns, an insignificant sum compared with the cost of the war to the belligerents. Furthermore, the Swedish debt was not a foreign debt. Before the war Sweden had been a debtor nation. During the war the great value of her exports as compared with her imports made Sweden a creditor nation. Moreover, Sweden had developed a strong merchant marine, which was able to take advantage of the shortage of ship tonnage created by the war.

The boom did not last long. Labor unrest and an unstable international currency, the penalities placed upon Germany by the Versailles Treaty, widespread discouragement of international trade by adoption of more vigorous protection for home industries, and intensified competition turned the Swedish boom into a serious depression. During the war the belligerents were the chief sufferers, but all nations shared alike in the ensuing chaotic international conditions.

As Germany was, next to Great Britain, Sweden's best customer, the economic effects of the Treaty of Versailles were keenly felt. Inflation in Germany caused Sweden to be flooded by German goods, while Germany, in turn, was unable to buy much from Sweden. In 1920 a depression had its effect on Swedish trade, both exports and imports dropping sharply. Manufacturers requested a reduction in the freight rates on railroads and increased tariff protection. The *Riksdag* of 1920 refused to grant the request, but the government decided to study the question. The minister of commerce consulted with numerous representatives of Swedish industries, whom he found to be divided as to what course the government should take. Many of them believed that tariff protection would lead only to retaliation by foreign countries. Lower freight rates and reduced production seemed the only solutions to a serious problem. Most of them, however, advocated increased tariff protection, and in 1921 the government recommended a drastic change in the tariff policy, granting an increased protection of 30 per cent to 100 per cent on goods most sensitive to foreign competition. The Social Democrats and most Liberals felt certain, however, that higher tariff protection would not alleviate the situation. But when the effect of war speculation threatened to ruin the farmer by the importation of German grain, the *Riksdag* could not escape granting the farmers protection.

One of the causes for the plight of Swedish industries was inflation, which was more than necessarily severe during the war. In December 1914 the amount of paper money in circulation was 304,060,000 crowns, while in December 1918 it amounted to 813,580,000 crowns. Though gold redemption had been stopped on August 2, 1914, it was not until 1917 that the government was able in a measure to control prices.

In spite of this, the cost of living in 1919 was more than two and one half times as high as in 1914. As there was no standard on which to base the actual amount of inflation in Sweden except the American dollar, it might be estimated that in comparison with the American dollar the Swedish crown had been inflated 40 per cent in 1920.

Meanwhile Swedish labor had secured an actual increase in wages. When employers sought to reduce wages, strikes and lockouts followed, and unemployment became a serious problem. By January 1922, 163,000 workers were unemployed, a number unparalleled in Swedish history.

The Swedish government decided that the only road to economic recovery was a return to the gold standard. The person largely responsible for this policy was the Social Democrat Thorsson. Such a policy would speed the decline of prices and in its wake would be bankruptcies, increased unemployment, a bank crisis, and unrest. The government, however, showed some inclination to soften its policy by rendering assistance to the banks, which were threatened by insolvency, and by extending unemployment relief.

Thorsson was handicapped, however, in establishing his policy because of certain political changes. When it was discovered in Sweden that two cabinet members had been heavily interested in the Swedish Import Corporation, which had failed, the Edén government rocked. The Liberals and Social Democrats had finally come to the parting of ways in the matter of communal taxation, the latter advocating a progressive feature which would have boosted the tax greatly. The Social Democrats had in the autumn of 1919 increased their strength in the First Chamber, until in 1920 they were the strongest single party in that chamber. Branting and Thorsson desired to continue cooperation with the Liberals, but other influential Social Democrats were growing restless and believed that the time had come for the party to try its own hand at governing Sweden. Edén was forced to resign, and on March 10, 1920, Branting formed his first Social Democratic cabinet.

It is doubtful if any cabinet since Louis De Geer's first one had included more intellectual prowess. The Branting cabinet included Thorsson, Palmstierna, Undén, Per Albin Hansson and as consultants, Richard Sandler and Torsten Nothin. The distrust of the Social Democrats was modified by the great popularity of Branting. The public was proud of the fact that no person in Sweden enjoyed greater respect abroad. Legends were spun around him. The mass of the people had forgotten his revolutionary Marxism. To them he was a leader with whom they were proud to associate. He was kindness personified, he was straightforward, he was refined and cultured, and he was a fluent speaker with enough pathos in his appeals to touch hearts without giving offense.

The mass of the people reasoned that inasmuch as the Social Democrats were in power in Germany, maybe the time had come for a labor government in Sweden. Branting succeeded in enacting the progressive communal tax law. The period of compulsory military training was drastically reduced to 165 days. A number of other pending reforms and measures prepared during his regime were approved by the *Riksdag*. Large appropriations encouraged the building trade. Tax laws on income and fortunes were adjusted upward, and taxes fixed on the sale of liquor. The departments of commerce, transportation, and social affairs were created. The two departments of defense were merged into one, and the old department of civil affairs was absorbed by the department of social affairs.

The tax reforms were in complete accord with the program of the Social Democrats and of themselves would not have led to the resignation of the Branting cabinet. But Branting had appointed three large commissions, one to study industrial democracy, a second to study socialization of industry, and a third to study the question of state control of trusts. The first two commissions frightened the public. It looked as if the Social Democrats really intended to carry out their Marxian ideals. Many Social Democrats doubtless

130

believed that Branting had acted unwisely, and his reputation as a legislator was seriously impaired. The war commissions had not yet been completely liquidated, and the people had by no means forgotten the chaotic conditions created by state regulation and control of almost every aspect of life during the war.

A study of the problems of a democracy such as found in Sweden made Branting's move significant, though for the time being politically unwise. The influence of communistic Russia on Sweden was growing stronger. Not only were the Socialist party and the Left-Wing Social Democrats flirting with Bolshevism, but the accusation that the Social Democratic party had deserted its Marxian ideals seemed justified. By the appointment of the commissions to study industrial democracy and socialization of industry, the wounds caused by the breach between the radical orthodox Marxists and the conservative unorthodox Marxists could be healed. Branting seemed to be flirting with the Left-Wing Social Democratic party.

The step taken by Branting was not, however, meant to be revolutionary, even if interpreted as such. It was intended rather as a lesson for the radicals. It was a costly lesson, for in the September elections to the Second Chamber the Social Democratic party had to pay the penalty exacted by a frightened public. The membership of the party in the Second Chamber was reduced from 86 to 75, the first electoral reverse of the party in its history. Branting requested the Liberals to cooperate with him, inviting them to join with him in the formation of a coalition cabinet. The Liberals refused. Gustav V, anxious not to damage Branting's international influence while the fate of the Åland Islands had not been decided, requested Branting to remain as prime minister with his cabinet.

Branting believed that the verdict of the people had not been decisive, but he was unable successfully to carry on without the cooperation of the Liberals. The economic crisis was assuming new proportions, and the Conservative party, which had made the greatest gains in the election, did not wish to assume the control of the government. The King then resorted to an old and rather unique Swedish practice. In times of great crises, the bureaucrats could always be depended upon, and the King, therefore, requested Louis De Geer, Jr., a former Liberal, to organize a nonpartisan cabinet.

As a stop-gap government, it performed a mission, but when it failed to secure added tariff protection for industries and an increased duty on coffee, De Geer resigned. The duty on coffee was aimed at balancing the budget, but the public had been deprived of coffee for so long during the war that a cup of coffee was far more important to them than a balanced budget. Oskar von Sydow was appointed prime minister, but no change in the character of the cabinet occurred.

Because of the adoption of the universal suffrage reform in the autumn of 1921, von Sydow dissolved the Second Chamber and requested a new general election. In this election the Social Democratic party gained 18 seats, and the King relieved von Sydow of his duties, whereupon Branting formed his second party cabinet in October 1921. In order to strengthen his government Branting had again unsuccessfully requested the Liberals to cooperate with him in the cabinet. His party had neither a majority in the First nor in the Second Chamber, even though it was the strongest single party. The economic depression had become by this time acute and unemployment serious. Branting believed that Swedish trade might profit by the recognition of Russia, but when both chambers of the *Riksdag* refused such a measure unless Sweden were compensated for the loss of capital in Russia during 1917-1919, Branting's position was weakened.

The Branting government suffered because he had taken upon himself too many duties. Besides being prime minister, he held the office of minister of foreign affairs and represented Sweden at the League of Nations. Even though the

H. M. KING GUSTAV V OF SWEDEN
Born on June 16, 1858; succeeded to the throne on December 8, 1907.

ORREFORS VASE

achievements of the *Riksdag* of 1922 cannot be attributed to the work of the Branting cabinet, it was in a degree responsible for the adoption of the referendum, a new sailors' law, discontinuation of state regulation of grain and sugar prices, large appropriations for the encouragement of the building trade and of home ownership, the appropriation of 1,000,000 crowns for the Swedish Red Cross for famine relief in Russia, and a higher duty on coffee. The last did not exactly please the Social Democrats, but the budget had to be balanced.

In this effort, the name of Thorsson looms large. Thorsson decided that the time had come when economy in government had to be introduced. Before the end of 1922, he had reduced the number of government committees from 162 to 70, and by 1924 only 26 government committees existed. The task of Thorsson, who in the absence of Branting was the director of this work, was gigantic.

Branting was so occupied by his many duties that the cabinet might just as well have been called the Thorsson cabinet. It was also the Thorsson policy of economic recovery which, though successful, caused the fall of the Branting cabinet. When prices began to fall in the United States, Thorsson insisted on a return to the gold standard, which, though it seemed to be Sweden's only logical recourse, had, nevertheless, some serious consequences. Swedish industry was hard hit by German dumping, and the quotation on the money exchange of the Swedish crown did not conform with the price declines. As a result, Swedish export suffered.

This hurried the decline in prices and caused much unemployment. The Swedish private banks were heavily interested in Swedish industries, almost 39 per cent of their loans being based on stocks as collateral. The value of the stocks tumbled even more rapidly than prices. Corporations failed, and the banks were in a precarious position. A number of banks were forced to reorganize at severe losses to stockholders. The government decided to aid the banks, and the Credit Fund Corporation of 1922 was created. The resources of this credit fund consisted of 50,000,000 crowns, contributed by the government toward the basic capitalization of the corporation, and the banks contributed 5,000,000 crowns as stockholders.

The purpose of the corporation was to facilitate reorganization of embarrassed banks by granting loans to banks on the basis of bank stock and corporation securities, on condition that the Credit Fund Corporation would be permitted to sign for a specified number of stocks in the reorganized banks. The Credit Fund Corporation assisted in the reconstruction of three large banks. It refused to grant help to a fourth, the Swedish Land Bank, whose financial position was so precarious that the Credit Fund Corporation did not care to jeopardize itself by aiding it. As it was a large bank and its failure would involve calamitous losses among farmers, the government decided to act independently of the Credit Fund Corporation. After the bank was forced to close certain business activities, the government recommended to the *Riksdag* that a new bank be founded to take over the business of the Swedish Land Bank. It was proposed that the government subscribe in behalf of the state for stocks in the new bank to the amount of 15,000,000 crowns, while the public should be invited to subscribe for stocks to the amount of 5,000,000 crowns. The *Riksdag* approved the proposal, and the Agricultural Bank was organized to take over the business of the Swedish Land Bank. Some of the banks were able to write down their assets without any aid from the government. The bank crisis in Sweden finally passed without involving the loss of a penny to the depositors. Yet, during 1920-1924, the number of banks was reduced from 41 to 32, and their assets had been written down from 472,500,000 crowns to 278,900,000 crowns.

The great crisis had been averted in spite of the fact that the decline in prices had been more rapid in Sweden than in most countries. Between June 1920 and November 1922 prices dropped by 57 per cent. At the beginning of 1922 the labor unions reported that 35 per cent of their members were unemployed. In April 1921 the National Bank began gradually to reduce the interest rate until by June 1922 it was fixed at 4½ per cent. The crown had nearly reached its old gold parity. A few protested against the Thorsson policy outlined in 1920 for a speedy return to the gold standard, but by the end of 1922 the trends were definitely toward a return to normal conditions. Widespread unemployment in 1921 and 1922 handicapped Thorsson, and sentiment gained ground for Sweden's cooperation with England, the Netherlands, Switzerland, and others in a common effort to check inflation. If Great Britain could have been induced to follow the example set by Sweden, success of the Thorsson policy would probably have been assured. In the autumn of 1922 the crown reached its former gold value, and in December it rose above the old gold parity. The National Bank was not forced to check the rise through the purchase of foreign currency. In January 1923 the National Bank had been successful by means of foreign currency purchased to control the value of the crown. The National Bank now sought to gauge the crown by the American dollar. This offered difficulties, for during the last part of 1922 there was a rise in prices of commodities in America, while prices were still falling in Sweden.

Some members of the *Riksdag* questioned the wisdom of the Thorsson policy, advising the National Bank that it would be unwise for Sweden alone of all European countries to return to the gold standard. Thorsson had by no means changed his mind, however, and the *Riksdag* agreed with him that a return to the gold standard was desirable as soon as it did not involve a risk. For a while the National Bank engaged in a dubious policy of trying to retain the parity of the crown and the dollar. It resorted to double quotations, necessitated by the rise in the value of the dollar. In 1924 the Banking Committee of the *Riksdag* recommended that the export prohibition on gold be repealed and the gold standard adopted. The National Bank felt that this would be unwise, for Sweden would then be flooded with gold. But when the *Riksdag* agreed to prohibit the importation of gold into Sweden except by the National Bank, the most serious objections were removed, and on July 1, 1924, Sweden decided to return to the gold standard.

It was no longer necessary for the National Bank to gauge the crown after the dollar. Norway and Denmark had been unable to follow the example set by Sweden, creating a rather difficult situation. The three Scandinavian countries had entered into a currency union several decades before the war, which allowed the currencies of the three countries to be freely exchanged and used in any one of the others. During the war, the inflation was more rapid in Norway and Denmark than in Sweden. In 1923 the currencies of those countries were worth only 44 per cent and 34 per cent respectively of the Swedish crown. The paper money of Norway and Denmark was not accepted in Sweden, while the silver currency freely circulated at par. As a result of these problems, the Scandinavian countries agreed in 1924 to dissolve their currency union.

Thorsson's policy had left bankruptcies and widespread unemployment in its wake. It had also been costly to the state. The state policy of aiding the banks through the Credit Fund Corporation involved a loss by the state of about two hundred million crowns and forced the state to revolutionize its unemployment policy. Unemployment might have been checked by a tariff law which would have prevented dumping in Sweden, but no such aid was given to the harassed industries. Instead, the government decided to encourage domestic industries by more government spending, and in 1922 the government placed orders with various Swedish manufacturers to the amount of 15,000,000 crowns. In addition, freight rates were reduced, and private railroads were compensated for losses. Otherwise, industry was forced to solve its own problems. This they did by greater economies, lower wages, and a reduction of personnel. The system of production was simplified, new machinery introduced, new markets sought, and capitalization reduced.

Thus, while the Thorsson policy was recognized as sound

by almost every economist in Sweden, it created increased unemployment for the time being. Under ordinary conditions unemployment in Sweden was chiefly seasonal, affecting unskilled workers in agriculture first, and then workers in the building trades. The agricultural workers, however, were usually able to find employment in the lumber, sawmill, tile, and sugar industries during the winter, and their unemployment offered no serious problem. The problem of seasonal unemployment was much greater in the cities, snow clearing and ice cutting providing not nearly enough work to fill the gap. Cyclical unemployment was most serious in the great export industries, lumber and iron being most sensitive to international conditions. The greatest stability was offered by agriculture, and as long as agriculture remained the chief industry in Sweden there was little danger of catastrophic unemployment, especially as Swedish farming was characterized by small holdings capable of taking care of a family.

The Swedish unemployment policy had been to grant appropriations to communities for relief work, without requiring the local governments to match the funds supplied by the state, until it was discovered that this policy caused local governments to be wasteful and extravagant in their relief program. To overcome this, the state decided to contribute only the amount matched by local governments. Local unemployment committees were created to cooperate with the Swedish Official Employment Agency. This cooperation was achieved through provincial unemployment committees, which supervised the local committees or agencies. The government policy was to grant aid only to those unable to work, i.e., the sick and the cripples. Poor relief and unemployment relief were thus two entirely different things. The initiation of unemployment help was left entirely in the hands of local authorities, a policy which had been in the main established in 1914 when the Unemployment Commission was created.

The operation of the system was very simple. The unemployed notified the nearest office of the employment bureau, telling the agent the kind of work the person was capable of doing. If the bureau found no employment in the open labor market, the local employment committee was notified that it must provide the unemployed with relief work or contribute to his support. The last kind of help could consist of food, clothes, tools, or cash. It was soon discovered that financial help by outright cash relief or even clothes and food was an undesirable form of relief, as it was no test of willingness to work. Authorities soon found government projects which offered plenty of opportunity for testing the willingness of the unemployed to work.

In order, however, to discourage labor from preferring public work projects to regular employment, it was decided in 1916 that the wage was to be only two-thirds of what the worker might earn through other employment. In 1921 and 1922 the powers of the Unemployment Commission were increased. Local communities were forced to secure special approval of the Unemployment Commission for local projects in order to regulate the amount the government would contribute toward these projects. This made possible greater coordination of national and local works projects and prevented more or less useless projects from being undertaken. The Commission was also authorized to reduce further the wages on public works projects to one half the regular wage of unskilled labor. This was a necessary step in view of the fact that agricultural labor complained that it received less pay on the farms than the workers employed on public works.

To make the wage scales scientific on the basis of the varied costs of living in different communities, a study of unskilled wages was necessary. Such a study even at its best would leave much to be desired, certain advantages necessarily attending work on public projects. If the public work project was situated at such a distance as to make it impossible for the worker to live at home, the state provided him with special compensation. Rainy days or illness did not stop the pay check. In addition, the laborer was paid for transportation to and from work. Special provisions were made for the worker to secure food, clothes, and lodging under actual cost. The tendency during the economic crisis after the war was to overpay rather than underpay the workers, because of declining prices.

Labor conflicts left the Unemployment Commission perplexed as to what course it would adopt in handling strikes and lockouts. In fact, the Unemployment Commission itself faced strikes and blockades of public works when it reduced wages in 1920 and 1921. The policy seemed to be to force organized labor to accept reduced wages offered by the employers, with the result that the Unemployment Commission became very unpopular among labor unions. The labor conflicts were particularly severe after the war because the collective agreements which did not contain a clause providing for a 48-hour week were made void by the Eight-Hour Labor Law of 1919. Labor wanted the same weekly wages for the shorter week as for the longer, while the employers wanted to reduce the wages.

Both employers and labor were in a stronger position than prior to the war. The employers had been strengthened by a series of mergers of employment associations, until the Swedish Employers' Association loomed as the undisputed giant of employers, ready to deal with organized labor. Furthermore, such large corporations as the Swedish Match Corporation and Stora Kopparbergs Corporation employed about 6,000 workers each. Six corporations employed 4,000 or more each, and a large number of corporations employed over 2,000. Of course, the National Federation of Trade Unions also had witnessed a rapid growth during the war. At the end of 1915 the Federation had about 110,000 members, while at the end of 1920 it had increased to 280,000. The total membership of organized labor in 1920 amounted to 400,000 in 1920 compared with 150,000 in 1915. The National Federation of Trade Unions did not have the power, however, that its membership indicated. Groups within the Federation believed that the time had come for the reorganization of the labor unions. Labor had been divided since 1910 when the Syndicalists established their own central organization.

In 1920 one group within the National Federation favored the retention of the old trade unions based on national trades; another group favored national industrial unions; a third group favored the combination of both types of unions on a national scale; a fourth group favored only local unions; and a fifth group favored the policy of a federation of national trade and industrial unions as represented in the National Federation of Trade Unions. In 1924 Branting predicted that it would be impossible for the National Federation to exist if labor continued to be thus divided.

The extreme radicals within the labor organizations knew no more efficient means of dealing with the capitalists than dynamiting. Sabotage became a word often used by the Syndicalists. In its less dangerous forms sabotage implied obstruction by doing careless work, wasting time, and accomplishing as little as possible for the wage received. In its more severe form sabotage implied obstruction through destruction of machines, plants, and material. The situation was so critical in 1922 that the Syndicalists were able to secure a hearing before the National Federation of Trade Unions, but the methods of Syndicalism were denounced by the Labor Congress. Supported by the Left-Wing Social Democratic party, the Syndicalists then threatened the continuation of the Inter-Scandinavian Labor Congress. In 1920 the Left-Wing Social Democrats were refused admission to the Inter-Scandinavian Labor Congress, causing Norwegian Revolutionary Socialists to refuse to attend. The Syndicalists called their own congress and declared that cooperation between capital and labor was impossible.

Yet the Syndicalists did not offer the National Federation of Trade Unions its gravest problem. The greatest danger came from the Communists, who were instructed to cooperate in all measures with the National Federation of Trade Unions, win the confidence of labor, and gradually gain control of the labor unions. Besides these troubles, conflicting interests of the trade unions and the industrial unions created friction. Even the National Federation of Trade Unions at one time found itself blockaded. In 1923 there were numerous lockouts in the iron, paper, sawmill, and building trades, and only with difficulty were the leaders of the National Federation able to prevent the radicals from winning the approval of a general strike. Again, in 1925, when about 130,000 workers were involved in lockouts, the Communists urged a general strike.

The fact that the National Federation of Trade Unions weathered this critical period was largely due to the leadership of Herman Lindqvist, who gained great personal prestige from both labor and employers as a result of his conservative policy. He was aided also by the fact that the legal status of labor unions had been clarified through the Act on Settlement of Trade Disputes of 1920. Through this law the civil responsibilities of employer and labor organizations were defined, and collective agreements were made legally enforceable by law. A Board of Labor Arbitration was created consisting of seven members, of which three were appointed by the government, two by the Swedish Employers' Association, and two by the National Federation of Trade Unions. The Board of Arbitration would consider a case only when both employers and labor consented to arbitration, and its authority was limited entirely to the problem of interpreting collective agreements.

The work of the National Federation of Trade Unions was also made less difficult by the fact that the Left-Wing Social Democrats returned to the fold of the Social Democratic party. The truth of the matter was that radicalism and individualism were very closely related. The schism within the Social Democratic party during the war, which led to the founding of the Left-Wing Social Democratic party, was the result of a desire not to conform. It was a revolt of the young against the discipline of their elders. When they grew older they discovered not only that some form of discipline was necessary but that they had by the schism exposed themselves to Russian influences far more demanding upon them than the discipline of the Social Democratic party. Realizing that they had greater freedom within the old party, they requested to be reinstated as members.

Syndicalism and Communism received a bad reputation and were effectively stamped by National Federation of Trade Unions and the Social Democratic party as "un-Swedish." Another illustration of the truth that radicalism and individualism were closely related was a split among the Communists in Sweden. Zeta Höglund became the leader of one of the Communist parties. A greater individualist than Höglund could not have been found. He would prefer to sit in prison any time rather than submit to dictation, and he was too Swedish to allow the Third International to influence him.

Despite the fact that neither the National Federation of Trade Unions nor the Social Democratic party was pleased or even partly satisfied with the position taken by the Unemployment Commission in the conflict between organized employers and labor, the government's unemployment policy greatly contributed toward helping organized labor during a troubled period. What was a fair attitude to take by the Unemployment Commission in a labor conflict? Was labor involved in a strike or a lockout unemployed? The employers maintained that labor under such circumstances was not unemployed and that, if the government gave work to labor under such circumstances, it gave active assistance to organized labor detrimental to the employers. What was the attitude of the Unemployment Commission when an employer involved in a strike offered work to men employed at public works? The employers insisted that when they offered work to men employed on public works these should immediately be classified as employed, even if they refused to accept the employment.

Organized labor took just exactly the opposite view. It maintained that the Unemployment Commission must be entirely impartial. This could only be done if the unemployed in a labor union prior to a strike continued to be classified as unemployed after a strike had ensued. Only those, the labor unions claimed, should be classified as employed that were actively engaged in a strike.

The Unemployment Commission sided with the employers and notified all its agencies that every opportunity for employment, regardless of labor conflicts, should be used to decrease the cost of unemployment relief. If work was offered, persons refusing to accept were to be immediately stricken off the records of the unemployed. The Unemployment Commission went so far in its partisan policy that when a strike broke out in an industry in a district, all persons engaged in the work of that industry were classified as employed even if many of them were, prior to the strike, engaged on public work projects. As the Thorsson economic policy aimed at the return of Sweden to the gold standard, and prices dropped, the cruelty of the Unemployment Commission may be realized.

Strikes and lockouts spread throughout the nation. The Social Democrats succeeded in appropriating large sums for unemployment relief work, but they failed in defining the scope of the activities of the Unemployment Commission. The Commission was allowed by the *Riksdag* of 1923 largely to determine its own policy on the basis of certain principles, already mainly recognized by the Commission. Thus, in case of general labor conflicts involving strikes, lockouts, or blockades within an industry or trade, all unemployment aid was to cease within the area involved in the conflict, if the industry represented in the conflict provided the chief employment of the majority workers within the area. If such conflicts, strikes, lockouts, and blockades represented only a minority of the employed in a given area, all unemployment work should continue undisturbed. If then an employer offered work to persons on public works projects and was refused, the case should be reported to the Commission, which would decide whether the refusal was justified or not. The state, furthermore, refused to recognize the right of labor to strike on public works projects.

Though cruel, this policy was sound and served the interest of both parties. It was not recognized as sound in 1923, however, and Branting's cabinet resigned when the policy of the Unemployment Commission was not modified. An adjustment was necessary after the war, and the less this adjustment was prolonged the sooner the industries would be in a position to return to a basis of sound production. High wages and rapidly declining prices gave labor an advantage. The government refused aid to industry by means of tariff protection, while the Thorsson policy exposed industry to severe foreign competition from countries with inflated currency. The return to normal conditions offered hardships to both employers and employees. When the adjustment had been made, Sweden was in a position to profit.

The farmers were given government aid in abundance, since the farmers were thought to be hardest hit by postwar conditions. The government retained grain price laws for a time to assure the farmers of a minimum price on grain, placed a graduated tariff on agricultural goods, made agreements with flour mills that a fixed amount of Swedish grain should be used in the production of flour, granted grain loans, and stimulated scientific farming, but nothing seemed to help. On top of it all, the farmers' livestock contracted the dreaded hoof-and-mouth disease during 1924-1925. Thus even the farmers were forced into bankruptcies, or compelled to make necessary adjustments, such as marking down the values of their land, livestock, and implements.

When the Dawes plan put an end to inflation in Germany, and other countries followed Sweden's example of returning to the gold standard, Sweden was in a more favorable position than any other country to take advantage of the return of normal international trade. The public works had provided Sweden with much needed improvements in communication and transportation; the banking institutions were sound; and the industries had been forced to make the adjustments necessary to face new obstacles in the tariff walls erected in America and Europe after the war.

CHAPTER X

NEW FOUNDATIONS FOR A SOCIAL DEMOCRACY

THE SUFFRAGE REFORMS of 1918-1921 gave democracy its triumphant entry into Sweden, even though, as the previous chapter has indicated, the road ahead was somewhat rough and the virtues of democracy were severely tested during the postwar crisis. Through 1918-1921 the following measures had invited democracy: All property qualifications for franchise in communal elections were abolished, and any person, regardless of sex, who had reached the age of 23 and paid a tax during any one of the three years preceding an election qualified for suffrage in communal elections. Universal suffrage was introduced in the general elections to the Second Chamber, the age minimum fixed at 23, tax requirements abolished, and only people who were the wards of the public authorities disqualified. The only undemocratic features remaining in the Swedish government were to be found in the long term of tenure, fixed at eight years for the members of the First Chamber, the thirty-five year age eligibility for membership in this chamber, and the income or property requirements. In 1933 the income and property qualifications for membership in the First Chamber were eliminated, and in 1936 the age qualification was reduced to 23.

The first reforms dealing with municipal elections had an immediate effect on the First Chamber, where the Conservatives' membership was reduced from 86 to 38, while the Social Democrats increased their membership from 19 to 49. After the constitutional change of 1921, which granted suffrage to women in the general elections to the Second Chamber, a new election was held. This did not bring about a significant change. If anything, women exerted a conservative influence on elections. There had been no strong

145

women's suffrage movement in Sweden as in England and the United States, but existing political organizations among women engaged in more active work were affiliated with the Social Democratic party. Furthermore, the excitement over women's suffrage in Sweden was not as great as in countries where women had not enjoyed suffrage in communal elections.

The election of 1921 was, therefore, almost uneventful. The Social Democrats polled 630,855 votes, the Conservatives 449,302 votes, the Farmers 192,269 votes, the Liberals 332,765 votes, the Left-Wing Social Democrats 56,241 votes and the Communists, for the first time participating in a national election, received a slightly larger vote than the Left-Wing Social Democrats. Minority representation entitled the parties to the following representation in the Second Chamber: The Social Democrats were entitled to 93 seats, the Conservatives to 62, the Liberals to 41, the Farmers to 21, the Communists to 7, and Left-Wing Social Democrats to 6 seats. Though the Social Democratic party and the Liberal party had fought minority representation, these parties never made an issue of a return to the old system of majority representation. In fact, Per Albin Hansson, who upon the death of Branting became the symbol of democracy and labor rule in Sweden, was a warm supporter of minority representation.

The party had also discarded its opposition to the First Chamber. In the elections to the provincial assemblies the Social Democrats constantly increased their majorities until in 1940 the Social Democratic party was able to control the First Chamber. Prudence, therefore, dictated to the Social Democrats not to attack what was once the fortress of conservatism, for it now safeguarded the party from political winds which might more suddenly influence the composition of the Second Chamber. Minority representation provided the party with an insurance against the fickleness of the voter. Every measure taken by the Conservatives to insure Sweden against labor rule had the opposite result, even though all the political parties through minority representation were provided more or less with a life and permanent disability insurance.

The great suffrage reforms of 1918-1921, instead of intensifying political party strife, created, after 1924, an era of good will. The most important political issues had been settled. Demilitarization of Sweden was in accordance with international developments and in harmony with the sentiments expressed in the Treaty of Versailles. The fact that Sweden had been able to remain neutral during the war also reduced the chances for the Conservative party to carry a program of national defense which would be looked upon as satisfactory by military experts.

The need for more effective social legislation was recognized by almost everyone. Sweden had no foreign policy beyond cooperation with the League. It was true that the Conservatives were not enthusiastic about the League, and any effort to alter the traditional isolationist policy of Sweden was doomed.

Thus the democratization of Sweden during 1918-1921 did not involve such radical changes as might be expected. The King no longer appointed the speaker of the Second Chamber and the chairman of the First Chamber, but this was no important change. Nor did the rise of the Social Democratic party check the influence of the bureaucrats. It was true that the growth of this party gave rise to a class of professional politicians, who as leaders in the party could always expect to be returned to their seats in the *Riksdag*. Rewarding political experience, however, was a sound development. Politics became a profession.

Furthermore, recognition within the Social Democratic party had to be earned the hard way, by evidenced leadership in youth organizations, study circles, labor organizations, and work within the party expressed in achievement. The one great fault in politics as a profession was the tendency of the politician to be careful in choosing a party that could assure him a permanent seat in the *Riksdag*. The strength of the Social Democratic party, for example, invited persons to join it for a purpose. Though the principles of civil service had been based on personal ability and permanency of tenure, a way was always found for awarding important offices to men who had performed special service to the kingdom, even though the qualifications of the appointee did not always justify such an appointment. Once appointed they could, however, not be removed. Civil service offered security, and the universities gave special courses for college students desiring to enter civil service. The promotion of civil servants was slow unless the civil servant was unusually capable. The disappointed civil servant sometimes decided to join the political party best able to serve his interest. There was no law against a civil servant having membership either in a political party or in the *Riksdag*. Large numbers of civil servants became leaders of political parties, for the parties realized the value of experts. In 1930 one-third of the members of the First Chamber and one-tenth of the members of the Second were civil servants. In spite of the reforms of 1918-1921, Sweden thus continued to be one of the most bureaucratic governments in Europe.

This, too, tended to insure political stability and discourage political experimentation. It freed the government from the influence of the street, and the *Riksdag* became a body of professional politicians, in the best sense of the term. There was no law to prevent the *Riksdag* from enacting legislation approved by any of its committees, which were chiefly permanent committees of experts on such matters as taxation, banking, and constitutional law. The *Riksdag* might have altered the proposals of the committees without consulting experts, but it rarely did so.

The real legislative branch of the government was neither the cabinet nor the *Riksdag*. The cabinet and the *Riksdag* merely approved or disapproved of proposals prepared by bureaus within the departments of the cabinet. On minor matters of a highly specialized nature the bureau through its department presented proposals, which usually were adopted by the *Riksdag* without any questioning, unless some expert in the *Riksdag* was capable of questioning the wisdom of the legislation. As the experts had a chance to voice themselves in committee before the question was discussed by the *Riksdag*, such questioning was rare.

Such a procedure was, of course, necessary, for thousands of small questions were raised and had to be settled by each *Riksdag*. On more important issues special committees were appointed to study problems which might require several years. These valuable committees were usually nonpartisan and directed by experts. As a result, political party platforms tended to become meaningless unless experts believed that their programs would meet with success. The value of civil servants, professors, and other experts as members of a political party was thus quite clear. When experts did not agree as to the wisdom of measures, the views of professional politicians became important to the *Riksdag*.

The most vociferous opponent of the economic policies of the government during the two decades after World War I was no less a person than the internationally famous economist, Gustav Cassel. His views, in turn, were challenged by persons of hardly less international fame, including Professors Eli Heckscher, Ernst Wigforss, Östen Undén, and others.

The very nature of the government discouraged radical experiments. Radicalism, expressed in orthodox Marxism by the Left-Wing Social Democrats, was doomed to fail. Yet such utterances as those of Fredrik Ström in the *Riksdag* of 1919 caused chills to creep up the spines of the people. "Soon," he shouted, "shall the red flag of the International and the Social Democratic party wave not only over Moscow, Budapest, Vienna, Berlin, Warsaw, and many other capitals, but over Stockholm, over this very building, and over the Royal Castle."

In 1919 the Left-Wing Social Democratic party joined the Communist International. Many members of this party objected to the International's twenty-one theses in 1920, and they formed the Swedish Communist party. The Left-

Wing Social Democrats were now a mere rump of the older organizations, and in 1923 they requested permission to return to the Social Democratic party.

The Communists were also headed for trouble. Höglund, the great individualist, could not submit to dictation at any time, and in 1920 it was apparent that all was not well between him and Lenin. Accusations in Russian newspapers that Höglund had gone from Lenin to Branting were the severest criticism that could be made by one Communist of another. In 1924 Höglund formed his own group of Communists, which was definitely anti-International. In 1926 he took the decisive step, and his group joined the Social Democratic party. The remnant of the Communist party, called the Kilbom Communist party after its leader, split again in 1929. At the outbreak of the war in 1939, the chief strength of the Communists was to be found in northern Sweden and the larger cities. Though not numerically strong, in 1940 they presented a serious problem.

Such able leaders as Fabian Månsson, Zeta Höglund and Fredrik Ström returned to the Social Democratic party. Månsson, it was said, turned from atheism to religion before he died. His gifts were recognized even by his severest critics, and few men enjoyed greater popularity. The great radical settled down, even entering into a bourgeois marriage, and wrote a most excellent novel based on the religious revival in Sweden. Höglund waited until after Branting's death to return to the Social Democratic party. Then the severest critic Branting had ever had made it almost his life work to write his biography. He also devoted his time to editing the works of Branting, and became editor-in-chief of *Social Demokraten,* the official organ of the Social Democratic party.

The World War was followed by an era of good will that cannot be easily explained. Doubtless the capitalists of Sweden learned much from the war and its aftermath and began to look upon themselves as fortunate in having a labor party which was definitely opposed to violence. During the 1930's the professional and business classes, or the so-

150

called white-collar classes, changed their attitude toward labor. In fact, the capitalists preferred to see the Social Democratic party in power. This might have been due to the fact that when the Social Democratic party was in power there was less labor unrest, for the party exerted an influence on the National Federation of Trade Unions. The capitalists also developed a profound respect for organized labor and its leaders through discussions of collective agreements and of labor difficulties. More important, almost every one in Sweden agreed that Swedish labor had waited long enough for a chance to enjoy life, and everything that could be done to make the laborer's life richer seemed worth the effort.

The change was not sudden. Labor itself had to show that it deserved the confidence of the people. At the Social Democratic Congress in June 1924, Branting clearly hinted at the evolution necessary within the party when he said: "It is true that our ideas of Socialism are not the same today as thirty-five years ago. We then had a very simple and schematic idea about it, namely, that if we would only acquire political power all that would be necessary would be to prepare for a new society. Now we understand that political power is not enough. There is so much that needs to be done. The process of remaking a society is a very slow process . . . and first in this process is educating the laboring class for increasing responsibilities."

The evolution hinted at by Branting was shown in the program of the Social Democratic party from 1911 to 1920. Within a period of nine years the program of state owner-ship of all means of production was changed to ownership of "necessary resources." After 1920 the party deserted a program of nationalization of production to favor national-ization of consumption, through the growth of cooperatives. The Social Democrats certainly did not speed the nationaliza-tion of production. In fact, leading members of the party in 1939 stated that there was no need for such measures, and that the chief aim of the party was a higher living standard for all people. Ernst Wigforss, the able minister of finance, stated that labor was not sure that the state could operate as efficiently as private capitalists.

Yet Wigforss, a noted economist, was one of the most radical members of his party. In 1939, when war clouds hung heavily over Europe, Gustav Möller, minister of commerce, proposed that the state should set aside 10,000,000 crowns for iron foundries in the rich iron fields of Lappland in order that Sweden might be freed from its dependence upon Germany as a market for the iron ore. Private capital could not be encouraged to enter the field, so Möller proposed state-owned foundries. His fellow Social Democrats were dubious about the venture, for the golden rule for state enterprise had been profit. The irony of the entire matter was that the Conservatives supported Möller, and his proposal was carried. To Americans it might seem paradoxical that the Conservative party in Sweden was almost entirely responsible for all the business activities in which the state was engaged.

Yet when Hjalmar Branting appointed the three large commissions in 1920 for the study of social democracy and industrial democracy, Sweden became alarmed. The value of the studies undertaken has often been belittled, for the commissions reached no final verdicts or conclusions on which to base a program, but their findings, represented by numerous volumes, were scholarly investigations into the problems of socialization of industry. Branting's motives for the studies might have been aimed at undermining the radical Socialists' opposition to the Social Democratic party. But Branting was no scheming politician. The conclusion was easily drawn that if political democracy was possible, industrial democracy should be possible. Branting, however, pointed out that the Commission on Industrial Democracy should seek to determine if the productivity of industries would be endangered by their being placed under a labor-capital management. His own doubts of the virtue of industrial democracy might also be seen in his instruction to the Commission to study to what extent a share in the management of industries by labor might be wise. When he appointed the Commission on Socialization of Industry, Sweden was sure, as expressed by Arvid Lindman, that in the "soft words of the prime minister it was possible to discern rumbling of a new and violent onslaught on private capital."

Cold water was thrown upon the study of industrial democracy from the very beginning, when at a conference of Scandinavian economists it was pointed out that industrial democracy had been tried only in a few countries during war, always with poor results. Those experiments, it was maintained, had greatly harmed the labor movement. Industrial democracy would deprive labor of the power of national organizations, their most powerful weapons. Swedish trade unions saw no need of industrial democracy so long as they had the right to strike. Furthermore, Syndicalists could do much harm in joint industrial organizations.

Many people in Sweden, as elsewhere, were apt to speak glibly about socialization of industry. When the Commission on Socialization of Industry was appointed, the confusion in the implications of socialization became evident. This commission had, therefore, first to agree on the meanings of the term. Was socialization a concept based on mere ideas of socialization or on actual experience? Experience as a basis of study would of course be of greatest value. But, as Russia was a world in itself, the Commission must go beyond Russia in its study to find a definition that would be acceptable. The Commission could not be satisfied by the definitions of scholars. It must try to find out why the public feared socialization. Ideas and realities baffled the Commission, and it plunged into a labyrinth of socialization in theory and socialization in practice until all its members seemed confused.

Branting's failure to carry the Social Democratic program for a more humane unemployment policy caused the second Branting cabinet to resign. The Conservatives were then given an opportunity to try their hands at government. But they failed shortly, and the Social Democrats assumed leadership again. It was not Branting, however, who was to solve Sweden's postwar problems. Branting's health was undermined by his heavy work, and in 1925 the great democrat died. Carl Lindhagen, elected for the first time to the *Riksdag* with Branting and Staaff in 1896, reflected in his memoirs over the fate of the three radicals, "the clover leaf," Branting, Staaff, and Lindhagen himself. He wondered who was the greatest democrat of the three, and at the grave of Branting he came to the conclusion that death was the greatest democrat.

Before Branting died in 1925, he had selected Rickard Sandler as his successor. Sandler was an able man, who had largely won his laurels as an educator in the service of the Social Democratic party. In 1925 the Sandler government drastically reduced the period of military training as an expression of the faith of the party in future peace. There was some criticism that the Social Democratic administration favored its own party members in making appointments in civil service, and thus did not strictly adhere to old practices in Sweden. But it was the question of unemployment that caused the Sandler government to resign in 1926.

The Liberal party under the leadership of Carl Gustav Ekman, who had inherited the mantle of Staaff and Edén, had embarrassed the Sandler government, and prosperity pushed politics into the background when Ekman formed his cabinet. The Ekman cabinet reaped the fruit of a very important reform prepared by the Social Democrats when in 1927 a new School Ordinance was approved by the *Riksdag*. This law made the primary schools preparatory schools for the secondary schools. Many of the private schools were closed or placed under direct state supervision and control. A Court of Arbitration for Labor was also established. This Labor Court was greeted with suspicion by labor, but it was soon discovered that labor preferred to make more frequent use of it than employers did.

In the election of 1928 the Liberals and the Conservatives sought to cooperate in checking the growth of the

Social Democratic party, which had been strengthened by the return of the Höglund Communists to the fold. The outcome of the election forced Ekman to resign. The Conservatives under the leadership of Arvid Lindman formed a cabinet, but when the Liberals showed no desire to cooperate with them they were helpless, as was strikingly illustrated by the savings bank crash of 1929. During April 1929, a number of the savings banks were forced to close their doors, and Sweden faced a major bank scandal. It was discovered that a number of prominent directors of savings banks had swindled their depositors. Though the state inspection of savings banks was much more rigorous than the inspection of ordinary banks, it was evident that state inspection had left much to be desired. During the bank crises of 1921-1925 the state had assisted a number of banks in reorganization, and there was no reason why the state should not act at this time. All the political parties agreed, and the *Riksdag* set aside 11,000,000 crowns for the savings banks in order to prevent any depositor from losing his savings. It soon became evident, however, that the Agricultural Bank was not liquid. It had come into existence as a result of state initiative in 1923, and most important agricultural groups and organizations in Sweden used this bank as a bank of deposit.

The state was its largest stockholder, and the state could not, of course, dispose of its stocks. The minister of finance, Professor Nils Wohlin, sought vainly to secure the cooperation of other banks in rescuing the Agricultural Bank. Wohlin then suggested that the Credit Fund Corporation should assume the ownership of the bad investments to the extent of 10,000,000 crowns. The Social Democrats criticized Wohlin for having appealed for the aid of the private banks, thus permitting them to check the investments of the Agricultural Bank. The Social Democrats hoped to use the crisis of 1929 to nationalize the banking institutions. The criticism became so severe that Wohlin was forced to resign, and the Lindman cabinet was thus weakened.

The Conservatives turned to the Farmers' party in hopes of securing cooperation by holding out hope of help for the farmers in their great distress. The farms were heavily mortgaged and it was believed that the Swedish tariff allowed a degree of dumping of foreign grain and flour in Sweden, which made the position of the Swedish farmers very precarious. The Conservatives believed also that the depressed agricultural conditions would have a bad effect on other industries and that therefore measures to aid the farmers were justified. A heavier duty was proposed on grain and flour, and the flour mills agreed to use only a very small amount of foreign grain in manufacturing flour. Thus the Swedish farmers were guaranteed at least the Swedish market for their grain. Carl Gustav Ekman and his Liberals held the balance of power in the *Riksdag* and when Ekman decided to oppose grain and flour duties proposed by the government, Arvid Lindman, the prime minister, resigned. The *Riksdag* did, however, approve regulation of the flour mills.

The King requested Ekman to form a cabinet, suggesting to him that he should try to cooperate with the Conservatives, but Ekman formed a purely partisan cabinet. This was the more unfortunate as the Ekman party was the weakest of the three major parties in the *Riksdag*. Ekman was trying to play the one party against the other and thus rule at the expense of the Social Democrats and the Conservatives. Of course, in a country where political parties were more important than in Sweden, the Ekman government would have been an impossibility. Under ordinary circumstances, it would have been an impossibility in Sweden as well, but an unprecedented industrial prosperity had created a spirit of well-being which could not be dampened by the petty political intrigues of Ekman.

The World War by no means altered the course of economic developments in Sweden, though it did both speed and retard certain developments characteristic of a prewar era. Shortly before the war the exports of Sweden were

156

increasing rapidly, until by 1913 the value of Swedish exports was estimated at 846,500,000 crowns. In 1915 the figure rose to 1,142,000,000 crowns but dropped sharply during 1917. Three years later the value of Swedish exports was nearly twice as great as in 1915. Even during the depression of 1921-1922, exports did not fall below 1,000,000,000 crowns in value. After 1924 Swedish export trade maintained a sound growth, not checked until the crisis in 1931.

In 1913 a preliminary plan was adopted by the state for the electrification of the state railroads, but the shortage of coal during the war made it necessary for the state to speed the electrification of railroads in order that Sweden might be less dependent upon importation of coal. But copper wiring rose to ten crowns per kilo in 1918, and this retarded electrification. In 1919 the price dropped to two crowns and again the work proceeded rapidly.

There were four distinct periods in the history of the utilization of water power for production of electricity. The first period, between 1893 and 1906, witnessed the building of a large number of small private power stations, usually constructed for the purpose of supplying an industry or a city or a district with power. Many of these were built by the manufacturing industries themselves, and were thus local. The second period extended from 1906 to 1920 and was characterized by the building of large power stations and the entrance into this field of large private utility corporations as well as the state. In many sections of the country, smaller power stations were built either by communities or by private corporations to satisfy their own needs for electrical power. This period witnessed a degree of competition, but during the third period, which lasted from 1920 until 1930, competition turned to cooperation and a more rational use of water resources.

Attention turned to the great water resources of Norrland, where 75 per cent of Sweden's water power was found. The water power of the central and southern parts of Sweden was found to be inadequate to supply even their own regions with electricity. This period inaugurated a series of mergers among the utility corporations.

During the fourth period, 1930-1940, these mergers continued, sometimes leading to cooperation of municipalities and joint ownership of power stations by private industrial concerns. Thus the Länforsen Power Works is owned jointly by the City of Stockholm and Sandviken Iron Works. The largest private utility company is the Southern Swedish Power Corporation, which virtually dominates the southernmost part of Sweden. The large state power stations were Trollhättan, Porjus, Älvkarleby, Lilla Edet, and Vargön. In spite of these developments, there were 1,069 power stations in 1936 producing 6,528,908 kilowatt-hours, showing a great deal of decentralization.

The World War necessitated a forced national saving. Consumption was reduced as a result of the blockade and the submarine warfare, and a large export surplus was created. The Swedish merchant marine was forced to engage in trade for the Allies, and Swedish shipping corporations accumulated assets abroad. Sweden thus became a creditor nation. This change would have occurred anyway, but it was speeded during the war. The forced savings during the war enabled Sweden to pay off its foreign debt.

The hourly wages of industrial workers had risen prior to the war and more abruptly, owing to the deflation, after the war. After 1924, the position of labor continued to improve. In 1929 the wage based on the cost of living compared with that of 1913 as 171 to 100. Yet higher wages did not bring about an increase in the cost of production. This was due to continued improvements in manufacturing, through labor efficiency, through nationalization, and through increased mechanization. In 1929 industrial production was probably nearly 50 per cent greater than in 1913, when Swedish exports were also about 50 per cent greater than in 1913.

For this latter situation the pulp, paper, and machine industries were largely accountable. All three of these industries had developed rapidly prior to the World War, and the market for these industries improved rapidly after the war. Wood pulp and paper industries doubled their production in volume during 1913-1929, and the machine industries increased their production at an even more rapid pace. Iron export declined, if measured by weight, below the prewar period. But reduction in the export of bar and pig iron was more than compensated for by the export of more finished products and greater home consumption of iron. The lumber industry suffered from greater competition of countries having cheaper labor, but cost-reducing mergers evident prior to the war continued. These did not, however, completely eliminate the competition of the sawmills and the wood pulp mills for raw material. Home industries dependent entirely upon the home market expanded. The building trade boomed after 1924, as did a number of industries dependent upon it.

The merger of business enterprises into large corporations and the formation of trusts and monopolies continued as before 1914. By 1931 there was hardly a field in which more or less monopolistic organizations did not exist. At that time, more than 200 combinations in the form of trusts or cartels existed. To overcome trade barriers an internationalization of certain large Swedish industries took place. In addition to the Kreuger match trust, this was true of the Swedish Roller Bearing Corporation, L. M. Ericsson, Separator, Gasaccumulator, Electrolux, and others. These corporations were more international than Swedish in some respects. What continued to make them Swedish was the fact that the leadership of these corporations has remained in Swedish hands. Their chief industrial activities were based on Swedish patents. Furthermore, Swedish law forbids that more than one-fifth of the votes of a Swedish corporation be held by foreigners. These corporations have extended their factories to numerous countries to overcome obstacles caused by tariff legislation, especially after World War I. The Swedish Roller

Bearing Corporation developed factories, offices, and agents in fifty-six different countries. Daughter corporations were organized in the United States, England, Germany, and Czechoslovakia. In 1933 the Swedish Roller Bearing Corporation employed more men outside of Sweden than in it.

CHAPTER XI

DEPRESSION AND RECOVERY, 1931-1940

THE CHANGE in the international economic situation during the autumn of 1929 did not have immediate serious repercussions on Sweden. As early as 1928 a notable restriction of international credit was evident, but because of a strong capital position Sweden was not adversely affected. The interest rate rose, however, from 3½ per cent to 4½ per cent, and the rediscount rate from 3 per cent to 4½ per cent. The Swedish discount rate was thus on a lower level than the Federal Reserve rate in the United States. When the Bank of England increased its discount rate to 5½ per cent in February 1929, Sweden did not immediately follow, but was forced to do so the following autumn to prevent undesirable movements of capital. For several months after the American stock market crash, it was believed in Sweden that the depression would not be serious. In 1930, however, Swedish export industries began to feel the effects of the depression in the United States and Germany. The depression was felt more keenly when the economic situation became acute in Great Britain.

The decline in prices, however, more severely affected imports than exports. Sweden's position in the world market was relatively favorable. Iron and steel showed a greater sensitiveness to the general world economic conditions than did other exports, and during the summer of 1930 unemployment rose. By the end of the year it was evident that Sweden was facing a serious unemployment problem. The industries producing for the home market rather than for export appeared from the first to be in a comparatively strong position. The decline of production of the home industries even through 1932 was not more than 13 per cent as compared with 1929. The production of the export industries dropped 34 per cent.

During the depression international attention was focused on Sweden's economic policy. Articles were written with such titles as the "Swedish Way out of the Depression" and "Controlled Currency," without much knowledge on the part of most of the authors of Sweden's relatively strong capital position. Certain Swedish export industries, such as wood pulp and paper, were not as sensitive to business cycles as were many others. In fact, Swedish export of paper and paper board was greater in 1932 than the average for the period 1926-1930.

Industrial efficiency and rationalization in the operation of industries had proceeded rapidly, making many economies possible. The productivity of the worker had been increased by 43 per cent in 1929 as compared with 1915. The use of machine power had increased by about 100 per cent. From 1930 to 1933, machine power rose 8½ per cent while employment decreased 13½ per cent. Combinations of related industries to control the price of raw material made for diversification of production and made large industries less sensitive to a crisis, which hit one type of production more severely than another.

Furthermore, agriculture was still the main industry. Though it had suffered severely after World War I, a recovery had been effected by 1930. Farm productivity had been increased, and various types of cooperative societies flourished. Not until 1930 did the government itself take a decisive step to help farmers. The State Grain Board was then created, and in September 1930 compulsory milling of Swedish grain was begun. In 1931 the state joined with the flour mills in the formation of the Swedish Grain Association, a grain import monopoly by which the import of grain could be effectively controlled. This form of protection for the farmer was far more effective than a tariff or direct subsidies, and in 1931 it was extended to other agricultural products. Under this system farmers were guaranteed a minimum price for their products, a circumstance which tended to encourage grain production to meet at least the demands of the home market. Soon, however, grain production came to exceed the demands of the home market.

The condition of the farmer had been greatly improved when the government launched upon its new monetary policy by leaving the gold standard in 1931. The international economic situation had gone from bad to worse, reflecting itself in a sharp decline in prices, until by the autumn of that year it seemed impossible to judge how far the prices might drop. Swedish exports continued to decline more rapidly than imports. For the time being the influx of foreign short-term capital offset the unfavorable trade balance. Sweden profited temporarily from the flight of capital, obtaining an ample supply of foreign exchange with which to finance investments abroad. But as the gloom of depression cast an ever darker shadow over England, the foreign exchange reserve of the National Bank was weakened. The National Bank had taken a step to discourage too great an influx of foreign capital into Sweden by lowering its discount rate to 3 per cent in order to encourage industry. This was merely following the example set by London and New York. When the Bank of England was forced, however, to raise the discount rate to 4½ per cent, Sweden had to follow. Sweden's success in this move became dependent upon whether or not England would be able to control the situation. The influx of foreign capital into Sweden prevented restriction of credit at an early date and lessened chances of remaining on the gold standard. At first the great foreign exchange holdings of the National Bank had been a source of worry. During August and September 1931, the National Bank was rapidly being drained of its foreign exchange, a situation which created a severe problem when England adopted a paper standard. The crisis then became so acute that on September 27 Sweden left the gold standard.

Sweden should have left the gold standard earlier, for when Sweden adopted the paper standard, the foreign exchange resources of the National Bank had been almost entirely wiped out. Indeed, it was not until March 1932 that the National Bank was in a position to make its influence felt on the foreign exchange market. As a result of the weak foreign exchange position of the National Bank, the adoption of a free currency caused drastic credit restrictions. The discount rate rose to 6 per cent and for a short time even to 8 per cent in order to preserve the internal purchasing power of the crown and prevent speculation in commodities and foreign exchange. Almost an entire year elapsed before the discount rate went below the level of the spring of 1931. Its decline was then temporarily checked by the Kreuger crash.

Speculators seem to have been inclined to believe that the crown would be linked to the pound sterling, but the National Bank at first did not interest itself in the fluctuations of the pound. It concerned itself chiefly with credit restrictions, aiming to prevent sharp rises in prices in accordance with the principles adopted officially when Sweden left the gold standard. The purpose of this policy was to maintain stability in the purchasing power of the crown within the boundaries of Sweden. In other words, the National Bank hoped to stabilize the cost of living. This was especially important in order that serious labor unrest might be prevented. In the spring of 1932 the program of the National Bank was expanded to attempt to encourage a rise in wholesale prices without greatly increasing the cost of living, until it was discovered that a general rise in the price level was desirable. The policy of the National Bank had thus been motivated first by fears of a sharp inflation, but it became apparent that the real problem was to counteract the decline in prices. Price trends indicated clearly that the most important result of the adoption of the paper standard had been to check the decline of export prices in terms of the crown. The advantages secured here for Swedish export were somewhat counteracted by actions taken by Norway and Finland, competitors in the wood pulp, paper, and lumber world market.

Both countries had adopted a paper standard which involved greater devaluation of their currencies.

The Kreuger crash temporarily undermined confidence in Swedish currency. It was an incident which gripped the public even more than the Ådalen unrest of May 1931. Both demonstrated that Sweden was not immune to the international depression. During 1931 labor unrest was even more severe than in 1928. In May the lumber industry at Ådalen was in the grip of a strike, and the sawmills began to hire blacklegs, who had to be protected by troops. When the soldiers arrived at Ådalen on May 13, they were greeted by the strikers with stones. Communists assumed leadership of a large labor demonstration, which attacked the troop encampment, and the soldiers were ordered to fire. Four people were killed and many wounded.

The demonstrators retreated and returned to their homes, but the troubles were far from settled. The governor ordered the soldiers to be withdrawn though threatening labor demonstrations occurred at Härnösand and elsewhere. In Ådalen the Communists actually established a form of "Soviet Republic," which ruled for a couple of weeks. All Sweden was excited. The Social Democratic party protested that public authorities had permitted the murder of striking workers. Stockholm witnessed a huge labor demonstration and in the Riksdag, Ekman was criticized sharply. The prime minister appointed a commission to investigate the Ådalen affair, with the right to make recommendations to the government or local authorities. The Conservatives criticized the action taken by Ekman because they saw in the instructions of the prime minister a possible indictment of the military authorities in Ådalen. On July 20 the commission reported that the firing on the demonstrators by the soldiers was not unavoidable, but that the situation was such as to make it impossible for the officers to judge the situation correctly. The captain and other officers were later exonerated by the courts.

The fate of the officers in charge of the Ådalen troops

had not yet been settled when news reached Sweden of the suicide in Paris of Ivar Kreuger. Kreuger had secured world-wide attention because he was thought to personify a new type of big business, the international trust. In 1921 he had secured the control of the L. M. Ericsson Corporation with vast international interests. He had thus expanded the interests of his holding company, Kreuger and Toll, beyond an international match trust founded on the Swedish Match Trust into an effort to control the telephone and telegraph industry on an international scale. The L. M. Ericsson Corporation, instead of organizing subsidiaries in foreign countries as had the Swedish Roller Bearing Corporation, had expanded its business through a system of cooperation with competing concerns, achieved through large stockholdings in competitor corporations and secured often by means of exchanging its own stocks for stocks of other corporations. In 1931 Kreuger and Toll secured control of the newly discovered rich minerals of Boliden.

To finance his expansion, Kreuger made use of participating debentures. This enabled him also to provide loans to Germany, France, Turkey, Greece, Hungary, and Persia, in return for which match monopolies were secured. He was generally looked upon as a financial wizard, although no one knew that his international match trust did not produce large profits. Kreuger was constantly in need of more and more credit, and to secure the confidence of bankers, Kreuger and Toll paid large dividends. This policy would have undermined the financial soundness of the company even if the principles upon which it worked were sound. It is doubtful that, even if the depression had not seriously interfered with international trade, Kreuger would have been able to overcome the difficulties in which he had placed himself by unwarranted dividend payments. The depression, however, made it impossible for Kreuger to secure more credit, and dividends, as a result, had to be discontinued. In 1931 Kreuger and Toll stocks dropped sharply.

Kreuger did not give up hope, and worked feverishly to

secure credit. For this purpose, he sailed for New York early in 1932. It was said that the Morgan banking interests had become dubious about his ventures. By bribing Ekman, however, Kreuger had secured credit from the National Bank of Sweden in October 1931 and February 1932, which for the time being postponed collapse. This credit was altogether inadequate, and when Kreuger failed to secure credit in America, his days as a financial wizard were numbered. On March 12, 1932, he committed suicide.

Panic hit Sweden. Swedish stocks dropped sharply. Kreuger's participating debentures, stocks in Kreuger and Toll, the Swedish Match Corporation, and L. M. Ericsson became worthless. Even the bonds of the Swedish government quoted on the Foreign Bond Exchange in New York dropped from over $100, which was par, to less than $70.

The value of the Swedish crown was also adversely affected. The Swedish government had become aware even before Kreuger's suicide that all was not well. On the day of the suicide, the government had granted to the Kreuger enterprises a moratorium which was put into effect the day after the suicide. One of the largest banks in Sweden, *Skandinaviska Kreditaktiebolaget,* had been very generous to Kreuger with credit. Had this bank been forced to close its doors, a bank panic could not have been avoided. The banks were none too sound, for they had speculated heavily in stocks, through creation of special corporations exempt from banking inspection. The government had been warned by the banking inspectors of the true conditions of the Swedish banks and realized, therefore, that it must come to the aid of *Skandinaviska Kreditaktiebolaget* immediately. The bank was provided with a loan to cover its losses from the Kreuger crash and to enable it to keep its doors open. In this way a run on the banks was prevented.

The government then ordered an investigation into the affairs of Kreuger. Among the most startling revelations was the discovery that Prime Minister Ekman had accepted bribes from Kreuger on at least two occasions. Another Liberal was appointed prime minister by the King, but his regime was to be very short. The Kreuger crash, as well as the Ådalen incident, played an important part in turning the public to the Social Democratic and the Farmers' parties, both of which made subsequent gains at the polls. On September 29 Per Albin Hansson was requested by the King to form a cabinet.

The personnel of the Hansson cabinet was essentially the same as that of the Sandler cabinet of 1926. The most notable difference was the fact that Sandler was made minister of foreign affairs and Hansson was appointed prime minister, indicating a change in leadership within the Social Democratic party. At the time, this change did not seem significant. In fact, not until 1939-1940, with the outbreak of World War II, did the full significance of the change become apparent.

Sandler had been selected by Branting as his successor. He shared Branting's views on international cooperation and was apt to look upon conditions in the light of international events. He was a cultured internationalist, representing Branting's pro-British sentiments.

Per Albin Hansson had risen from the ranks of labor. He was well built, with a round and open face and large eyes that sparkled with humor. He looked, if anything, over-fed and prosperous. Cautious and unimpulsive, he lacked a thorough understanding of international developments. He had little of the fighting spirit of Branting, exuding rather more of the solid, careful temperament of the Swedish peasant. As such he was slow to anger and sure of himself. Branting's impressive figure and his firm features had led Sweden to accept him as a symbol. Sandler obviously could not serve as such a symbol, but Hansson could. Long before he became prime minister, the workers had called him "our Per Albin," and soon he was Sweden's "Per Albin," about whom the people liked to spin their yarns. The King also liked him and the two became good friends.

The election of 1932 was so favorable to the Social Democratic party that the public expected much from it. The party had won so much support in addition to that of organized labor that it was almost a people's party. The electorate had evidently tired of the impotence of the Conservatives and Liberals, and of a political situation which had allowed a weak party under the leadership of Ekman to bring international disgrace upon Sweden through the Kreuger crash. Depression required positive leadership, and it was believed that Per Albin Hansson could provide what previous Swedish governments had lacked — public confidence.

The Kreuger crash was, fortunately, far less serious to the Swedish credit system and foreign exchange policy than had been expected. When Kreuger had been unable to secure credit abroad, he had been forced to rely more and more on Swedish credit, a situation which created strong pressure on the government credit and foreign exchange policy. This pressure was now removed. By November 1932 the National Bank had strengthened its foreign exchange reserve to about 200,000,000 crowns. The export of Swedish goods still continued to decline, but less rapidly than imports, and Sweden's trade balance became more favorable. By April 1933 the National Bank's foreign exchange reserve had been increased to 260,000,000 crowns and the gold reserve strengthened by 60,000,000 crowns. This was achieved in spite of fluctuations in the pound sterling, which the National Bank made no effort to follow. But the National Bank had not succeeded in raising the general levels of wholesale prices, for in April 1933 these were lower than they had been in September 1931. A general downward trend of prices was noted outside of Sweden as well, and there was a degree of instability and uncertainty which was far from beneficial to industry.

To check this trend of declining prices, the National Bank made large purchases of foreign exchange and, during the summer of 1933, sought to gauge the crown after the pound sterling, which had become more stable. The National Bank continued this policy of making large purchases of foreign exchange, until by the end of 1936 its gold and foreign exchange reserve had reached a value of 1,715,000,000 crowns. The price decline had been definitely checked.

The influx of foreign exchange was undoubtedly due to the purposeful undervaluation by the National Bank of the crown in terms of the pound. Yet it would be foolish to believe that controlled currency performed magic. Sweden could not escape feeling a notable business revival in England and other countries as well. This revival alone could stimulate the Swedish export industries.

The favorable foreign exchange situation in which Sweden found itself made it possible to pursue a more independent economic policy than before and effectively to combat depression without adversely affecting the foreign exchange. It enabled Sweden to adopt the Social Democratic party's unemployment policy, without which a more speedy recovery would have been impossible. To believe that this policy was scientific and its success not a link in the chain of good luck would be wrong.

In theory, the policy of the Swedish government was not very much different from Kreuger's policy of paying dividends before they were earned. The Swedish government, however, lived to witness the return of prosperity and could then accumulate earnings which were sufficient to take care of the unwarranted dividends.

If less fortunate countries than Sweden had tried the same depression policy, the results might have been quite the opposite. These countries might not have succeeded in accumulating the foreign exchange reserves which Sweden had and might have faced a serious foreign exchange risk. Mere undervaluation of the crown certainly might soon have depleted the reserves of the National Bank if Sweden had not had articles of great international demand. The whole Swedish system was built on the idea that export industries would be able to restore prosperity in Sweden, if not immediately, then at a time when international conditions improved.

The Swedish industries dependent upon the home market had great power of resistance to outside depressing influences. These were chiefly the highly diversified home-consumption industries. It was important that the interests of these industries not be stimulated at the expense of the export industries. A reduction in the cost of production for export industries in terms of wage reduction would lessen home consumption. It would also have caused the labor unions to start strikes which would have seriously injured Swedish trade. Nor would wage reduction have been possible, for labor unions were stronger than ever and collective agreements dominated the labor market, especially in the manufacturing, mining, transport, and building trades.

The Social Democratic party's unemployment policy, adopted by the *Riksdag* in 1933, provided for financial expansion as a means of stimulating home consumption. This implied that the government must discard both its attempts to balance the budget during the depression and the limitation of its financing to productive investment. The Conservatives sought to defeat the new unemployment policy, but the Social Democrats had entered into an agreement with the Farmers' party by which the latter promised to support the Social Democratic unemployment policy on the condition that the farmers would secure better prices for their products in the home market. The agreement was called the "Cow Deal" or "Sköld's Smörgåsbord." Per Edvin Sköld, one of the leaders of the Social Democratic party, had promoted the agreement.

The underlying idea of the new unemployment policy was the belief that increased government expenditures would increase public purchasing power. It involved the transfer of income from one group to another. There followed higher taxes on incomes of more than 10,000 crowns, higher inheritance taxes, higher property taxes, increased taxes on tobacco and liquor, and increased tariff protection. These taxes were levied quite frankly in order to allow greater government expenditures. Prior to 1933 the government had tried exactly the opposite policies in an effort to decrease government expenditures, ease taxes, balance the budget, and limit the government debt expansion to productive undertakings.

In 1933 and 1934 large government loans were floated to secure funds for its unemployment policy. The government had spent only 28,000,000 crowns in 1932 for unemployment, a sum increased in 1933 to 215,000,000 crowns. During the years 1933-1935, the total government expenditures in combating unemployment reached 832,000,000 crowns.

At the peak of the depression in 1933, it was estimated that about 250,000 people were out of work. These could not, of course, be taken care of by large public works projects, which frequently involved the severance of family ties by the unemployed. Instead, an extensive system of outright dole was resorted to. The government further reasoned that large public works such as road building were always needed and should not, therefore, be regarded strictly as unemployment projects. The government felt that it should encourage a larger number of smaller projects that under ordinary circumstances would probably not be undertaken. These would employ more people and at the same time involve fewer hardships on the unemployed. Local communities were encouraged to build city halls, recreation centers, swimming pools, athletic fields, new sewage systems, and other civic improvement projects. Schoolhouses were built by state aid in the poorer districts of Norrland, Vesterbotten, Vesternorrland, and Bohuslän. Government aid in encouraging civic projects varied with each community's wealth, in many instances from 30 to 90 per cent of the cost being assumed by the government.

Many of these projects were closely related to the building trades, the government believing that the building industry was the most important. If this industry could be encouraged, the iron and steel, cement, lime, brick, glass, plumbing, heating, furniture and numerous other industries would be stimulated. Loans were provided for contractors; funds increased to encourage home ownership, and the government's own building program, planned to cover a period of six years, was stepped up to cover only two years. Industrialists or business men who were unable to secure loans from any other source were granted loans from the government to make possible greater employment in industry.

Though the chief aim of the new unemployment policy was to encourage projects that would not reduce the income or purchasing power of the worker, the Social Democratic party was forced to modify its program in the "Cow Deal" with the farmers. If, however, the above unemployment policy is carefully studied, its effects appear to be essentially the same as those desired by the Social Democrats. Numerous other trades dependent upon the building trade were encouraged, and these industries prospered.

The state, however, was somewhat restricted in the wages it could pay. Wages paid on the so-called reserve projects under the supervision of the Unemployment Commission were adjusted in 1933 to conform to wages paid unskilled labor in the various localities. Previously the wage had been slightly below this rate. This principle was also applied to state communal reserve projects. The state reserve projects provided, chiefly, work for the unmarried unemployed, as these projects were usually located at some distance from the home of the unemployed, while the state communal reserve projects offered employment for those with family obligations.

It may be said that, on the whole, the unemployment policy of 1933 never received a real trial. Conditions were definitely improving before the policy could be put to a serious test. Improvements appeared first in Great Britain and reacted favorably upon Sweden. The economic ties between the two countries had become stronger than ever before when in July 1933 the National Bank of Sweden fixed the sterling rate of the crown at a level maintained up to World War II. Finland, which had been more speedy than Sweden to tie its currency to the pound sterling, also experienced a more rapid recovery than Sweden. Finland's more rapid recovery may be attributed also to two other circumstances: first, Finland exported nearly twice as much of its total imports to England as did Sweden, and secondly, Finland was more dependent upon the sawmill industry than was Sweden, and this industry was among the first to experience improvement. Sweden, on the other hand, took more rapid advantage of the market provided by economic improvement in the United States and Germany and in the international market in general.

Sweden's economic policy during the depression, especially its unemployment policy, was nevertheless definitely significant in turning recovery into an industrial boom. There was every indication prior to World War I, and again after 1924, that under normal international economic conditions, Swedish industries were in a position to expand production. This was true also in 1934. But the government's unemployment policy gave an unprecedented impetus to the expansion of the home market and turned recovery into a boom. This boom made it possible for the government to balance its budget and make arrangements to reduce indebtedness accumulated during the depression.

The resulting prosperity must, in the main, be attributed neither to the dole system nor to more liberal unemployment relief work, but to certain other features of the unemployment policy. These features were those which aimed to stimulate consumption at home. The two most important ones were the reduction of interest rates on loans and aid to agriculture in a form of price fixing which later amounted almost to a bonus. When loans could be secured at 3 to 3½ per cent interest, the foundation was laid for an unprecedented building boom. Although the guarantee of fixed prices considerably above market prices for the farmers increased the cost of living, this was offset by the farmers' ability to purchase more goods.

In 1937 the production of industries dependent upon the home market was 10 per cent higher than in 1929. Unemployment was no longer a problem. It dropped in 1937 to about 35,000 and a year later unemployment was probably no greater than 18,000.

In 1935, the state introduced a new feature in its unemployment policy by granting state subsidies to unemployment insurance funds created by the labor unions. These funds had to be approved by the Social Board and to meet specific requirements laid down by the Social Board. The contributions of the state in the form of subsidies varied, contributions being greater to those insurance funds on which the strain of unemployment was greatest. It might be said, however, that in addition to sharing in the expense of administering the funds, the government contributed from 50 to 60 per cent of the unemployment benefits paid by the funds. It is to be noted that employers did not contribute anything toward this form of unemployment insurance. The payment of the members of the insurance funds varied from .20 crowns to 1.40 crowns a week for unemployment benefits of 2 crowns to 4 crowns a day. Benefits were fixed at from 2 to 6 crowns a day.

No benefits were paid until after the sixth day of unemployment, when the unemployed were to register at the State Unemployment Bureau, and no benefits were paid to members during a labor dispute. Furthermore, before benefits were paid, the member must have made 52 weekly payments to the insurance fund, of which at least 26 must have been made during the previous 12 months. All of the labor unemployment insurance funds were eventually placed under the supervision of the Social Board and made eligible for state subsidies. About half of those who registered for unemployment insurance secured government subsidies.

The Kreuger crash demonstrated the need of serious amendment of previous banking legislation to discourage the banks from dangerous speculation, but in the midst of all the social legislation the importance of the banking reform of 1933 and 1934 was lost sight of. The banks were placed under stricter government regulation and limited to what

175

might be called strictly banking functions, in an effort to sever the close relationship between banks and industries. Banks were forbidden to own stocks, and the granting of loans on the basis of stock security was drastically curtailed. They were also forbidden to enter into any relationship with an organization which might be used by the bank to cover its stock speculation, thus outlawing bank holding companies.

Improvement in business was noted in almost every industry except that of stone cutting. These improvements might be illustrated by a few figures. The annual value of manufactured goods was estimated at 3,812,383,000 crowns in 1925, which was a very prosperous year. In 1935 the annual value of manufactured goods rose to 5,548,445,000 crowns. In 1936 the main Swedish industries produced goods in values as follows: iron manufacture, 753,628,000 crowns; wood pulp industry, 390,000,000 crowns; lumber, 241,000,000 crowns; paper, 204,000,000 crowns; textile, 239,000,000 crowns; electrical machine, 182,900,000 crowns; flour mill, 147,900,000 crowns. The iron ore export had dropped almost catastrophically during the depression. Prior to the depression, the average export of iron ore had been nearly 10,000,000 tons a year. In 1932 it was about one-third of this amount. Five years later nearly 14,000,000 tons of iron ore were exported at an estimated value of 212,000,000 crowns.

In spite of this, Sweden did not have a favorable balance of trade. Since the close of World War I, the value of Swedish export exceeded the value of imports only in 1922, 1927, and 1929. Sweden was, however, more than able to maintain her position as a creditor nation because of the growth of her merchant marine. During 1928-1931, Götaverken Corporation built more ships than any other corporation in the world, about 100 at a total gross tonnage of 450,000. Few Swedish industries witnessed a more rapid growth after the war than shipbuilding. Between 1920 and 1936, the total tonnage of Swedish ships increased 500,000 tons. In 1938 only five other nations in the world had a larger motorized merchant fleet than Sweden, namely, Great Britain, Norway, Japan, the

Netherlands, and Germany, in the order given. Götaverken retained throughout the 1930's its position as the largest builder of ships in the world. This enabled Sweden not only to build for its own needs but for other nations as well.

The "Cow Deal" rescued the farmers in 1934, and it was planned to restore agricultural prices to 75 per cent of the 1925-1929 average. In 1936 the "Cow Deal" was further strengthened by the invitation of the Farmers' party to share leadership in government with the Social Democrats. The leader of the Farmers' party was made minister of agriculture, and it was decided that since farm expenses, especially agricultural wages, had risen, the average prices on agricultural goods during 1925-1929 were inadequate to afford the farmer a reasonable return on his investment.

The steps taken by the government to aid the farmers in 1934-1936 were of utmost importance. The number of farmers who had been forced into bankruptcy during 1930-1932 had doubled. The price-fixing policy of the government increased their income by 838,000,000 crowns in the three years prior to 1936, but the government had been forced to assume a rather severe loss because of its grain policy. Grain production was encouraged beyond the needs of home consumption, and in exporting the grain the government had to assume the loss in the difference between the fixed price and the world market price. This at times amounted to as much as $1.25 per 100 kilos of wheat. Wheat production in 1936 was more than twice as great as in 1920.

The dairy industry also was encouraged, but to make price fixing effective on butter the oleomargarine prices also had to be fixed by law. Though grain price fixing was not necessary after 1936, when the world grain market improved, the butter industry remained distressed, forcing the government from time to time to adjust its price. Though this implied that the Swedish consumer was forced to pay much more for his butter than the English consumer, who used almost 19,000,000 kilos of Swedish butter, no one seriously objected to government paternalism toward agriculture.

This government paternalism did not lessen the efforts of farmers to improve their own economic conditions by means of agricultural cooperatives of various kinds. These were in the main of two general types, marketing and purchasing cooperatives. Both types antedate World War I, but their growth became more marked after 1920. Among the oldest and most progressive were the creamery cooperatives. Between 1920-1930, the number of such cooperatives increased by about 100. In 1937 they numbered 727, many of them being much larger than the earlier cooperatives because they represented extensive mergers of earlier dairy cooperatives. The amount of milk weighed in at these creameries rose sharply, and their importance might be more readily realized when one considers that creamery production alone, excluding pork and poultry sidelines, accounted for about 43 per cent of the farmers' total income. The cooperative creameries were organized into a National Creamery Association, which in 1936 handled better than 88 per cent of the total milk of all creameries, and 99 per cent of the export of butter.

Another cooperative society which had grown rapidly since World War I was the Swedish Meat Packing Federation, which in 1936 had 34 member societies with a total membership of nearly 200,000 engaged in a volume of business which may safely be said to have exceeded 20,000,000 crowns in 1940. The Swedish Meat Packing Federation in 1933 had been formed by combining various cooperative packing associations.

This cooperation of these packing associations was brought about by the General Agricultural Society, which had been organized in 1917 mainly to study the problems of economical operation and management of farms. The initiative in the formation of the General Agricultural Society had originally been taken by the provincial agricultural societies, individual farmers' societies, and other related organizations. In 1939 it was reorganized to concern itself chiefly with problems of marketing and purchasing, and as such became the central organization of national cooperative farmers' associations. In 1936 there were seven of these, namely, the Swedish National Creamery Association, the Swedish Meat Packing Federation, the National Union of Swedish Farmers, the Swedish Egg Marketing Union, the Swedish National Fruit Association, the National Federation of Forest Owners, and the Swedish Agricultural Credit Bank.

The General Agricultural Society cooperated closely with the government and suggested legislation. Through an affiliate, the Agricultural Society Publishing Company, it carried on an extensive program of education. As a coordinator of the seven national farmers' cooperative associations, it also exerted an important influence in checking certain unsound developments. It owned large warehouses and elevators, mainly for storage purposes. The functions of the other national farmers' cooperatives were largely described by their names. In 1937 the various cooperatives handled about 60 per cent of all agricultural production.

As a result of government measures in maintaining domestic price levels on agricultural products and the constant growth of farmers' cooperative market associations, the farmers greatly improved their economic conditions prior to World War II. A series of good crops, rationalization of operations, and access to credit at a low rate of interest made the farmer more satisfied with his lot. The scarcity of agricultural labor, however, created a serious problem. Labor preferred to work in factories. The *Riksdag* of 1936 and 1937 adopted an eight-hour working day for agricultural labor. This legislation applied only to farmers employing three or more farm hands, and it was applied in such a manner as to allow the farmer to secure 54 hours of a work week from his employees during the summer, while the working week was shortened during the winter.

To encourage agricultural labor to remain on the soil, the government took measures to improve the housing conditions of rural labor. Between 1933 and 1938, about 50,000,000 crowns were allotted for rural housing improvements, of which the great majority went for grants without repayment obligations. About 60,000 new homes were built or remodeled as a result of these grants and loans. The government also encouraged farm ownership by tenants, creating for this purpose in 1934 the Tenants' Home Ownership Fund and the Tenants' Loan Fund, both of which aimed to assist persons without means to become independent farmers. The state began a policy of purchasing large farm estates in southern and central Sweden, dividing them into smaller farms to increase opportunities for ownership among tenants and agricultural laborers. The two funds above permitted the future farmer to secure working capital up to 400 crowns as an interest-free loan to be repaid in 16 years.

One special type of rural labor was badly in need of help, namely, the seasonal laborers who depended upon fishing, stone cutting, lumbering, or agriculture. These were assisted through a special fund created in 1933, called the Worker's Subsistence Homestead Fund, which granted loans up to 6,000 crowns exempt from interest payments during the first five years.

To believe that either the farmer or the rural laborer was entirely satisfied with his lot would be false. The lure of city life was strong, probably more so because modern means of transportation, the automobile and the bus, and excellent highways placed the rural population at the very doors of the cities and towns. Of course, better farm wages and better prices for farm products permitted the rural population to dress and act more and more like the city population. Furthermore, 78 per cent of the entire kingdom of Sweden was electrified prior to World War II, and it brought greater comforts to all parts of the country.

If, however, the rural population lived better and enjoyed life more in 1939 than at any previous time in Swedish history, the lot of the urban population had improved even more rapidly. An investigation between 1933-1936 of the general housing conditions in Sweden uncovered the fact that though there were no slums in Sweden, 15 per cent or about 120,000 of the rural homes could be classified as inferior, while in the cities only 30,000 homes were so classified. It was found that 700,000 people in the rural areas and 450,000 people in the cities lived in overcrowded quarters. When the government, therefore, decided in 1933 to enter upon a credit expansion program to fight unemployment, it was soon discovered that it could not spend money for a better cause than that of improving living conditions. Unsanitary and crowded conditions were found to be worse among the large families. The expense of feeding and clothing a large number of children often forced such families to live in smaller units than the small family, which could afford to pay more for better housing accommodations.

For years Swedish authorities had been worried over the practice of birth control and the nationwide use of contraceptives, and sociologists worried over possible race suicide. It was, therefore, important not only from the point of view of sanitation to improve the living conditions of the large families, but because of its biological significance. In 1935 the government inaugurated a policy to encourage the building of larger homes. Loans were granted up to 45 per cent of the cost of the material to communities willing to undertake a building program for large family accommodations. These loans were in the form of subsidies, as the communities were forced to pledge reductions in rent from 30 to 70 per cent, depending upon the size of the family. Thus a family with three children was entitled to a 30 per cent reduction in rent, a family with five children a 50 per cent reduction, and a family with seven or more children a 70 per cent reduction.

This program could be applied only in cities, towns, and villages where local authorities were willing to cooperate with the state. By 1938 only about 4,000 dwellings had been erected for large families in accordance with this plan. In rural sections an entirely different policy had to be pursued. Here, the government had to aid the large family directly by providing it with a loan, of which 20 per cent was exempted from any interest payment. When the house was completed, the state would make annual grants to the family in the form of deductions on the loan, which depended upon the size of the family.

This policy did not originate with the Social Democrats, though they were responsible for its broad extension. A decade before World War I broke out, the government had created the Home Ownership Loan Fund, and in 1918 the government seriously entered upon a program for the colonization of Norrland. Liberal homestead loans were granted. From 15 to 37 acres of land were given to the homesteader, on which he was exempted from any rent or interest during the first five years. During this time, however, he was obliged to place three acres of land under cultivation, in return for which the government paid him 500 crowns. The government also supplied the settler with building material at cost. In 1923 it established a fund by which the settler could secure loans to enable him to purchase cattle. The problem of meeting the cost of building was solved by another loan, which was not to exceed 4,500 crowns, on the condition that buildings on the farm would be completed within ten years. At that time the settler had the right to purchase the farm. If he lacked money to do so, the government assisted him by providing him with a loan at 3.6 per cent interest. In 1938 it was possible to secure a loan up to 75 per cent of the value of a 10,000 crown home at 4 per cent interest and a loan for the purchasing of a farm not exceeding a cost of 20,000 crowns at 3.6 per cent interest. In 1935, this Home Ownership Loan Fund had extended loans to home owners to the amount of 325,000,000 crowns. Though both the colonization program of Norrland and the Home Ownership Loan Fund were designed to combat emigration, their goal was essentially the same as that of the housing policy inaugurated by the government after 1932.

CHAPTER XII

A SOCIAL DEMOCRACY

THE ENTIRE ECONOMIC SYSTEM of Sweden had long been built on close cooperation of the state with private enterprise, the one supplementing the other rather than providing competition. The Commission on Socialization of Industry filed its report in 1932. Then strangely it seemed as if all agreed that the sooner the work of the Commission was forgotten the better. The Social Democrats were not eager to have the state extend its enterprises.

The state controlled and owned the postal, telegraph, and telephone systems, and the canals. The state was the sole owner of the National Bank, the Postal Savings Bank system, and through the Farmers' Mortgage Association had the oversight of the Farmers' Mortgage Banks. Through the Credit Fund Corporation the state became a large stockholder in banks, a position which it strengthened in every bank crisis. The state held three-fourths of the interest in the Agricultural Bank after this bank had been created upon the ruins of the Land Bank.

Through its constantly growing railroad net, the state also dominated the Swedish railroad system. All the key railroads were owned by the state, though the total mileage of these key railroads was only 6,641 kilometers compared with the private railroads' mileage of 10,168 kilometers in 1930. When the state believed that a reduction in freight rates was necessary to encourage industries, private railroads were sometimes granted subsidies to prevent them from operating at a loss. When the state absorbed a private railroad through purchase, it was motivated almost in every instance by the desire to save the investments of private capital. This policy caused capitalists to unload their bad investments on the state, until the private railroads remaining were those which were financially sound. The state also owned a passenger and freight bus service system, which were coordinated with the railroad system. Competition between railroads and busses, and various bus systems was not permitted by law. Communities served adequately by a railroad system were not served by bus lines. Rates on bus service were made the same as on railroad service.

In 1936 the investment of the state in railroads was estimated at 1,350,000,000 crowns. The returns to the state on this investment amounted to 40,000,000 crowns. This sum allowed the state, upon the payment of interest on indebtedness, a net surplus of 7,400,000 crowns. The large investment of the state in railroads was in part due to their costly electrification. The first road to be electrified was the Kiruna-Riksgränsen Railroad, completed in 1915. By 1937 the state had electrified 3,356 kilometers of its railroads, and by 1939 it was expected that about 50 per cent or 4,000 kilometers of the state railroads would be electrified. The electrified roads carried about 80 per cent of all the freight carried by the state roads. The cost of electrification by 1937 was estimated at nearly 300,000,000 crowns, but the speed and efficiency of the service were vastly improved. The express trains on the main trunk lines averaged a speed of 74 to 75 kilometers per hour.

In 1935 the state and local governments owned 23 per cent of the forests, while 27 per cent were owned by private corporations, and 50 per cent by private individuals. In 1936 the state owned crown parks to the extent of 5,366,121 hectares, providing a gross income of 51,597,000 crowns or a net annual profit of 17,698,200 crowns. The state owned all important waterpower sites, and in 1937 its net revenue from these amounted to 21,328,461 crowns. No direct competition existed between state and private power lines. The state extended its system into areas that private corporations could not profitably serve. The state compensated private utilities for services which were not profitable but were deemed necessary by the state in the interest of the general welfare.

The underlying motivation of state utility service was the encouragement of industries. In spite of this, even the telegraph system provided the state with net revenue of 35,082,703 crowns in 1937, and the postal service provided a net income of 18,251,554 crowns. In the same year the National Bank provided the government with a net income of 3,889,008 crowns, and the total revenues from state-owned and operated industries supplied the state with a net revenue of 151,738,358 crowns. This did not include the revenue secured from state monopolies, such as those from liquor and tobacco. The state profit from the sale of liquor in 1937 amounted to 189,595,686 crowns, while the revenue from the tobacco monopoly amounted to 94,179,082 crowns.

The state became the largest pension and invalid insurance company, virtually "the medical association"; it owned the public schools and higher institutions of learning; it subsidized and controlled all private schools; it owned the Svappovaara minefields; and it held stocks in the main mining corporations, thus assuring it of the eventual ownership of these mines through special agreements with the corporations. Between 1920 and 1937 the investments of the state in all its varied enterprises rose four times in value, an expansion involving great cost. Yet the revenues from state enterprises increased three times.

The control of trusts by the government was rigid, as in the case of the giant Swedish Sugar Trust. However, this control was difficult when a trust grew from a national to an international trust, as in the case of the Kreuger and Toll trust, which in 1924 controlled one-third of the entire world's production of matches. As a holding company built upon pyramiding of ownership of far-flung match corporations throughout the world and incorporated under the laws of Delaware, its business could not be checked on beyond the boundaries of Sweden. When Kreuger failed, it was discovered, however, that the parent organization, the Swedish Match Corporation in Sweden, was financially sound.

The failure of Kreuger revived the question of the necessity of nationalization of industry. The repercussions of the Senate Committee's revelations in regard to extension of American credit to the Allies and the sale of arms and ammunition as a cause of America's entry into World War I encouraged a group of Social Democrats in Sweden to nationalize the banks. Senator Nye became overnight one of the best known personages in Sweden; and in good American style Frans Severin uncovered sensational evidence of the far-flung power of Swedish capitalists. In 1936 he published a pamphlet, financed by the Social Democratic party for campaign purposes, called *The Empire of Big Finance* in which he maintained that 58 persons virtually controlled all industries in Sweden. As propaganda it was excellently timed. Banking institutions in Sweden had been rocked by the Kreuger swindle, and throughout the world the public had lost confidence in private banks.

In no field had concentration been more marked than in banking. In 1908 there had been 84 private banks, all of which were branch banks. Less than 30 years later this number had been reduced to 28. Of these, four controlled more than 60 per cent of all the assets, the members of the boards of these banks constituting the 58 persons referred to above. They had 590 seats on boards of 394 corporations. The capitalization of these corporations amounted to 2,776,500,000 crowns. The reserve funds of these corporations amounted to 590,000,000 crowns, and other funds to 483,000,000 crowns. These corporations were responsible for 80 per cent of all the taxable income in Sweden. Furthermore, the 58 bank directors controlled the savings and deposits of their banks, estimated at 1,905,000,000 crowns, and they controlled 50 per cent of all public investments.

Although nothing happened immediately as a result of these revelations, a logical step seemed to be the nationalization of the banks. In many of them the state was already heavily interested. Even the most radical adherents of socialization of industry realized that such a step could not be taken rapidly, but they thought that economic crises from time to time would cause the banks to fall into the lap of the state. The process of an extension of state ownership would then involve no radical departure from a long established policy. Nor would it greatly increase state control of industry, as might be indicated from *The Empire of Big Finance*. A banking law which prohibited banks from owning stock in corporations, except when ownership was necessary to safeguard investments of the banks, discouraged them from entering into risky businesses. A nationalization of the banks should, therefore, not greatly change or increase state ownership of industrial corporations.

In 1937 the state had no foreign debt, and its total national debt was 2,237,000,000 crowns. Since World War I, the Social Democrats and other parties had adopted the principle that any increase of the national debt must not be the result of unproductive investments, a position which was altered only in the case of unemployment aid during the depression of 1932. The Swedish government then also spent more money than its revenue warranted and had an unbalanced budget. During the fiscal years 1936-1939 the government, enjoying a surplus which corresponded to the deficits of 1933-1935, proceeded to set aside funds for use in emergencies. The national income of Sweden in 1939 exceeded $2,500,000,000. Considering the fact that the country had a population of only 6,300,000, Sweden must be regarded as one of the wealthiest countries per capita in the world. High taxes both on individuals and corporations prevented the accumulation of huge fortunes without placing serious handicaps on the development of industries. The worldwide economic depression of the 1930's caused the Swedish government to recognize the need for reserve funds by both the state and industrial corporations which might be used during an economic crisis, and the latter were extended tax exemptions for plant expansion and reserve funds.

187

Of slightly less significance than government paternalism in creating a higher standard of living was the work of the cooperative movement. It was another method of socializing industry and it had a greater appeal to the public than an expanding program of state ownership. The cooperative housing movement can be traced back two or three decades prior to World War I, although it was the war which, in 1917 gave impetus to the organization of the Stockholm Tenants' Union, which became the foundation for the modern cooperative housing movement. At that time the war had created an acute housing problem, and the landlords did not hesitate to take advantage of the situation. To combat the landlords, the Tenants' Union was created; but it had at first a rather precarious existence because of certain measures taken by the government to check the abuses of the landlords.

The Tenants' Union had considered the possibility of entering into a building program, but lack of funds prevented such action. In 1923 the reorganized Tenants' Savings and Building Society was organized in Stockholm for the specific purpose of entering into a program of cooperative housing construction. Similar organizations were founded in other cities, and in 1926 a national organization was set up. The purpose of the National Tenants' Savings and Building Association was to provide legal advice, to assist in placing loans, and to supervise activities of local societies. It also purchased building materials at wholesale prices, ran its own sawmills, owned numerous supply houses, operated a savings fund for members, and sold building loan certificates.

The pillars of the national association were the district or city societies, of which there were 69 in 1939. They collected savings from members and placed loans for building credit, helped to obtain building sites and directed building operations, managed the accounts of subsidiary societies and the sale or exchange of apartments, and assisted the societies in purchasing supplies and fuel at wholesale rates. For every cooperative house there was a separate society. They represented the owners of the building and concerned themselves with the details of management. Each subsidiary was a legal unit.

Through the cooperative housing movement about 20,000 apartment houses were built between 1923 and 1938 at an estimated value of $62,000,000. The cooperative housing movement was largely responsible for the fact that nearly 30 per cent of all homes in Sweden have been built since 1927. These homes were substantial, sanitary, and inexpensive. The planning of the projects of the cooperative apartments indicated thoughtful study of ways to eliminate superfluous luxury and yet provide every modern convenience. The low cost of these cooperative apartments was due to a number of causes. The savings fund of the National Tenants' Savings and Building Association had grown rapidly. Since 1935 the rate of interest paid on savings was only 3½ per cent. There was no difficulty in disposing of building loan certificates. The certificates provided ready cash, thus reducing the cost of material. All purchasing was done on a wholesale scale, and the national organization owned its own mills and warehouses. Most of the risk of private landlords was not present in the constructing of cooperative housing units. All planning and building was done on a large scale.

Both municipalities and the government granted credit on very liberal terms, because the cooperative housing movement was in accord with the government's own housing policy. This aimed at providing adequate housing conditions for families with very limited financial means, an ideal which the cooperatives were able to carry out in their planning. They provided their members with cheerful, up-to-date apartments, and unfolded a new and happier world in playgrounds, recreation centers, nurseries, parks, and lawns.

The laborer was also able to increase his purchasing power through the growth of consumers' cooperatives. These grew rapidly prior to World War I, and in 1920 the Swedish Cooperative Society had nearly a thousand member societies. After 1920 the Swedish Cooperative Society developed, however, along different lines than it had before. It consolidated its position and entered into manufacturing. In 1936 the results of consolidation were especially noticeable in a reduction in the actual number of member societies to 811. The membership of these societies more than doubled in sixteen years to reach 637,000 members.

Meanwhile the number of cooperative stores more than doubled. In 1936 the sales total of some 4,560 cooperative stores reached 461,876,000 crowns. In 1920 the cooperative stores' assets amounted to less than 50,000,000 crowns. These had risen, by 1936 to 205,855,000 crowns. The net profits of the Swedish Cooperative Society in 1936 amounted to 31,097,000 crowns. Prior to World War I producers' cooperatives produced goods valued at only 4,000,000 crowns. In 1936 they accounted for a production of 50,503,000 crowns.

As we have noticed, Swedish industry had from time to time tended to develop in the direction of trusts and monopolies. Some of these were under strict government control and might be called legal monopolies, while other trusts acquired a virtual monopoly of the Swedish market by sheer strength of organization and capital resources. Two striking examples of these two types of monopolies were the Swedish Sugar Trust, which enjoyed a complete monopoly on sugar production, and the Swedish Cement Trust, which controlled about 90 per cent of cement production. When a number of corporations failed to acquire a monopoly on the home market, they organized into a cartel to prevent competition. These cartels were able to regulate prices as effectively as if a monopoly existed. These developments were discouraged neither by the government nor by labor. The larger organizations were more easily controlled and regulated by the state, which readily recognized economies and efficiency achieved through the growth of big business. The state was principally interested in greater production. The labor organizations, too, preferred to deal with strong corporations rather than with small ones, and labor could expect to profit, at least to some little extent, from economies involved in greater mass production.

The state had gone so far in encouraging these trends as to make it possible for one producer to make legal claims against another for unsound competition. Because the cost of production had been standardized as the result of collective agreements between labor and employers, it was easy to determine if unsound competition existed. This, it would seem, would encourage more and more people to enter into business. Two considerations, however, prevented such a trend. In the first place, large amounts of capital would be necessary to enter profitably into an already established line of business. In the second place, the various cartels co-operated with one another, and they might refuse to sell goods to a newcomer. The danger of this development was evident, in that the trusts and cartels might charge exorbitant prices for their goods.

To check or minimize this danger, the capital resources of the Swedish Cooperative Society provided a sound weapon. In fact, it might be said that the Swedish Cooperative Society offered a more restraining and healthy influence on trusts and monopolies than any legislation against abuses. Since 1921 the Swedish Cooperative Society, in order to drive down prices of goods, had entered into the manufacture of oleomargarine, flour, galoshes, light bulbs, glassware, and a number of other products. It alone had enough capital to challenge the trusts, and usually a mere threat by the co-operative that it would start into another manufacturing venture brought a reduction in prices of goods manufactured by monopolies or controlled by trusts.

So much has been written in America about the Swedish Cooperative Society that the American public believes that Sweden is just one huge cooperative society. Only about 18 per cent of all retail business was done by the cooperative stores in 1938. To credit Sweden's prosperity to the cooperatives would be unjustifiable. They were, to be sure, important. But any country with the rich natural resources of Sweden and as favorably situated geographically would be prosper-

191

ous. Sweden had the natural resources, except oil, which are characteristically identified with the present civilization.

Sweden was blessed with what some democracies regard as a curse, a bureaucratic government, which without regard to politics guarded against harmful exploitation of the natural resources. Prosperity in Sweden was not the result of any political party, or of economic planning by any group at a given time, but was due, rather, to a government paternalism which antedated the twentieth century. For at no time throughout the nineteenth or twentieth centuries did any one seriously challenge the right of the state over its citizens. The right of the state to care for, protect, and foster the citizen was an inheritance from the age of the absolute monarchy antedating even the Age of Enlightenment.

Sweden has also been blessed with intelligent and able leaders of organized labor. The state never questioned the right of labor to organize, and since 1880 it has taken definite measures to provide labor with intelligent leaders through education. In combating drunkenness, the state performed an especially valuable service to labor.

The Swedish banks would have suffered the fate of many American banks if the state had not from time to time come to their rescue. The number of pennies that Swedish depositors have lost in banks since 1830 can easily be counted. Even the great crisis after World War I did not involve the loss of money by depositors.

Sweden had never believed in the racial superiority of its people, and for centuries invited brains, regardless of nationality, to immigrate to Sweden. Its indebtedness to Belgium, Germany, England, and especially Scotland was great. It was the wholesome influence of the Scots, with their thrift and sobriety, that really began to make things hum in the early part of the nineteenth century. The Jews became valuable citizens too, though forming a very small number. Through the veins of such persons as Wallenberg, Mannerheim, Bonnier, Lamb, and others, Jewish blood flows in more or less diluted form.

The benevolence of the paternal state reached into all areas. Not long ago a Swede wrote that the people of his country had confidence in God and "Per Albin," but as they did not wish to bother God too much they relied on "Per Albin" most often and only in the face of great danger sang "A Mighty Fortress Is Our God." Children born out of or in wedlock had the same rights. When a child was born, the state, if the parents desired, provided for baptism. If the parents had limited funds, the state provided for maternity help. If unemployment hit the parents, the state helped; and when the child reached the age of seven the state provided for an education. When there were too many sisters and brothers, the state supplied a bigger and better home. The Board of Health watched over sanitation and tried to prevent the spread of contagious diseases. The state and local governments provided the children with recreational centers, encouraged athletics, and fostered interest in the work of temperance societies. When the child reached a certain age, the state completed his religious education by means of confirmation, if the parents so desired. When manhood was reached, the state performed the marriage ceremony and helped in establishing a home. Regardless of what profession he chose, the citizen was aware of the state's watchful eye. In old age, the state provided care, and at the grave the state pronounced the final blessings.

The extension of social legislation has been so significant after 1933 that a separate study would be necessary to clarify the exact relationship of the state to the citizen. More recently even domestic servants' working hours have been regulated; and, according to a law effective in 1940, every employee is guaranteed two weeks' vacation with full pay. Provision has even been made for summer resort vacations for housewives, who are provided with lectures by expert dietitians, child nurses and home economics experts.

The state railroads have made it possible for anyone to travel throughout Sweden at very low cost, and special rates are provided for large families. A great deal has been done also to care for the aged in attractive homes.

The expansion of social legislation after 1932, however, did not amount to a new policy. It was based on a century-old principle that the people must be taught how to care for themselves. This policy was characteristic of the government's war against venereal diseases, its housing policy, its encouragement of cooperatives, its unemployment policy, maternity aid, labor legislation, old age pensions, extension of the public school system, and temperance. It was only those who were unable to help themselves that remained the wards of the communities. The government tried its utmost to prevent the accumulation of such cases.

The major political parties after World War I were the Social Democratic, the Conservative, the Liberal, and the Farmer parties. All of them except the Social Democratic party became weaker in the postwar period. The Communists, tired of being dictated to by Russia, returned in large numbers to the Social Democratic fold. The inability of the Conservative party to hold its own against the Social Democrats caused division within that party. The older members of the party grew more tolerant and liberal in their views, while a few of the younger members leaned toward National Socialism. The Nazi party in Sweden, however, had no future, economic conditions being such as to discourage its growth, and it was almost entirely ignored by the public.

Chapter XIII

THE FOREIGN POLICY OF SWEDEN
BETWEEN TWO WARS

S WEDEN, AFTER WORLD WAR I, might be taken as a
typical small European country which looked toward
the United States to assume leadership in building a better
world. Though it was true that few people in Sweden looked
upon Wilson as a Messiah who would inaugurate a millenium,
the Fourteen Points appealed to their sense of justice.
Sweden, as well as the other Scandinavian countries, was
disillusioned by the fact that she was not allowed to cooperate with the victors in laying the foundations for European
peace. Swedish desire and ability to remain neutral during
the war were in part caused by a desire to serve Europe
after the war. This was especially true of the Social Democrats, who believed that a neutral Scandinavia would be
able to contribute far more toward the establishment of a
just international order after the war than would a belligerent. The creation of the League of Nations seemed to be
a significant step toward the establishment of international
peace. When the neutrals were invited to a special conference by Colonel House on March 20, 1919, to discuss the
organization of the League, Scandinavia was jubilant.

The Scandinavian countries considered the invitation
seriously and began to prepare a program, including a study
of the nature of the League and its aims. Sweden assumed
the leadership of the neutrals, and requested that the date
of the conference be postponed in order to give it greater
significance. But postponement was not granted. The neutrals
had no chance whatsoever to outline a program for the
League of Nations.

The excitement over the invitation of January 11, 1920,

to join the League, in spite of the fact that the League already appeared to be something entirely different from what Sweden had hoped for, was soon dampened. It seemed certain that neither the United States nor Russia would become members. The fear grew that the League, in the absence of the United States, would become an organization designed to maintain the articles of the Versailles Treaty. Furthermore, if it were to be merely an organization directed against Germany, it would not become the instrument of international peace for which Sweden hoped. In 1920 many believed that it was Sweden's isolation policy that had enabled her to remain neutral during World War I and that to join the League would be a venture in another direction, the results of which no one could predict.

The Edén government, however, reasoned that Sweden's acceptance of membership in the League did not pledge Sweden's support of the maintenance of the *status quo* created by the peace treaties after the war; nor did it imply, according to Edén, that Sweden would be forced to participate in any military action. The Conservatives wanted Sweden to delay action in joining the League until the United States had taken a definite stand. They criticized the League as an alliance to enforce peace treaties. They warned of the dangers of becoming involved in future wars. Some Conservatives even believed that membership in the League meant the loss of complete independence. The main objections were that adequate guarantees had not been given for the membership of Germany and Russia, that representation of smaller states in the Council was not satisfactory, that a court of arbitration was not immediately established, and that the means of arbitration of disputes were not clearly described.

The advantages of a League of Nations to a small nation outweighed by far the disadvantages, in the opinion of Liberals and Social Democrats. It would afford the small countries a security which strong fortifications and a strong army could not provide. They declared that Sweden, in cooperation with other nations, could eventually prepare the way for membership of the excluded nations. Once within the League, they could strive successfully for a more satisfactory representation of the small nations in the Council, speed the organization of an international court of justice, secure a clearer definition of the duties of the delegates, and urge universal disarmament. Edén believed that the United States would certainly enter the League, and Branting rose to new heights of oratory as he pleaded before the *Riksdag,* in a speech filled with pathos and power, that Sweden accept the invitation to join. He said: "It is not the desire of the majority of the people of Sweden to look with mistrust upon a work built by men under a thousand and one difficulties aimed to safeguard the peace of the world. We wish to be along when this work is done."

The vote in the *Riksdag* was almost entirely along party lines, Conservatives voting against Sweden's acceptance of the invitation to join the League, and the Liberals and the Social Democrats voting for the acceptance of the invitation. The Liberals and Social Democrats won, and Sweden formally accepted in March 9, 1920

Sweden was represented by Branting, Ernst Trygger, and Marks von Wurtenberg at the first meeting of the League at Geneva in the fall of 1920. The majority of Swedish people placed great hopes in the future of the League as an instrument for international peace and justice. The League was accepted more as a legal than as a political institution.

Sweden's influence in the League was out of proportion to the size of the country, but might be attributed to the international reputation of Branting and to the close cooperation of the Scandinavian countries. Branting's chief task was to give labor confidence in its work. He did not share Georg Brandes' view that "progress is a sick snail," but he nevertheless believed that in a world torn by war progress must of necessity be slow. He, therefore, did not believe that he could immediately correct the injustices of the Versailles Treaty, but rather that he must exert every bit of his energy to its modification first in one particular and then in another. He had little desire to spare Germany from indemnity payments; but he believed care should be taken that "justice does not become injustice." He realized more clearly than most people the difficulties faced by the Social Democrats of Germany in maintaining the German Republic.

The German Social Democrats, as well as all Scandinavian Social Democrats, had a common ideology. The Danish Social Democrats probably had more intimate contact with German leaders than Swedish, but the problems faced by the Germans won Branting's heartfelt sympathies. He saw in the indemnity payments over an indefinite time a factor that would engender hatred and bitterness; and he perceived that it would make the Social Democrats' task in Germany impossible. Branting burned with a zeal to change the League from a tool in the hands of the victors into a shield for the oppressed.

The great confidence in Branting was shown by his appointment as chairman of the Disarmament Commission of the League of Nations, and by the election of Sweden as a member of the Council of the League of Nations in 1922. This was especially significant, for Branting had led the fight against the Council because he believed that Great Britain and France would use it as an instrument with which to minimize the influence of small nations in League affairs. Under the leadership of Branting, Swedish representatives to Geneva worked to free the Assembly from any influences of the Council, and the increase of the nonpermanent members from four to six in 1922 was undoubtedly a measure intended to overcome Swedish objections to the Council, which were shared by many if not most of the small nations.

Ever since the autumn of 1917 Sweden had hoped that the people of the Åland Islands might be reunited with Sweden. Geographically, historically, and racially the people of these islands are Swedish. Also, the islands have important strategic value to Sweden, for they command the entrance into the Gulf of Bothnia and are within easy reach of Stockholm. Sweden had joined with the people of Åland in petitioning the Great Powers at the Peace Conference to consider the question of the disposition of the Åland Islands. Sweden was of the opinion that the Peace of Paris of 1856, which forbade Russia to fortify the islands, had made the Ålands an international question rather than one which must be settled between Sweden and Finland. The people of the islands had petitioned the United States, France, Italy, and Great Britain that the fate of the islands should be determined by a plebiscite. The Swedish government sought to influence the government at Helsinki for a peaceful settlement of the Åland question upon the basis suggested by their inhabitants. The excitement of the people on the Åland Islands was great, and in January 1919 a special deputation of the people of these islands appeared in Paris to plead for a plebiscite. Hopes ran high for a reunion with Sweden from which the islands had never been separated in spirit, in spite of the fact that a hundred and ten years had passed since Sweden had been forced to cede the islands to Russia.

Finland claimed that the Åland Assembly did not truly represent the wish of the people. To disprove these claims a plebiscite was taken in June 1919, when 9,735 out of 10,196 citizens expressed their hopes for a reunion with Sweden. Clemenceau expressed his personal hope in September 1919 that the Åland Islands would soon be reunited with Sweden. The relationship between Finland and Sweden became so strained that it was necessary to recall the Swedish minister from Helsinki. Finland maintained that Sweden was taking an unfair advantage of a situation created by the war, which had made the people of the islands apprehensive of both Russian and Finnish rule. It was fear of the uncertainties of Finland's future as an independent country and fear of falling again into the hands of Russia which caused the people of the Åland Islands to seek a haven under the Swedish flag. At least, this was the Finnish position, and it is true that few people had suffered greater hardships during the war than the people of the Åland Islands. Finland maintained that the Åland Islands had for centuries shared the fate of Finland, and that the destruction of its fortifications was an adequate indication of Finland's desire to please Sweden. Sweden, however, stubbornly clung to the idea recognized by Wilson in his Fourteen Points, the principle of self-determination.

The strained relations between Finland and Sweden were not a serious threat to peace. However, when two of the islands' leaders were arrested by Finnish authorities for their part in inveigling the people into a refusal to obey Finnish laws, and when Finland refused to release them, a war-like sentiment developed in Sweden. The Swedish Social Democrats proposed a conference for the purpose of settling the Åland question peacefully by the labor organizations of the two countries who were to agree on a program which they could present to their respective governments for adoption. The Finnish Social Democrats refused, however, to cooperate with those in Sweden.

The relationship between Sweden and Finland remained strained throughout 1920. The feeling spread in Sweden that the government had betrayed the confidence of the people of the Åland Islands, who had repeatedly expressed their devotion. The Swedish government had been unable to secure a settlement of the Åland question at the Peace Conference, despite Clemenceau's promise of September 1919. However, the League of Nations at its first session in the autumn of 1920 gave the people of the Åland Islands a new hope. Finland had consented to have the question settled by the League, although it expressed the opinion that it would not be bound by any decision that it might render. Upon the initiative of Great Britain, the Council decided in September 1920 to study the Åland question, and a commission of three was appointed, which made a hurried visit to the islands and reported to the Council the result of its fact-finding mission. It reported in part as follows. "To concede to minorities, either of language or religion, or to any fractions of a population the right to withdraw from the community to which they belong, because it is their wish or their good pleasure, would be to destroy order and stability within states and to inaugurate anarchy in international life; it would be to uphold a theory incompatable with the very idea of the state as a territorial and political unity . . ."

The Commission recommended that the Åland Islands be awarded to Finland outright. It completely ignored historical and geographical factors and the wishes of the people of the Åland Islands. It ignored the fact that Sweden might have gone to war with Finland in 1920, at a time when international chaos would have made it impossible for any nation to interfere or arbitrate. Finland had not recuperated from its War of Independence and would have been no match for the Swedish army. Yet it was Sweden that pleaded for peace and understanding, and the people of Sweden were sincerely happy over Finland's independence. Nor was it a happiness based entirely upon selfish nationalistic interests which regarded an independent Finland as a bulwark against future Russian expansionistic policy. Rather it was a happiness based upon a common history of two people over several centuries.

Sweden could not go to war against Finland. Her feelings were those of a mother sorrowing over a wayward son. She had been deeply wounded by the uncompromising attitude of Finland. She had recognized Finland's independence unconditionally, and this had formed the basis of the Commission's recommendation to the Council of the League of Nations. Sweden had been eager to be the first nation to recognize the independence of Finland.

The Commission had recommended, and the Council had approved, certain mitigating measures in awarding the Åland Islands to Finland. These were that the people of the Åland Islands were not to be compelled to learn Finnish; that non-residents of the islands were not to be domiciled until after a residence of five years; that the governor of the islands was to be appointed by the President of Finland upon the recommendation of the Åland Assembly; and finally that the

201

League of Nations was to be the guarantor of those provisions which gave the Åland Islands a degree of autonomy.

This was the first dispute to be settled by the League of Nations, and it raised serious doubts as to the impartiality of that body's decisions. A serious dispute between two nations had been avoided without recourse to war; but the credit was more Sweden's than the League's. The settlement of the Åland question was undoubtedly in no small measure the result of the desire of the Great Powers, especially Great Britain and France, to reward Finland for its heroic war against the Communists of Russia. At the same time, it rebuked Sweden for its unwillingness to join the allied powers in a blockade against Russia after the World War.

This policy had been consistent with Sweden's neutrality policy throughout the preceding war. Although the situation created in the Baltic after the World War was a godsend as far as Sweden was concerned, she was not sure that things would always be so ideal in the Baltic. Sweden could not afford to offend Russia. She had recognized the independence of Poland in 1919, and two years later that of Estonia, Latvia, and Lithuania. Sweden desired no policy which might involve her at a future time in difficulties either with Russia or Germany. Branting sought to have Sweden recognize Russia officially in 1922, but he failed because the *Riksdag* desired to await the results of action taken at Geneva. When, therefore, the Soviet Union was recognized by Germany, Turkey, and Great Britain as well as by Italy, the *Riksdag* in the spring of 1924 followed the example set by these nations.

The decision of the League in regard to the Åland question in 1921 jarred Sweden's confidence in the League; but, strangely enough, it did not alter her position in regard to the need for compulsory international arbitration. The seriousness with which Branting viewed the work of the League caused the public, even the Conservatives, to admit that the League represented an ideal. More and more the League came to be looked upon as a world parliament, rather than as a permanent congress of diplomatic representatives from various nations. Sweden seriously assumed its League obligations, and during the depression the Scandinavian countries were almost the only nations that continued to meet their financial obligations to the League. Sweden's chief interest was the League's potential power to preserve the peace.

During 1920-1921, the Scandinavian countries made every effort to amend the Covenant of the League of Nations. Sweden was especially alarmed over the sanction obligations of members, which she desired to have reinterpreted to weaken their importance; but at Geneva the position of Sweden, free from any war hate, was not appreciated.

The Scandinavian countries were more successful in changing the rules pertaining to the Council and to the rotation of membership of the non-permanent members of the Council. Sweden's policy at Geneva would appear to the casual student to be contradictory. Though she sought, on one hand, to reduce the obligations of the members of the League, she believed, on the other hand, that the theoretical duties should be increased. She believed that the war and human suffering, endured by neutrals as well as by the nations at war, had created such an impression that these alone could provide the foundation for a lasting peace. On September 8, 1921, Branting said: "The high principles which form the foundation of the League . . . shall . . . even if slowly step by step . . . win in the struggle over force and selfishness."

After 1922 Branting tried to influence the Council in such a manner that it would not become the spokesman of a great power or a group of powers. When Ernst Trygger became prime minister of Sweden in 1923, Branting retained his seat in the Council; for every one in Sweden recognized the fact that it was Branting and not Sweden who had been elected a member of the Council. Branting personified Sweden's Geneva politics. The year 1923 witnessed unrest in Europe, and on June 1 Branting expressed his views in writing to the League on the question of guarantees, maintaining that it was easier for newly created states dangerously situated geographically to offer guarantees than it was for older and more favorably geographically situated countries. To some countries, guarantees did not increase the risks of war, but for Sweden to enter into a general guarantee of the territorial integrity of independent countries involved danger.

Branting suggested as tactfully as possible that European conditions created by the peace treaties after the World War were not and could not be regarded as permanent. In spite of the view voiced by Branting, the League again, as in 1922, took up the question of mutual guarantees. Branting's position was further weakened when Edward Benes was made a member of the Council. Benes was a spokesman for the French *status quo* policy. Branting suffered another defeat in 1923 when he wanted the League and the Council to take upon themselves the question of Italian occupation of Corfu. Again the Great Powers showed that their conceptions of the functions of the League were not at all the same as Branting's. They decided to settle the question among themselves.

Branting was, however, the international optimist. He was happy over the outcome of the general election in England in December 1923, which carried the Labor party to power. He was more than pleased with the elections in France in May of 1924, which brought Edouard Herriot to power in France. Ramsay MacDonald and Herriot enjoyed the confidence of Branting, and he approved of their conciliatory policy toward Germany. Neither MacDonald nor Herriot, however, was to be in power very long. In October 1924, the Labor party in England suffered a reverse which carried the Conservatives into office. Branting did not live to see the Geneva Protocol doomed. On February 24, 1925, he died, remaining to the very last optimistic about the future of Europe and world peace. He died before the League of Nations had a chance to test its real worth. He had attended the session of the Council at Brussels in October 1924 and had proposed a settlement in the dispute between Great Britain and Turkey over Mosul. He came home very tired, fell ill in November, and died the following February. In Branting's passing, the League lost one of its noblest friends.

The Scandinavian countries had been zealous in their efforts to secure membership in the League for both Germany and Russia. In 1924 Germany petitioned for membership and a permanent seat in the Council; and immediately Spain, Poland, Brazil, China, and even Persia raised claims to permanent membership. France promised to support Poland, her ally, while Great Britain had promised to support Spain. At the Locarno Conference of October 1925, Germany had not been made to understand that her membership in the League and a permanent seat in the Council were to be dependent upon a general increase in the number of permanent seats. When, therefore, the Assembly of the League met in the latter part of March to discuss the admission of Germany into membership of the League, it seemed as if Germany would suffer another humiliation.

Sweden made it clear that she would oppose any increase in the number of permanent seats in the Council except one for such a nation as Germany, and offered to turn over her temporary seat to Poland in the Council in order to overcome that nation's objection to not having a voice in the Council. Brazil, however, was unyielding; she insisted upon a permanent seat in the Council. Chamberlain and Briand conducted a number of private "conferences" in order to reach a satisfactory solution, a method which greatly offended the Scandinavian countries. The Assembly broke up without reaching a decision. Nansen of Norway said: "The League itself cannot be blamed for what has happened. The machinery of the League did not even begin to work; no use has been made of it. What has happened is that there have been private conversations. There has been no meeting of the Council and no meeting of the Assembly to discuss the question." Not until September 1926 was Germany admitted to membership in the League and allowed a permanent seat in the Council.

Sweden's contributions to the reorganization of the

205

Council in 1926 have been greatly exaggerated. The Locarno negotiations had laid the foundation for a better understanding in Europe, and Germany's membership in the League was inevitable. But 1926 marks a change in Sweden's attitude. As stated before, Branting had looked upon the League as a legal organization, an international parliament supported by a World Court. Sweden had been a strong advocate of compulsory arbitration. After 1926, however, the sentiment gained ground that the League must be looked upon as a diplomatic organization; in other words, it was a bargaining agency.

Sweden's position in 1926 represented a last feeble effort to make the Council an impartial judicial agency. She believed that the Council would be better balanced if Germany were a member. It was the first time that Sweden took an important part in international affairs after the war. By her generosity Sweden offended Poland more than was necessary in spite of the fact that she was eager to remain friendly to Poland. She similarly offended Spain. The *Riksdag* did not really know what the excitement was all about, and Professor Östen Undén, who represented Sweden, was puzzled by the rumpus created by Sweden's attitude. Sweden had been caught in the net of international intrigue and she was not comfortable. The relinquishing of her temporary seat was no sacrifice at all, as the term was soon to expire for Swedish membership in the Council; and it might not have been renewed.

Sweden's interest in the League dwindled considerably in 1926. With the death of Branting the optimism about the future of the League as an institution of international justice ebbed. Its value was still appreciated in a sense, however, for Sweden hoped that the rubbing of elbows by diplomats would create a better understanding among nations, and that the League might influence disarmament. Only the Scandinavian countries, however, took disarmament seriously. It was they who encouraged the adoption by the Assembly of the General Act of 1928 encouraging an extension of international arbitration, a move in complete harmony with their policy of arbitration treaties.

Sweden was also one of the first countries to subscribe to the optional clause in the statute of the Permanent Court of International Justice, which authorized the Court to settle any controversy between Sweden and any other country which had signed the clause. Treaties were signed by Sweden with Denmark, Finland, Norway, Switzerland, Estonia, Latvia, and Lithuania, by which Conciliation Commissions were created during 1924 and 1925. Through the arbitration agreements among the northern European countries a "Northern Locarno" had been created by 1925. Sweden extended her program to include compulsory arbitration treaties with Germany in 1924 and with Norway in 1925. The following year, similar compulsory arbitration agreements had been reached between Sweden and Austria, Belgium, Czechoslovakia, Denmark, and Finland. Few countries have had a better record in promoting international peace. The Kellogg Pact won the approval of Sweden, as it fitted admirably into Swedish Utopian pacifism. It can be said that Sweden had no foreign policy outside of its relations with the League.

Though Sweden had been dubious about the use of economic sanctions by the League, Rickard Sandler in 1935 supported the economic blockade of Italy, and Sweden's and Italy's relationships were strained. Sweden had strong economic interests in Ethiopia, and the loss of life in a unit of the Swedish Red Cross as a result of Italian bombardment there brought forth anti-Italian demonstrations in Sweden. The return of the Social Democrats to power in 1932 had strengthened Sweden's interest in the work of the League, an interest in part motivated by fears created by the rise of Hitler in Germany. Sweden was seriously worried over the situation in Germany, seeing in Hitler a real threat to European peace. The Hoare-Laval plan brought forth severe Scandinavian criticism of the British-French conciliatory and vacillating policy in regard to Ethiopia. That Great Britain and France could not be trusted entirely seemed quite evident.

Swedish interests in the Baltic were threatened by British flirtation with Germany. In spite of the fact that the minister of Swedish foreign affairs, Rickard Sandler, was president of the Assembly of the League of Nations and enjoyed the confidence of Great Britain, this power had decided on the dangerous policy of playing with Hitler. By a naval treaty with Germany, Great Britain allowed Germany to build a fleet in the Baltic which was to be equal to 35 per cent of all other fleets in the Baltic, and she tried to induce Sweden to sign a naval building program, but naval experts believed that the specifications of this treaty served only the interests of Germany.

Public opinion wondered in 1935 if the time had not come for Sweden to look elsewhere than to Great Britain for leadership in international affairs. Though Sweden had been relentless in its criticism of France's postwar foreign policy, she now wondered whether after all France, rather than England, should not assume the leadership of Europe. Sandler, however, urged the ratification of the naval treaty between Sweden and Great Britain, and rumors circulated that Sandler was mere putty in the hands of England's rulers.

This was hardly true. Sandler was realistic, and in 1935 he began strongly to urge that Sweden and Finland should cooperate in fortifying the Åland Islands. In the first place, this required a preliminary agreement between Sweden and Finland as to a common defense and, in the second place, permission from the League of Nations to undertake such fortifications. Sandler's realistic foreign policy brought about an increase in Sweden's military appropriations in 1935, now a necessity as a result of the failure of the Disarmament Conference of 1934 and of Germany's denunciation of the military clauses of the Versailles Treaty. All hopes for disarmament had vanished. The increased military appropriations were not used to increase the period of military training but to modernize the army, navy, and the air defense. After

1935 Sweden's expenses for national defense mounted rapidly.

The Sandler plan for joint fortification of the Åland Islands did not materialize until 1939. Sandler had worked energetically in Sweden and Geneva to overcome opposition. In Sweden opposition was especially strong because of the great unpopularity of the Sandler plan on the Åland Islands. The people of these islands believed that Sandler had sacrificed their interests, and if any one was disliked more than a Finn on these islands in 1938 and 1939, it was Sandler.

The Conservatives in Sweden had made the most of the strong spirit of nationalism in Finland, which had led to the discouragement of the preservation of the Swedish language and culture in Finland among a strong minority group of Swedes on the eastern coast. Swedes in Finland adopted Finnish names in order not to be discriminated against, and persons more capable of speaking Swedish than Finnish refused to admit that they understood or were able to speak Swedish. Finnish students wanted to address in Finnish the Scandinavian students' conferences at which they were represented and tried, vainly, to persuade the Scandinavian university students to adopt a resolution that Finnish was a Scandinavian language. Sandler succeeded, however, in convincing Finland that the joint fortification of the Åland Islands was desirable. By the summer of 1939, he had made all the preliminary arrangements, and the matter was ready to be presented before the League of Nations for approval. In sounding the views of the various members of the League, Sandler must have been assured of success. It therefore surprised him to find that Russian opposition made the realization of the plan unattainable. Germany was silent on the question of the fortification, but expressed her appreciation of Russia's views.

This implied that both Russia and Germany had suddenly changed their minds, for Sandler certainly would not have brought a question before the League that he was not sure he could carry, especially a question on which probably both Russia and Germany might be sensitive. Both these nations must, at one time, have assured Sandler of their support. Sandler's reverse must have been the direct result of the negotiations between Germany and Russia which led to a treaty between these nations in August, a treaty which more than any other factor contributed to the German invasion of Poland. The failure of Sandler to gain approval for the joint fortification of the Åland Islands by Sweden and Finland clearly indicated the nature of the German and Russian alliance, which later became evident in Russia's attack upon Finland.

The summer of 1939 was fatal for European peace. Sandler was criticized severely in Sweden for having undertaken a task which he could not carry out successfully; but perhaps he was not greatly to blame. Great Britain had seemingly been willing to go almost as far as Germany in making concessions to Russia and Germany, at least in the Baltic, as a price for Russian friendship. It was possible to believe that Great Britain was willing to sacrifice the interests of Finland in the same manner. The negotiations between Russia and Great Britain, which had been carried on simultaneously with the German-Russian negotiations, suddenly broke down. Finland enjoyed more international good will than could safely be sacrificed by Great Britain. This good will extended far beyond the Scandinavian countries to the United States.

In Sweden, the diplomacy of the Great Powers was neither understood nor appreciated, with the result that Sandler's prestige suffered. It was not only the Conservatives who criticized Sandler, but many prominent leaders within the Social Democratic party. They believed that Sandler was playing a dangerous game and playing right into the hands of Great Britain. There was little doubt that Sandler was pro-British, but like the English diplomats he had been too slow to act. No one in Sweden was better acquainted with international developments than he, but during the summer of 1939 the international theater changed too rapidly. More fatal for Scandinavia was Sandler's inability to secure Denmark's interest in a joint Scandinavian defense of the neutrality of the North. Though the Conservative party had flirted with such a thought in 1926, the Social Democratic party did not begin to consider seriously the question of the cooperation of Scandinavian states and Finland in the defense of their neutrality until after 1936. But unwillingness on the part of Denmark to join in this program, as well as Norway's hesitancy, crippled the defense of Scandinavia and Finland. In the spring of 1937 Prime Minister Stauning of Denmark said in an address delivered at Lund: "Denmark is not the watch dog of Scandinavia." With Denmark unwilling to strengthen effectively her national defense, leaving all of Scandinavia vulnerable to attack from the south, Sandler's policy had to be focused on keeping all four countries of the north free from any European controversy, a policy on which they agreed in April 1938 at a conference in Oslo of the ministers of foreign affairs of Sweden, Norway, Denmark, and Finland.

Sandler was not cheered by the Munich Conference. He said on December 9, 1938: "After the armies and navies had been made ready for war, peace or an armistice was concluded (who can be sure which term is the right one?) without resorting to the burdensome, time-wasting and uncertain procedure of war. In the political history of Europe, Munich is a turning point . . . A new power situation has been set up. Versailles now belongs to the past." He was skeptical about the Peace of Munich. As long as Italy had not come to terms with Great Britain and France, there could be no stability. He looked upon Russian and Polish agreements in 1938 as an effort aimed to check German expansion toward the Ukraine. In view of the events in Europe, Sandler believed that Sweden, in conjunction with other small nations, had acted wisely in freeing herself from sanction obligations under the Covenant of the League of Nations. Late in 1938 Sweden resigned from the Non-intervention Committee's executive section in another effort not to become entangled in the politics of the Great Powers. Sandler felt that all reliance upon collective security had to be abandoned, and that if the League were to be revived and become an agency of international peace, the United States had to lend its prestige. In other words, he thought that the interest in the League must be universal.

The Munich Conference of September 1938 caused Europe to fall into a dangerous mental state, from which even the violation of the Munich agreement by German occupation of Bohemia could not completely arouse it. The occupation of Bohemia caused great excitement in Sweden, and the *Riksdag* of 1939 proceeded at an unprecedented rate to make appropriations for strengthening the national defense. Preparations were made for air defense. and precautionary measures were taken to decrease the hazards of fire resulting from air raids. Women were encouraged to take up work and learn duties which are usually done by men. The Swedish Cooperative Society advised the people to purchase certain supplies of food for storage. But by August 1939 few people had stored goods, and most of them had again fallen into a state of mental lethargy. Many believed that the government's precautionary measures were unnecessary. It was believed that Germany would have no other claims on Poland than the right-of-way across the corridor; that the city of Danzig would perhaps elect Hitler as its president; and that neither Poland, the League, Great Britain, nor France would be greatly concerned over such a step. If nothing had been done to prevent Hitler from occupying Bohemia, the people reasoned, nothing would be done over German annexation of Danzig. Furthermore, some kind of friendly relationship between Poland and Germany did not seem impossible. Not only had Hitler repeatedly assured Poland of his friendship; Poland had been a partner in the German crime against Czechoslovakia. In the month of August, Europe believed an immediate war improbable. No nation was fully prepared for what happened. Germany undoubtedly believed that Poland would yield to German demands and that France and Great

Britain would, if anything, encourage Poland to yield to a compromise.

When the war broke out with the German invasion of Poland, the world was stunned. It seemed as if no one could believe what had happened, and Sweden was probably less prepared mentally for the war than was almost any other nation.

CHAPTER XIV

THE DILEMMA OF A NEUTRAL NATION
DURING WORLD WAR II

O N September 1, 1939, the church bells tolled for hours
throughout Sweden. Germany had invaded Poland.
World War II had begun and Sweden ordered partial mobilization. The *Riksdag* proceeded to strengthen Sweden's defenses, not only increasing appropriations for defense itself
but also taking measures to compensate families whose
income had been jeopardized by mobilization. Sweden's social
legislation was thus carried into her program of preparedness. The Farmers' party felt that the time had come when
party politics must be put aside. It recommended a coalition
government, and Prime Minister Per Albin Hansson did not
object, though his party controlled both the First and the
Second Chamber. The Conservative party saw no need for
such a coalition government, as no crisis had been created to
make such a coalition necessary. Professor Gösta Bagge,
leader of the Conservatives, stated that his party could best
serve Sweden by remaining in opposition to the government.
He believed that nothing was more dangerous than the absence of opposition in the *Riksdag,* and that a wide-awake
and intelligent opposition could prevent many mistakes in
government. He stated that the Conservatives would pursue
a policy designed to serve the interests of the kingdom, and
that if a coalition government became necessary to show that
Sweden was united, the Conservatives would cooperate.

The government declared its neutrality immediately, and
ordered export prohibited on almost every kind of goods in
order to prevent a repetition of the sad consequences of
Sweden's trade policy in World War I. The *Riksdag* was
called into special session, and the government was given the

right to confiscate all private property should an emergency require such a drastic measure. Preparations were made immediately for rationing gasoline, and the government proceeded to check the rise of prices on various goods. There was no run on the banks, as in August 1914, and in less than two weeks the crown was tied to the American dollar.

The sinking of a number of Swedish ships by the Germans was the first evidence that international trade was to be seriously interfered with and that Germany had an effective system of espionage in Sweden. The people were warned over the radio not to speak or to reveal secrets to strangers. Still every one was sure that Sweden would be able to stay out of the war.

Several misconceptions prevailed. It was believed that the war would develop mainly into an economic one, and that Sweden must, therefore, take immediate measures to encourage the importation of raw materials and other essentials. War risk insurance was offered Swedish shippers and there was no immediate interruption of the international trade. During the first month of the war, it was believed that, except for a severe gasoline shortage, Sweden was well prepared to face an economic blockade. Restrictions on the use of automobiles and trucks were the first severe war restrictions. By October and November, these restrictions were made more liberal. Numerous oil tankers had reached Sweden, and automobiles were again for a time seen on the streets and roads during the month of October. The shortage of coal first appeared to be serious during December, and measures were taken to limit the amount of coal consumption.

During September and October 1939, the nature of the German-Russian agreement of August was gradually revealed. Sweden was alarmed over Russia's demands upon Finland, and on October 17 and 18 King Gustav was host to Finland's President Kyosti Kallio and the kings of Denmark and Norway. He had invited them and their secretaries of foreign affairs to a conference in Stockholm.

The purpose of the Stockholm Conference was not known. Various rumors circulated. Among others it was believed that a visit by Sven Hedin to Berlin prior to the Conference had laid the foundation for a peace proposal by the Scandinavian countries. Thus, the Swedish king was to serve as a tool of Hitler and a medium through which a peace proposal was to be presented the nations at war. There was little doubt that at that time Germany was eager to have Scandinavia serve this purpose, and on the two days of the Conference a full-page advertisement was published in a number of newspapers requesting the Conference to draft a peace proposal.

The fact that it was the Finnish minister to Stockholm, Juho Paasikivi, who led the Finnish negotiations with Russia indicated that cooperation between Finland and Sweden was a close one. On their numerous journeys to and from Russia, the Finnish delegates were greeted by the diplomatic representatives of the Scandinavian countries in Moscow and Helsinki. This created a feeling that the Scandinavian countries had made common cause with Finland. Such was not the case. Finland intended to yield, but sparred for advantage, and was greatly surprised over the sudden end of negotiations.

Even should the Swedish King have desired at the Stockholm Conference to make common cause with Finland, neither Denmark nor Norway desired to pledge aid in case of war.

Denmark, in fact, was not an asset in a military alliance. Denmark's entire defense program had been built upon the idea that her geographical situation made a strong national defense worse than none at all. A strong national defense would, it was believed in Denmark, be an invitation for German invasion or might invite the enemies of Germany to turn Denmark into a military base. As a result of Hitler's and Roosevelt's war of words during the summer of 1939, Denmark had accepted a non-aggression treaty with Germany. Denmark was completely at the mercy of the good

217

will of Germany, and could not afford to enter into a military pact with Finland and the other Scandinavian countries. The vulnerability of Denmark exposed all of Scandinavia.

Norway, furthermore, had fears neither of Germany nor of Russia and could not appreciate Sweden's fears. Finland and Sweden had both begun more seriously to strengthen their defenses, especially after 1936. Norway had not been similarly aroused. Of course, Norway had a better army and navy than Denmark, but it was far too weak to permit a venture into a dangerous foreign policy.

It was, therefore, very doubtful that the King of Sweden had even speculated upon the possibility of a military alliance. He knew that the Swedish army and navy were not strong. The Social Democrats had been consistent in their demilitarization of Sweden, and in 1936 they had fought successfully against an increase in the period of compulsory military training. Appropriations in Sweden for military purposes had been increased mainly to speed the mechanization of the national defense. Though King Gustav was old, he knew that the military experts in Sweden did not believe the Swedish defense to be satisfactory. The reason for the Stockholm Conference was, therefore, a desire on the part of the King to keep Scandinavia from embroilment in war.

The aged monarch was over 80 years old, and the Bernadotte dynasty had brought peace to Sweden, a peace that had lasted for 125 years. After World War I, the sovereign had allowed many burdens of the state to be assumed by others. He had discontinued his struggle over royal prerogatives and he had become a democratic monarch. Then suddenly, at the age of 82, he came to a realization that his own reign might witness the end of the long peace. His one and only thought was to keep Sweden out of the war. The Stockholm Conference was a peace conference, aimed at preventing the spread of war into Finland, which might also involve Sweden.

It can be said with a degree of certainty that the Stockholm Conference pledged no other aid to Finland than moral support. If anything, Finland was encouraged to yield,

218

although the Scandinavian countries were pledged to exert themselves in such manner as to reduce the severity of the Russian demands. The Stockholm Conference stirred the spirit of nationalism as never before. The public liked to imagine that Finland and the Scandinavian countries were a united people, and that the fate of Finland was the fate of Scandinavia. Some were drunk with the prospect of Finnish and Swedish armies fighting side by side as they had for centuries prior to 1809. Tears were shed as Sibelius' "Finlandia" was played, and voices grew hoarse from singing the Swedish national anthem. No one knew what had happened when the Conference was over except that President Kallio had left on an airplane in the same manner that he had arrived, and that old King Gustav had kissed King Haakon of Norway on both cheeks, just as he had King Christian of Denmark. This was significant, as he had greeted King Haakon only with one kiss at the Malmö Conference in 1914. People believed that Scandinavia was inaugurating closer cooperation than that which had been made necessary by World War I. Of course, there was much loose talk and speculation. Some believed that Finland could not yield to the demands of Russia, and that in such a case Sweden would send an army to the aid of Finland. These people maintained that both the United States and Sweden had encouraged Finland in resisting the demands made by Russia, and that the United States would sooner or later be dragged into the war and Germany would be vanquished. Others maintained that Sweden could not send an army to Finland, for Sweden was helplessly exposed to a German attack through Denmark. Many criticized the Social Democrats sharply, feeling that they had exposed Sweden to new dangers by their antimilitarism. Sweden hurried its air raid precautionary measures, and strengthened the army and the navy, but was too slow in realizing the necessity of a strong defense. By November 1939 most people admitted that Sweden's air defense did not at all meet the requirements of modern warfare.

When the war between Russia and Finland broke out, Sweden found herself in a helpless position. The Stockholm Conference had failed. Russia had not been impressed by the moral support given Finland by either Scandinavia or the United States. There were demonstrations against Russia in all the capitals of Scandinavia. Young men volunteered to serve in the Finnish army, and Communist newspaper offices were stormed. During the Russo-Finnish negotiations, a Swedish Communist said that he hoped that Russia would extend the benevolent protection of the Russian bayonet to Sweden. The Communists, though not strong, posed a serious problem in Sweden. They had one representative in the First Chamber, and it was feared that he would divulge state secrets to Russia. Some newspapers suggested that the King should dissolve the First Chamber and order a new election, as it was certain that no Communist would be elected.

But this alone would not solve the problem. The Communists were strong in the northern part of Sweden, where Sweden was vulnerable. The Social Democrats did not believe that it was wise to make martyrs of the Communists. One thing only was certain, namely, that Sweden was not prepared to aid Finland. It had neither the trained men nor the airplanes to fight a modern war.

An emergency was created that called for the cooperation of all the political parties in a coalition government under the leadership of Hansson. The fact that Hansson remained prime minister was in itself a token that Sweden intended to stay out of the war. It was around his neutrality policy that the Conservatives and the Liberals were willing to gather. Sandler was retired as minister of foreign affairs to appease Germany, and he was succeeded by Christian E. Günther, a career diplomat. It was also significant that Günther had held the position as envoy to Oslo, and that Sweden's foreign policy might thus be more fully in accord with Norway's.

Sandler had grown more and more restless, and believed that the time had come for discarding Sweden's traditional neutrality policy. He feared especially that the Russians might occupy the Åland Islands and that Russian aggression might not cease with occupation of Finland. He believed that Finland was fighting Sweden's war. He also realized that this policy would invite German invasion, a danger which he was willing to risk. He had never made a secret of his anti-Hitler sentiments. Sandler was, therefore, looked upon as a very dangerous man to the peace of Scandinavia. In November 1939 he had doubted that there would be a Scandinavia twelve months later.

The removal of Sandler in December 1939 was thus not only to appease Germany, but to remove the worst fears of Denmark and Norway that Sweden by its foreign policy was on the point of endangering the independence of these countries. The policy of the new government, the Hansson coalition government, was outlined at the opening of the *Riksdag* of 1940. The King in addressing the *Riksdag* stated that the time had come for Sweden to think first of her independence, and that thoughts of social legislation must for the time being be put aside. The old monarch stated that the policy of Sweden was to give Finland all help possible without directly taking part in the war. He stated that Sweden had not obligated herself to help Finland. Hansson stated on January 17 that there had been neither pressure brought to bear on Sweden from the Western Powers nor threats from Germany. "Every attempt to violate our neutrality will be averted by every means at our disposal. All unneutral acts, such as permitting troops of belligerent powers to pass over our territory, or use of Swedish territory as bases for action, will not be tolerated . . . We feel no hostility toward the Russian people. The government is deeply anxious to help Finland, though great care is required if we want to escape being drawn into the area of the big conflicts. We need no instruction from the outside as to our relations with Finland. We ourselves can best decide how to serve the interest of both Finland and the whole North." He spoke of the generosity of the Swedish people toward Finland, how workers gave their wages, the young men their lives, and the poor their last penny.

But in the *Riksdag,* Sandler spoke of "the wreckage of northern collaboration." He accused the government of lacking courage and charged that in the war between Russia and Finland "Scandinavian collaboration suffered a defeat." He said: "I accept this defeat. However, it is no capitulation and the last word has not yet been said. If the Red Army of this war should defeat Finland, that would mean the complete Bolshevization of Finland with the consequence that the Finnish race must take refuge in Sweden and Norway. Real help to Finland would be the most effective limitation of the danger that Sweden might be drawn into a great war."

Frederik Ström urged the formation of a northern defense league and expressed his belief that if such a league had existed in the autumn of 1939, Finland would not have been at war with Russia. He believed that it was not too late to save the rest of the Scandinavian countries by the formation of such a league. But the prime minister called Sandler to task and stated that there was a difference between what Sweden would like to do and was able to do.

Though Sandler was applauded in the *Riksdag,* most members agreed that the prime minister was correct. The *Riksdag* decided to appropriate 1,000,000,000 crowns for national defense. Steps were taken for the manufacture of airplanes in Sweden and the purchase of airplanes in America. Plans were made for the purchase of other war material in America and for a loan to meet these additional expenditures.

Hansson encountered difficulties. The people became more and more restless as it became apparent that valiant Finland was fighting a losing battle. The unrest was most notable in military circles, and there were rumors that Hansson might be overthrown by force. In *Svenska Dagbladet* the peace-loving religious leader, Manfred Björkquist, wrote: "It is now our fatal hour. Our leaders have Sweden's fate in their hands. Whether they know it or not they stand face to face with the Lord of History. May God save Sweden — not only its life but also its soul." Many of the people in Sweden believed that honor compelled Sweden to come to the rescue of Finland even if the cost would be her very existence. The press was critical of the Hansson policy, and though the *Riksdag* was more or less immune to public opinion, Hansson's position was not secure. The Swedish government had received a direct appeal from Finland for military aid on February 13, which Hansson refused to grant. He outlined the reasons for his government's attitude on February 15, and the following four days witnessed a great public indignation, which might have brought an end to the Hansson government and hurled Sweden into the war against Russia if King Gustav had not made a public appeal on February 19 in which he urged support for the Hansson neutrality policy. He said: "From the very beginning Sweden has tried to help Finland by means of volunteers and in numerous other ways, but at the very start I informed Finland that, unfortunately, no military help could be expected from Sweden. With sorrow in my heart I have come to the conclusion after serious reconsideration that we must hold fast to this decision. For I am definitely of the opinion that if Sweden were now to intervene in Finland we would run the greatest risk of being involved not only in a war with Russia, but also in a war between the Great Powers, and such a responsibility I have not been able to assume. In such a situation, moreover, it would probably be impossible to render the not inconsiderable help which Finland now receives from us and which it so much needs and which we are prepared to continue to give with the warmest of hearts. Sweden's vital interests, her honor and peace, are the goals I have ever in mind. With the help of God I hope that by following the route we have chosen we shall be able to escape all the misfortune of war."

Since that time it has been revealed that Germany had troops ready to occupy Scandinavia. Had Sweden thus decided to aid Finland, it was believed Denmark would immediately have been invaded. Southern Sweden was not strongly fortified, and Sweden would have been forced to concentrate on its own defense and the situation in Finland would not have improved. Professor Östen Undén, Chancellor of the University of Uppsala, summed up the official position in February when he said that Sweden's foreign policy was neither shortsighted nor immoral, but realistic.

Great Britain could have sent her fleet with telling effects to Petsamo during the first weeks of the war. This would have enabled Finland to hold this vital port at the same time that Great Britain could have cut off the shipping between Germany and Murmansk. Troops could also have been brought to this region. This would have given the Scandinavian countries confidence in Great Britain, a confidence sadly shaken by the German invasion of Poland, when Great Britain and France watched the butchering of their ally. Sweden and Norway would have been encouraged to aid Finland without feeling that Great Britain was trying to make Scandinavia the battle ground.

Britain was gambling on Swedish and Norwegian aid to Finland, which would have meant that Germany would have been forced to help Russia. Furthermore, Great Britain believed that the more Germany expanded her conquests and the more the theatre of war was widened, the weaker Germany would become. It was also desirable that Sweden should be won for the cause of Great Britain, for Germany in 1940 was more dependent upon the iron ore of Sweden than in 1914.

Sweden knew the intentions of Great Britain, for England made no effort to hide them. Britain was fighting for western civilization, and any nation which refused to cooperate with her was the enemy of democracy. Sweden was severely criticized. False rumors were circulated in the press that Great Britain was ready to give help to poor Finland, but that Sweden stood in the path of her errand of mercy. These rumors were entirely false. Great Britain and France were not ready to offer any help to Finland, until it was too late. From fairly reliable sources, it is indicated that Sweden would have ventured into the war to aid Finland, if it could have been assured of adequate help from Great Britain and France. Sweden wanted assurance that the Western Powers were ready to send at least 120,000 men to Norway and Sweden. This was made clear when Finland was belatedly offered help by the Allies. Then Sweden refused to allow a mere 50,000 men to pass through Sweden. This she did not do in her own behalf, but in conjunction with Finland, for the position of Finland was desperate, and 50,000 men would not have turned the tide.

It was of paramount importance that the war in Finland should come to an end. Though Sweden hoped Great Britain would be victorious she was too realistic not to perceive the dangers of British policy in Scandinavia. Public opinion was too pro-Finnish to make it possible for Sweden to immunize herself from the danger of British pressure.

The Scandinavian countries had refused to vote on the question of Russia's expulsion from the League of Nations on December 14, 1939, and had made reservations in regard to the application of sanctions. Fear that Great Britain, on the basis of League action, would request permission to send troops through Norway and Sweden to Finland and thus turn Scandinavia into the battleground of Europe was the reason for caution on the part of the Scandinavian countries. The position taken by the three countries at Geneva somewhat counterbalanced Sweden's short-of-war aid to Finland, and diplomatic relations between Sweden and Russia were not brought to a breaking point.

The minister of foreign affairs, Günther, had been in close contact with Finland's minister of foreign affairs and both agreed that it would be fatal for Finland and for all Scandinavia if Sweden entered the war on the side of Finland. Finland from the very outset of the war made it clear that it desired to resume negotiations with Russia, and the aim of Günther was to find a basis for such negotiations. In January, probably as a result of German pressure, Russia indicated her willingness to Sweden to consider peace negotiations. Sweden did not, however, bring any pressure to bear on Finland to consider Russian peace proposals and after Sweden had made the preliminary arrangements for peace negotiations between Russia and Finland, the government of Sweden was stunned by the severe terms insisted upon by Russia.

For the time being, it seemed that Sweden had saved Scandinavia from being drawn into the war. Her help to Finland had been real. *The New York Times* of March 19, 1940, made the following intelligent comment in an editorial. "Some observers in this country and in England have been critical over the role played by Sweden during the invasion of Finland. To them it seems that Sweden should not only have sent her own troops to defend her neighbor but should have opened the way for the passage of Allied contingents. She should, according to this argument, have made herself a part of a conflict which almost certainly would have involved her with Germany as well as with Russia. She would have offered herself as a flank for maneuvers in a general war.

"The reason given by Sweden for her failure to follow this course is that it would have been futile. Finland would have been completely overrun and Sweden herself would have faced the Russian armies, backed by whatever German aid was needed with no adequate outside help. Whether this would have happened, there is no way now of knowing. But a glance at the map is enough to dispel the notion that the Allies would have found it easy to put into Scandinavia a large enough force to decide the issue in their favor, or that they could have supplied such a force if they had managed to get it there. It seems highly probable that the battle for the independence of small nations could not have been won in Finland or in Sweden. If it is to be won, it will be won on the major fronts and embodied in a peace which will restore the reign of law in Europe.

"So much for Sweden's failure to enroll herself as a

combatant in the struggle. What she did do ought to be written in letters of gold. A dispatch to this newspaper from Stockholm estimated that her aid to Finland, in money and supplies, has amounted to the remarkable total of $125,000,000. This total is growing with every day that passes. It is growing every hour as the Swedish food trucks roll in a steady stream over the Finnish border. It already amounts to $20 a head for every man, woman and child in Sweden the equivalent, per capita, of a gift of more than $2,500,000,000 from the people of the United States. In the presence of this superb generosity we do well to take our hats off to the Swedes."

The war in Finland had greatly weakened a none too strong Swedish national defense. Sweden gave Finland 90,000 rifles, 42,000,000 rounds of ammunition, 80 anti-tank guns, as well as much of Finland's artillery ammunition. Sweden's already weak air force was reduced by one-fifth as a result of donations of airplanes.

Before the end of the war the Fredrick Ström plan for a Northern Alliance between Sweden, Norway, and Finland had won many adherents. Günther and Halvdan Koht, Norwegian minister of foreign affairs, had come to a preliminary agreement with their respective governments and Finland's that the territorial integrity of the three countries demanded such a defensive alliance. This indicated that Finland, Sweden, or Norway looked upon the peace between Finland and Russia as an armistice. Sweden also proposed to help Finland in rebuilding fortifications, and numerous cities in Sweden adopted a Finnish city for reconstruction, assuming the cost of this work.

The prospect of an alliance gave Finland a certain amount of confidence in the future, and Swedish authorities had seemingly succeeded in convincing Russia that the alliance was not directed against her. At any rate, Russia offered no objections to the defensive alliance proposed by Sweden. But it nevertheless ran into snags. The president of the Norwegian *Storthing*, Carl Hambro, led the opposition against the alliance for he believed that such cooperation would bring Norway into war. The alliance proposed by Sweden was aimed at any nation that attacked either Finland, Sweden, or Norway. In reality, of course, it could not have been aimed at any other nations than Russia, Germany, Great Britain, and France. Germany had already made plans to invade Scandinavia and she brought pressure to bear on Russia to oppose the formation of the alliance. But it was Hambro, who had delayed its consummation and made it possible for Russia to change her mind.

Scarcely was the peace concluded between Finland and Russia before Denmark and Norway were invaded on April 9, 1940, by Germany. Norway would indeed have appreciated the help of Sweden and Finland. But the swiftness with which Germany occupied all of Denmark and the strategic ports of Norway made it rather dubious whether Sweden could have rendered effective aid. Had the defensive alliance existed between Finland, Sweden, and Norway, however, German tactics would have had to be modified, and from Denmark, Germany would have attacked Sweden. Sweden was better prepared, although it could not have made a long stand against Germany. Finland was in no position to give any real help. If she had tried, there was every reason to believe that Russia would have occupied Finland, and Finland could have offered little or no resistance. The defense alliance, so badly wanted by both Finland and Sweden, would thus have been fatal to both countries.

Even though no formal alliance existed between Sweden and Norway, Sweden could, of course, have moved her troops into Norway swiftly, and might even have succeeded in driving the Germans out of Oslo. But the triumph would have been only temporary. German troops would then have driven directly into Sweden, and Sweden, inadequately prepared, would have suffered the fate of Norway. In fact it was impossible for Sweden to pursue a policy in regard to Norway identical with that followed during the Russo-Finnish war. The war in Norway was interpreted by Swedish statesmen as

228

a war between Germany and Great Britain. As long as military resistance existed Sweden refused all requests for the transit of war materials to the belligerents in Norway. Economic interests compelled Sweden to attempt a pacification of the northern part of Norway with the consent of the belligerents, but this measure failed.

The defense of Norway had been neglected, and the discontent of the army with the Social Democrats in Norway was serious. The officers of the army, in some instances, had been trained in Germany. They were part of a class of bureaucrats, distrusted by farmers and labor alike.

Norway lent itself admirably to any type of espionage system. It may be said that Norway's chief fault was that nowhere else in the world had democracy so completely conquered a country. Greater personal freedom existed nowhere. Democracy in Norway was not a recent development, but was perhaps the oldest in Europe. This democracy was built on anti-militarism. The Danes were anti-militaristic of necessity; the Norwegians, by choice.

The *Altmark* incident, with its violation of the neutrality of Norwegian waters by Britain, had excited the public even though it was predominantly pro-British. When the German troops arrived, the people were confused, shocked, and bewildered. The people of Poland, Belgium, and the Netherlands, and even of France expected the war, and had prepared for it in a sense, but the Norwegians were caught entirely off guard.

Few countries had been spared to the same degree as Sweden the ravages of a rabid nineteenth century nationalism. Although the militarists had succeeded in establishing an army modeled after the Prussian army before World War I, the people were dominantly antimilitaristic. This was true especially of the farmer and laborer. The people believed that the militarists were never satisfied in their demands for stronger and stronger defenses. They believed that a strong army was a factor in bringing about war. They realized that from time to time nationalism might exert itself and that the country might be thrown headlong into a war if it were prepared to fight. The fact that Sweden had not waged a war for more than 125 years was not due so much to a desire to stay out of war as to the fact that the nation had not been prepared for war. Unpreparedness had been a very strong factor in keeping Sweden out of the Russo-Finnish war of 1939-1940.

The Swedish people were deeply suspicious of all great powers. Some of their principal laws indicated this, for instance, those passed to prevent foreigners from gaining economic control of Sweden. Sweden had refused to be entangled in the diplomacy of the Great Powers. Its program of national defense was aimed mainly to make it unpleasant for any nation to attack.

Three days, therefore, after the German invasion of Denmark and Norway, Hansson stated: "Our country is again living through an hour of trial, perhaps the most severe in a century. War has come close to our borders. Our sentiments in regard to our Scandinavian sister nations I do not need to put into words. Everyone must understand that in spite of our own peace, our minds are deeply shaken. It is now, however, a question of ourselves, and our possibilities of protecting our own peace, freedom, and honor. Hitherto Sweden has done everything in reason to uphold her policy of neutrality as originally proclaimed. Sweden is, furthermore, firmly determined to follow the line of strict neutrality, which means that we must retain in every direction our independence of judgment and freedom of action. It is not consistent with strict neutrality to allow any belligerent to use Swedish territory for its own enterprises. Fortunately, no such demands have been made and if they are made, they must be rejected.

"To maintain neutrality means also to defend it when necessary. To make sure that Sweden would be able to do this the government has had to keep up throughout the war an extensive military establishment adjusted to our judgment of the requirements. The extensions of the war to our own neighborhood has made necessary a further strengthening of our defenses. This means added interference with normal living conditions, new difficulties for our business life as well as for individuals. I know these difficulties are heavy for many families, but I also know that they are borne with equanimity in the knowledge that they are necessary for the welfare of the country. Obviously, this uncertainty and insecurity is a nervous strain, even for such a balanced nation as Sweden, but in times of war it is necessary more than ever to keep up a calm confidence and above all we must check the dangerous spread of false rumors.

"You can rest assured that our watchfulness and supervision have been increased, especially in regard to such elements as may be suspected of being willing to serve the ends of foreign powers. I feel assured that the Swedish people are prepared to make heavy sacrifices for peace and independence, and I am convinced that by unity and resolve we shall be able to pilot our country through the difficulties. Should, however, misfortune come to our borders, the Swedish people will surely prove itself able to protect that which is most precious — Sweden's freedom and independence."

The German occupation of Norway and Denmark established a complete blockade to the west by cutting off Swedish trade with Great Britain and the Western Hemisphere. Sweden was compelled to reorient her trade or face acute unemployment. This realization, combined with other considerations, caused her on July 5, 1940, to consent to German transit of war materials through Sweden. Fighting had ceased in Norway on June 10, and the crumbling of the Dutch, Belgian, and French defenses had caused despair. Russia had aggrandized herself at the expense of trouble-torn Rumania, and it was feared that Russia's appetite had merely been whetted by Estonia, Latvia, Lithuania, Poland, and Finland. Conditions in Finland were appalling. The people were suffering from exhaustion and the threatening shadow of Russia grew darker and darker. A realistic Swedish

231

policy dictated that the friendship of both Germany and Russia must be cultivated in the hope that the aspirations of one power might be checked by the ambitions of the other. Whether the average Swede was willing to recognize the fact or not, his country was at the mercy of Germany and Russia. Later, Sweden followed the example set by Finland in permitting German soldiers stationed in Norway to travel through Sweden while "on leave."

Trade treaties were entered into by Sweden with Germany, Russia, and German-controlled or occupied countries for the purpose of finding markets for goods which under normal conditions would have found their way to Great Britain and across the Atlantic. New sources of supply for goods formerly secured from England and the United States had to be found. Germany had long been one of Sweden's best customers, but with the occupation of Belgium and the northern part of France, Germany no longer was as dependent upon Sweden for iron ore. The concessions which Sweden had made in regard to the transit of war material and soldiers "on leave" were important in reaching a favorable trade agreement with Germany. The latter country promised to continue the import of Swedish iron ore and to increase the purchases of wood pulp and paper in order to alleviate the distress of industries particularly dependent upon export to Great Britain and the United States. Germany also promised to supply Sweden with coal, coke, dies, chemicals, and certain metals. A greater German market, however, could not compensate for the loss of other markets; in fact, the value of Swedish imports from Germany exceeded the value of exports. Especially hard hit by the war and the blockade was the dairy industry, which was dependent upon the importation of fodder and oil cakes. In September 1940, Sweden provided Russia with a credit of 100,000,000 crowns, which became the basis of a barter treaty by which Russia was to purchase goods in Sweden valued at better than 60,000,000 crowns during a period of two years and, in turn, was to export to Sweden grain and fodder. Finland was also granted a loan of 60,000,000 crowns for the purchase of goods in Sweden needed for reconstruction. These and other trade treaties were built upon the principles of barter, which led to the establishment of clearing systems for export and import.

It should not be believed that Sweden had found a way out of the economic dilemma which she faced as a country practically hemmed in by Germany. The barter system of trading with her neighbors might not have involved a financial risk, but actually these countries could not supply many necessities. The result was that almost all vital goods, especially foods, were rationed. During 1940, the value of exports declined 30 per cent and the imports 20 per cent in spite of the fact that the war had brought an increase in prices. The cost of living rose during the last five months of 1940 by about 20 per cent, and in January 1941 the people were paying 8 per cent more for their commodities than during the previous month.

Under ordinary circumstances the loss of such vital Swedish markets as Great Britain and the United States would have implied much suffering from unemployment. But the blockade encouraged new industries engaged in the production of substitutes for goods no longer available through the normal channels, and the national defense program of Sweden, unparalleled in her history, caused an industrial activity during 1940-1941 which was unsurpassed in any boom year. The government was then spending more for armaments in three weeks than was spent for defense during the entire year of 1936. An American reader would understand the extent of the sacrifices made by the Swedes, if the cost of Swedish neutrality were translated into dollars. The cost of the national defense program of the government from July 1, 1940, to June 30, 1941, was estimated at $600,000,000.

This clearly indicated that Sweden was determined to maintain her independence and was prepared to fight for her ideals. But it would be presumptuous to assume that any country, regardless of how deeply rooted its people might be in the principles of democracy, would not under similar circumstances find its faith in democracy tested. The gravest dangers might come from within if the war was prolonged and the shortage of essential goods approached an acute state. Though the German press was vociferous in protesting against the nature of news and editorials in Swedish newspapers, the government was able to maintain a freedom of the Swedish press which was essential. Of course, a type of censorship was imposed immediately upon the outbreak of the war, a censorship aimed at controlling public opinion, although it was far from being a vigorous one. The press stressed particularly the misfortunes of the occupied countries; Norwegian, Danish, and Dutch discontent; and unrest caused by German authorities. The nature of the news published in Swedish newspapers was intended to inspire a will to resist aggression and to unify the people in the support of the government's policies.

Although this propaganda pleased neither Germany nor Russia, the suppression of voices out of harmony with the form of government could hardly be called democratic in the strictest sense of the term. It was a program made more necessary by the concessions Sweden had made to Germany after July 5, 1940 and by her commercial reorientation. Although German soldiers "on leave" were not permitted to carry arms and were forced to travel on special trains under Swedish military guard, these soldiers might have been dangerous carriers of a philosophy which could have been contagious. The increased German trade with Sweden led to the establishment of a large number of German business agencies in the larger industrial centers, and these merchants sought to undermine the confidence of their Swedish friends in a democratic form of government.

Sweden was able to meet these dangers because of the success of her social democracy and partly, perhaps, because she enjoyed the leadership of two great men: the aged King, who had the confidence of the people, and Per Albin Hansson, the popular labor leader and democrat.

The immediate political effect of the first Russo-Finnish War was to weaken the Communists in Sweden. The interventionists were strong, and old fears of Russia found a fertile soil. For the time being, these fears dictated Sweden's policy. The invasion of Denmark and Norway by Germany could not eliminate them, and if the Swedes had no other choice they did prefer German control over Russian. The sympathies of the people for their Scandinavian brethren could not have been more real; yet fears of Russia must have been important in the Swedes' analysis of the international situation.

The Swedish people were no less confused than were the people of other countries. The future relationships between Russia and Germany were not clear. These were clarified after the German occupation of France and the German attack on Russia in June 1941. It became clear at that time that Russo-German cooperation had been one of necessity as far as Russia was concerned. When this necessity passed, Russia was ready to resist German demands for further collaboration. Russia became an ally against aggression, and opinion in Great Britain and even neutral America changed. But this complete reversal of opinion was impossible in Sweden. Many interventionists, who had insisted that Sweden should make war upon Russia during the first Russo-Finnish War, saw in Germany a bulwark against Russian westward expansion and the spread of Communism. Finland sought to regain her lost territory by joining in an alliance with Germany. This confused the issues. Some persons, like Sandler, recognized at once the full implications of the sudden change in the European scene.

Outrages in Norway by the Nazis and the Japanese attack upon Pearl Harbor clarified the atmosphere. The doom of the Axis powers became certain, but while Japanese and German successes continued for a time uninterrupted, the Swedes rallied behind the government's policy of neutrality. The failure of Sweden to aid Norway and Denmark in April 1940 found an expression in a penitent sentiment. Curious apologies were offered as Sweden was compelled to explain her concessions to Germany. To cover up what many regarded as a national dishonor, Sweden spoke of future Scandinavian collaboration after the war and to ease her conscience engaged in extensive charitable activities to alleviate the pains and sufferings in both Finland and Norway. Most people understood the causes which had again led Finland to war, but they refused to give aid to Finland at this time. Instead, Sweden sought to bring pressure to bear upon Finland to get that country out of the war in order to make Sweden's position more secure and make possible a stronger sympathy for the cause of the United Nations.

The concessions which Sweden had been compelled meanwhile to make to Germany were real indeed and in violation of her neutrality. In the occupation of Norway by German troops, Sweden was at the mercy of Hitler, whose power had been further demonstrated by German successes against the Netherlands, Belgium, and France. The most important concession, which called forth a just protest from the United Nations, dealt with the transportation of German troops to and from Norway "on leave." A specified number of special trains were to take German soldiers from or to the nearest point on the border from Oslo, Trondheim, and Narvik or from or to the most southern part of Sweden or the port nearest Germany or Denmark. The soldiers were not to be armed, though they could be equipped with bayonets and the officers with revolvers. The transport privilege did not permit an increase in the number of German troops in Norway. Germany was permitted, however, to transport an entire division of troops from Norway to Finland where it was to participate in a German-Finnish offensive against Russia. Sweden was also compelled to grant a limited credit to Germany.

These concessions were cancelled as the fortunes of war changed and as Sweden's own defense was made stronger. During the summer of 1943 the transit of German troops through Sweden was halted. A year later the shipment of ball bearings to Germany was reduced, and in October of 1944 it was stopped entirely. These changes might have come as a result of pressure from the United States. The Swedish government labored hard to terminate the war between Finland and Russia and was successful in bringing about the initial negotiations which brought Finland to terms with Russia. In the spring of 1945 the government planned to send an army into Norway in order to drive the Nazis out, but the collapse of the Third Reich came so quickly that Sweden did not have a chance to break off her relations with Germany until May 7, 1945, the day of capitulation. Sweden had thus escaped involvement even during the last stage of the war. When at last she was ready to sacrifice her traditional policy of neutrality and peace, fate deemed it unnecessary.

Expediency and self-interest had been her guiding policy. A series of circumstances more closely associated with accident than a skillful diplomacy of neutrality had made neutrality possible. Sweden emerged from World War II unscathed and more prosperous than any other European state.

The Swedish people had suffered much less during World War II than during World War I. The war economy had been carefully organized and maintained. Cooperation and coordination among war commissions had discouraged profiteering and black marketing. Sweden had not exported such amounts of foodstuffs after 1939 as to create a shortage similar to that which existed in 1917. Prices and wages were effectively frozen. Even inflation had been partly controlled though military preparedness had doubled the national debt by 1944.

The Swedes continued after the war their generous aid to Finland, Norway, and Denmark, and by 1950 Sweden's aid had amounted to 3,000,000,000 crowns, or 500 crowns per inhabitant. At first the aid consisted chiefly of foodstuffs, clothes and drugs. But Sweden also cared for 300,000 refugees, and after 1945 granted extensive credits to her neighbors. Thus Sweden played an important role in the reconstruction of Europe with the return of peace.

The outlines of Sweden's domestic and foreign policies had been well laid out before the Cold War began, but every hope for a Scandinavian alliance was shattered when Denmark and Norway joined NATO. Sweden then proposed to walk alone, and to fight only if her independence were threatened.

Whether Sweden's policy of neutrality and peace is an illusion or not must be told by others. One thing is certain, namely, that the matter hardly rests with Sweden, but in her lone role she has sought moral support from her emigrants and their children.

CHAPTER XV

EMIGRATION AND AMERICANIZATION

THERE IS UNDOUBTEDLY A RELATIONSHIP between emigration and the Americanization of Sweden. It is not a simple one of cause and effect, though the emigrant probably played a role. Many patriotic citizens came to recognize that emigration represented a serious loss to the economy of Sweden and that it could best be combatted by making Sweden into a Little America. Therefore, the transformation of Sweden into a democracy was not unrelated to emigration. Here an effort will be made to discuss these relationships and some interesting aspects of Americanization.

It can hardly be doubted that emigration was one of the most important manifestations of the political, religious, social, and economic unrest that gripped Sweden when the old social and economic orders tumbled. A student of emigration would have no difficulty in finding numerous significant causes for mass migration of Swedes. Prior to 1900 these could be identified with a series of adjustments in Sweden's major basic industries of agriculture, lumber, iron, and fishing. After 1900 many emigrants would have said that they left Sweden in hopes of escaping compulsory military training. But no list of causes at any one time would be satisfactory in explaining why Sweden lost one-fourth of its population from 1840-1924.

In the study of emigration a number of factors must be kept in mind. If emigration is to take place, the population must have freedom to move. The right to emigrate and immigrate was not fully recognized in Sweden until 1860, when the old "pass regulations," designed especially to stop the emigration of skilled labor, were abolished. Emigration could not take place until transportation was accessible and within the financial resources of those who wished to emigrate. Before the time of railroads in Sweden, the problem of reaching a port was in many instances almost as trying as the journey across the ocean; and it involved even greater hardships in America for those eager to settle in areas not reached by water transportation. Swedish railroad building did not begin until the fifties, and did not proceed rapidly until in 1870. It was not until after the Civil War that the United States began the building of the transcontinental railroads which offered opportunities for work as well as new territory for settlers. By 1865, the sailship was giving way to the steamship, greatly reducing the hazards of the sea voyage. However, before emigration could reach such proportions in Sweden as actually to give rise to fears that Sweden was being "depopulated," the desire to emigrate had to be stimulated.

Prior to 1830, America was virtually unknown in Sweden. Probably only a few intellectuals were acquainted with the travel account of Fanny Wright and the letters of Count Klinckowström. A more serious study of conditions in America was stimulated throughout Europe by the rise of liberalism and the reaction to the Metternich system. Europe became divided into two camps, those who believed in the *status quo* and those who desired political reforms. America became a leading topic of conversation. Europeans visited America for the express purpose of spreading either favorable or devastating propaganda about the United States. The literature on America suddenly became popular, and to Fanny Wright's travel accounts were added those of Hall, Hamilton, Mrs. Trollope, Marryat, Stuart, Harriet Martineau, de Tocqueville, Beaumont, Dickens, Combe, Chevalier, Power, Lyell, and the travel accounts of Swedes like Arfwedson, Gosselman, Housewolff, and Fredrika Bremer.

Interest in America was so great that the liberal newspapers copied letters published in German newspapers written by German emigrants and from Norwegian newspapers written by Norwegian emigrants. An anonymous Swedish author tried his hand at writing novels about America.

Through the pages of the *Spectator* the letters of Martineau were read with much interest, and her travel accounts were translated into Swedish in 1843. De Tocqueville's work was translated from 1839 to 1846. In contrast to the favorable accounts of conditions in America given by some travellers and emigrants, the liberal press painted Sweden as drab in order to arouse opposition to the government. The result of all the pro and con discussions was that the United States became an "Eldorado,"

"Where goodly farms for almost naught are sold,
And honest men are worth their weight in gold."

During the Civil War Swedes had learned a great deal about America through letters from emigrants in the uniform of the Blue. Immigrant letters stressed the low taxes, the virgin soil, the mild climate, and the sober, honest, religious, and industrious characteristics of the American people. When such letters were written by a father to a son, by a son to his parents, or by some friend to a friend, who could doubt their truth?

These "America letters" often compared the conditions in America with those of Sweden. The entire bureaucratic system of government, state and local, had become unpopular. The letters pointed out the many advantages of living in America, where there was no hated bureaucracy and no class distinctions.

Too much stress can hardly be placed on the social cause of emigration from Sweden, a country which before 1907 was more class ridden than most European countries. The Swedes had failed to recognize the value of the individual for his own sake. Birth and wealth were the criteria in evaluating individuals.

Employers abused their servants and often referred to them as "dumbbells" or "devils." A favorite expression was, in fact, "The devil but you are dumb." In America, on the other hand, it was said that the worker held his head as high as the employer and, that, when a laborer searched for work, he was addressed by the employer: "What can I do for you, sir?" If unable to give the worker employment, he would usually say, "I am sorry that I cannot use your services at this time. Call again." No effort was made by the employer to impress the worker that there existed a social gap, based on either wealth or "culture" between him and the worker. In America there were no "titles."

In Sweden some types of labor were looked upon as "degrading." A college student did not wash dishes or dig ditches to earn his way through college, but borrowed money and lived like a gentleman until his credit was exhausted. A man in a prominent social position did not think it possible to economize, even when he realized that he was headed for bankruptcy. His social position had to be maintained, he borrowed from friends or relatives, until he was forced into bankruptcy.

But as autocrats or tyrants began to tumble in the nineties, emigration caused both the liberal and conservative press to begin a war on social injustices in Sweden. However, the press was handicapped by libel laws, and when one newspaper defended a poor woman from mistreatment by a local autocrat, the editor was fined several hundred crowns for libel. The newspaper editor refused to give up the cause and succeeded in having the autocrat fined fifty crowns for mistreating the poor woman. But it was not until after the suffrage reforms during the first two decades of the twentieth century that it was possible for the worker to demand and secure respect.

Class snobbery was at its worst when steamship companies, American land companies, American railroads, and various states began to compete for emigrants. In efforts to attract people to America, maps, books, pamphlets, and illustrated brochures were scattered over the country. Before the Civil War the Illinois Central Railroad was the only agency that had seriously sought to attract emigrants from Sweden; but after 1865 Minnesota, Iowa, Wisconsin, Maine, Nebraska, Kansas, and other states began to advertise their respective advantages. The Union Pacific and the Northern

Pacific Railroads, eager to dispose of their land grants, entered into competition with such land companies as the American Emigrant Company, the American Emigrant Aid and Homestead Company, the Great European-American Emigration Land Company, the Columbia Emigrant Company, the Scandinavian Emigrant Agency, and the Swedish-American Emigrant Company. Railroad and land companies and states sometimes worked in close cooperation with steamship lines, and before 1875 the Hamburg-American Lines, the North American Lloyd, the Packet Lines, the Cunard Line, the Inman Lines, the Allen Lines, the Anchor Lines, and the National Steamship Company had established offices in Sweden. Their subagents were found throughout the country.

Even the Federal Government of the United States did a great deal to encourage emigration to America. The passage of the Homestead Act was only a phase of this encouragement. American consulates tended to become emigrant agencies; and the creation of the office of the Commissioner of Emigration in 1864 was intended to gather information regarding economic conditions in the United States that might be useful in spreading propaganda about America, and emigration of contract labor was sanctioned.

Some land companies offered free transportation from New York to their land; others offered free transportation to those who were willing to indenture themselves for a year; others, to indicate that their work was "philanthropy," secured prominent persons on their Board of Directors. Intense competition among the steamship companies caused a considerable lowering of transportation charges.

Friends and relatives in America often sent for their dear ones. Emigration had been made a possibility for most able-bodied persons. Soon there was hardly a family in all rural Sweden that did not have a friend or a relative in America. Pictures and knickknacks from America were found in almost every Swedish home, and the most treasured mail was that from America. No day was more important in

243

the humble Swedish home than when visitors came from Chicago or Minneapolis. The Swedish children virtually grew up wanting to emigrate.

The provincial governors and the clergy reported "America fever" was spreading. The governors, from 1865 to 1890, analyzed the causes, stressing the activities of the emigrant agencies, of which there were nine general directors and hundreds of subagents as early as 1870. At that time there were fifty-eight subagents who worked on a commission basis in one single province. When a local official or clergyman warned the people against emigration, a letter from a relative or friend in America was brought forth, and the people had far greater confidence in the opinion of a friend or relative than in the warnings of a none-too-popular local official.

The governors observed that the abolition of emigrant restrictions in 1860, and the development of railroads, the telegraph, and the steamship had by 1865 brought Sweden closer to the rest of the world. Obstacles in travelling had been reduced, and time and cost of travel had been revolutionized. The family and communal ties had been strained by the enclosure movement. Better educational facilities, the public school, and the parish libraries stimulated reading of popular magazines and journals as well as newspapers containing articles about America. One governor wrote in his report from 1866 to 1870: "Emigration represents a stage in culture and civilization that must touch every country, and its intensity will depend upon the state of culture and individual freedom . . . The hope of exchanging the old home for a new country must always appeal to those whose fight for existence at home has been difficult and has caused them to appreciate individual worth and to underestimate danger." Emigration was thus a stage in a modern materialistic civilization prompted by a desire for a higher standard of living.

The specific reasons for emigration were numerous. A large growing agricultural population was dependent upon seasonal labor which farmers could supply only during spring, summer and early fall. Abundant historical sources testify to the suffering of an agricultural proletariat. Home crafts recuperated somewhat from the effect of the American Civil War, when the import of cotton had been restricted; but spinning and weaving in the home of the small farmers, crofters, and cotters had really been doomed. Large farm owners, to economize, placed their land under one manager and after 1865 began to replace crofters with agricultural day laborers or cotters.

Though there was a migration to cities and industrial centers, Swedish industry was unable to absorb the increasing agricultural population. The seventies was a decade of railroad building on a large scale, and employment opportunities as well as wages rose, but in 1878 railroad building was hit by a severe depression. The farmer was burdened by high taxes, post and road repair duties. The price of grain dropped sharply. He enjoyed no tariff protection, and American grain, bought and transported from the region west of the Mississippi River, could be sold cheaper than the Swedish farmer could produce it. If the farm was mortgaged, the farmer was unable to pay his taxes, and the voice of the auctioneer was heard throughout Sweden during the severest agricultural crisis in Swedish history during the eighties. The credit system was not flexible. Many farmers were paying a higher rate of interest on their mortgages than the money was worth.

There has been a tendency to over-emphasize the re-parceling and division of land. It has been stressed by Professor Nils Wohlin, on the basis of much statistical data, that emigration was greatest from the areas where enclosure and the division of land had been carried furthest. Undoubtedly, it is true that the small farmer found the problem of paying taxes more difficult than did the larger farmer; but the small farmer, nevertheless, had some advantages over the larger farmer. He and his family could farm the land when the wages of the agricultural laborers rose to become prohibitive and he was less likely to invest in expensive implements. The value of the small farm rose more rapidly than that of

245

the large farm because there was more competition in the purchase of the small farm. However, this was also an encouragement to emigration, for the small farmer could dispose of his farm more readily and secure means with which to purchase a farm in America. The Russian and American competition in grain brought on the agricultural crisis from 1881 to 1885 which made certain adjustments necessary. But the change to dairy farming was not as pronounced because the government decided to protect the grain farmer by a protective tariff. The high wages demanded by farm laborers who threatened to emigrate to America or to move into industrial centers forced the use of labor-saving farm machinery. Farmers' sons were no longer satisfied to remain at home where an agricultural worker earned only three hundred and twenty crowns a year and board and room, working twelve hours a day. Standards of living had risen, and, as long as rural and city laborers were forced to live below the standard they desired, emigration to America, where wages were higher, continued.

In 1883 the Royal Academy of Agriculture successfully petitioned the government that ten million crowns be appropriated by the *Riksdag* for larger drainage projects in order that more land might be placed under cultivation. Thus, the opportunity to become an independent farmer had but slightly increased. The *Riksdag* adopted a more just system of taxation. A progressive income tax was adopted. The capital resources of the Central Bank of Mortgage Associations was increased to thirty million crowns, and credit was made more flexible. Short term loans made it possible to adjust interest rates. Later when the lumber industry suffered, the small farmers of Norrland were especially hard hit for they were dependent upon that industry for sale of lumber and for seasonal labor. Emigration after 1890 from northern Sweden shows a clear relationship of emigration to the temporary decline of the lumber industry. Both the lumber and iron industries were sensitive to general world conditions. Even after 1895, unskilled workers did not earn more than sixty-five cents a day in the city of Stockholm, where the cost of living was high. In America, on the other hand, unskilled workers earned from $1.25 to $2.00 a day, and a farm hand could earn $20.00 a month plus board and room.

After 1885 the number of industrial strikes in Sweden increased. Socialist propaganda spread, and the relationship between employer and employee became strained. Many workers who had participated in strikes lost their jobs. The government showed a great intolerance toward organized labor, and a few Socialist dreamers joined in the move to America. Of these, Erik Nordman was the only one who made a significant contribution to the cause of organized labor in America. The others were dreamers, extremely sensitive to reverses.

The World War checked emigration in general, and after the war the United States adopted a more restrictive emigration policy. This policy did not seriously affect Swedish emigration up to 1924.

The Swedish industrial workers who emigrated from Sweden after World War I did not find conditions in America to their liking. America was more intolerant toward Socialism than Sweden. It was said that truth and justice were "but little respected in America," and the people were "slaves to the dollar." Eugene Debs had spent more time in prison than any Swedish Socialist leader, and it was said that the Sacco-Vanzetti and the Dayton trial cases were examples of how justice and liberty had been trampled under foot more cynically than in gangster-ridden Chicago. Organized labor, which was becoming increasingly powerful in Sweden, began to discourage emigration to America. Unorganized labor might still have preferred to emigrate, but such emigration was unimportant in numbers.

Thinking men in Sweden had long realized how serious it was for Sweden to lose hundreds of thousands of strong men and women between the ages of fifteen and forty. Emigration could not be dismissed by calling the emigrants "trash"; this they definitely were not. Propaganda by the

Church and press against emigration was not very effective. It was said that America lacked culture and refinement and had no traditions. Emigrants returning to Sweden for visits were ridiculed for their manners and clothes. America was only a big "humbug," a term which became synonymous with America. Truthful accounts of emigrants and of their experiences in America became fewer and fewer in the press during the seventies and almost disappeared during the eighties, but the Church and press continued their anti-American propaganda for a long time in an effort to combat the "America fever." At the turn of the century they were joined by the National Association Opposed to Emigration. In spite of these endeavors, Sweden lost over a million people as a result of emigration, of which at least eight hundred thousand emigrated to the United States prior to 1914.

It is no wonder, therefore, that Sweden has become one of the most Americanized countries of Europe since World War I. It is a process which has proceeded rapidly. The attitude toward America in Sweden prior to 1914 in official circles was an unfriendly and perhaps even contemptuous one. The psychological reasons for the situation are easily understood. The danger of mass depopulation, however, demanded the creation of a Little America in Sweden.

Emigration to America was related to almost every aspect of Swedish history. America gave new dimensions to the concept of the dignity of man, and this was a significant factor in the transformation of Sweden into a democracy. The earlier chapters in this volume must be viewed in the light of the impact of the concept of America upon the Swedish mind.

The folk movements of the nineteenth century had profoundly influenced ideals and concepts of a good life. It is not possible actually to evaluate the results of a great religious awakening of a significant temperance movement, of concepts of human progress associated with liberalism and humanism, or inevitable repercussions of emigration, but all of these must have sharpened the criticism directed against social and political injustices and heightened economic discontent during a period of great economic changes.

During World War II Sweden discovered more and more the significance of enjoying the friendship of the United States and the importance of fostering closer contact with Swedish emigrants. The age-old fears of Russia refused to subside and the friendship of America became a matter of utmost importance. The emigrants were no longer regarded as "traitors" or "deserters" but became instead an important asset. They would more readily appreciate Sweden's continued policy of neutrality and non-involvement in power politics than other Americans. The United States became popular, and the visiting emigrant was received as a dear and close relative.

But it would be false to assume that this is a sudden pragmatic change, an act of expediency, related entirely to the international situation since World War II. Throughout the entire period of emigration America loomed large in the Swedish mind and there was a more or less conscious effort by Swedes to Americanize. Maybe, at first, it was not a pleasant thought, but gradually it became a part of a mass psychology. Of course, revolutionary changes in communication and transportation, the growing interdependence of nations, and the impossibility of erecting barriers against ideas must certainly have contributed to the Americanization of all Europe, not to mention Sweden.

The strongest outside influences upon recent Swedish life and thought have been coming from the United States, influences intimately associated with the great folk movements. Two of those were Anglo-American or purely American in origin—the religious awakening and the temperance movement. These forces of piety and sobriety had leavened Swedish life since the nineteenth century and were not weakened by World War I. Though the Bratt System with rationing of liquor had been adopted, there was a growing feeling after 1920 that it had not solved the liquor problem. Therefore, sentiment gained ground that Sweden must adopt

249

a policy of prohibition similar to that in the United States. A prohibition proposal was defeated in 1922 by only a very small vote.* Though sentiment in favor of such a drastic measure declined, the temperance movement flourished, and the work of the temperance societies was encouraged by the state through liberal subsidies.

George M. Stephenson in *The Religious Aspect of Swedish Immigration* has stressed religious discontent as a factor in emigration as has Wilhelm Moberg in his novel, *The Emigrants,* which, shocking as it may be in its realism, has succeeded nonetheless in capturing remarkably well an authentic historical setting of the economic, social, and religious conditions of a Sweden not yet affected by important American influences.

Changes occurred, to be sure, in the Established Church. It experienced a rejuvenation under the direction of the great primate Nathan Söderblom, whose ecumenical contributions are well known. He recognized the wholesome American influence upon the life of the Established Church, particularly in broadening the point of view and interests of the clergy. The Church grew more tolerant under Söderblom's leadership and non-German influences became significant. A greater interest was evidenced in the Sunday School, the Church discontinued its opposition to social reforms, and in the Sigtuma Institute a serious effort was made to arouse an interest within the Church in the labor movement. The Y.M.C.A. and the Y.W.C.A. and the Christian Student Movement were Americanizing agencies of importance.

In some ways, the most important agency in the Americanization of Sweden was the returning emigrant himself. More than 200,000 immigrants in America returned to Sweden to live. Some of these had failed to make a success in America. Others, who had made a financial success, took advantage of business cycles to purchase farms in Sweden when land could be secured favorably. Their influence was frequently held in contempt by those who looked upon them

*Rationing of intoxicating drinks has recently been repealed:

as persons ill-acquainted with modern methods of farming. This was undoubtedly true in many instances, for the returning emigrant had not always been a farmer in America. But these "Swedish-Americans" had a great moral influence. Not infrequently they had been active in religious and temperance organizations in America. They implanted a certain cocksureness sadly needed among Swedish farmers. They dressed better; their sanitary and food standards were higher than those of the ordinary Swedish farmer; they influenced rural architecture, painting their houses in more varied colors and introducing the American sun porch. The yarn-spinning influence of the American frontier and the cow country was transplanted to Sweden, though without the vaudeville and the minstrel show it lost a great deal of potency. The white fleet of the Swedish-American Line with its constant flow of human cargo became a significant link between the old and the new.

As stated earlier, the government did not discourage Americanization. Much of Sweden's social legislation can be traced to a desire on the part of the government to combat emigration from Sweden to America. The introduction of the protective tariff system between 1888 and 1892 was aimed to improve the economy of the farming class which contributed the largest number of emigrants. Liberals had early advocated universal male suffrage as another step to "move America to Sweden." The foundation of the Home Ownership Loan Fund of 1904 and the colonization of Norrland after World War I resulted from efforts to discourage emigration. In Swedish industry and business, American methods were very widely adopted, though in Sweden natural developments were not restrained through anti-trust legislation. Americanization of Sweden was stimulated by the wide acceptance in Sweden of Frederick Winslow Taylor's theories of industrial efficiency.

Sweden, like the United States, had confidence in education. The adult educational movement, so important in the United States a few decades ago, touched a large portion of the population in Sweden. After World War I, the Workers' Educational Association secured important subsidies from the state. In 1938 this association had about 1500 libraries with a total of 549,131 volumes. During that year about 130,000 people made use of these libraries. Both state and local governments contributed toward the building of the educational institutions of the Workers' Educational Association. The Collaborating Educational Association had its own publication and sought to bring about greater cooperation and coordination in the work of the various educational societies.

Troubles within the ranks of labor were minimized by the rapid growth of the Social Democratic Youth Association, which since the schism of 1917 remained loyal to the Social Democratic Party. In 1936 it had 1796 clubs with over 100,000 members. The membership of the Social Democratic Youth Association undoubtedly rose to 200,000, of which nearly all were members of study circles in 1940 or at one time or another belonged to such circles.

Though closely cooperating with the Workers' Educational Association and its school at Brunnsvik, which on the average trained about 400 study circle leaders a year prior to World War II, the Social Democratic Youth Association purchased a country estate, which was turned into a school for the Stockholm district of the Society. The youth movement in Sweden grew strong, largely owing to the stress placed on education as a means to train leaders. It provided youth with a miniature world of its own in which qualities of leadership were molded, but a world that was not separated from the real problems of society. The youth movement in Sweden was an integral part of the work of mature men and women. To what extent these developments are related to the influence of William James and John Dewey would be difficult to say.

Education must always remain the pillar of a democracy. The public schools of every country have their shortcomings, and the Swedish system had one in particular. It stressed the fundamentals of an education, reading, writing, and arithmetic, but beyond these, it was removed from the realities of life. When a young man finished his education, he was almost entirely ignorant of many problems of society.

In fact, it was possible in Sweden as in the United States, to acquire a high school and university education and yet be abysmally ignorant of social, political, and economic problems. The gradual recognition of this condition stimulated adult and youth educational movements in Sweden. Youth discovered that a mere formal public school education left much to be desired, and the Workers' Educational Association represented an important influence in overcoming the shortcomings of the public schools.

Teachers in public schools were civil servants and could not be removed. On the other hand, as civil servants, the teachers had greater freedom in teaching and had no fears that they might lose their positions. The Swedish system was superior to the American in that the idea of democracy in education had not been carried to the same extremes as in America. A dullard had no chance of continuing his education beyond the period of compulsory education, and he was not advanced from one grade to another unless able to meet the requirements prescribed for each course. Able and promising young students were enabled by recent educational legislation to transfer from the regular primary public school to the *Realschule*. After World War II the public primary schools were made the foundations for higher education. The recent reform of the Swedish schools arose from American influences, and as a result the school system of Sweden was made more democratic. American influences upon the educational system of Sweden have been most noticeable from 1937 to 1950.

The trends have been part of a great cultural readjustment involving what may be called a "de-Prussification of Sweden after World War I." But the strong German cultural influences upon Sweden's educational institutions have made the process a slow one. British and American influences in the voluntary educational associations were, therefore, more significant in counteracting the German influences, which were especially strong in the institutions of higher learning. The decline of German culture since World War I was so noticeable, however, that it did not escape the notice of Swedish scholars and educators, who were forced to re-orientate themselves.

Swedish scholars in particular became aware of progress made in America, especially in the fields of medicine, surgery, dentistry, and the pure sciences. Certain American institutions, such as the Massachusetts Institute of Technology and the Carnegie Institute of Technology, became virtual meccas for graduates of Swedish technical and engineering schools. The American Scandinavian Foundation performed, largely under the leadership of Henry Goddard Leach and Hannah Astrup Larsen, a valuable service in strengthening the cultural ties between Scandinavia and America. This work was matched in enthusiasm by *Sverige-America Stiftelsen*, a sister institution of the American Scandinavian Foundation. American scholarship won greater recognition. Many Swedish scholars visited America on lecture tours, and were surprised at the growth of American educational institutions. Their admiration was not dampened by the fact that they were unable to appreciate the American combination of teaching and research.

The awards of Nobel prizes to numerous American scientists and a number of literary figures indicated a definite cultural interest in, and appreciation of, America. The Swede undoubtedly read more than the average American, but it was doubtful if uneducated classes in Sweden read more discriminately than the average American. A great deal of trash appeared in print in Sweden, much of it imported from all corners of the earth. Some Swedish Sunday newspapers reminded one not a little of the Hearst Sunday newspapers, and much of the cheap literature in popular magazines is of American origin. *Pic* and *Look* have their counterpart in *Se*. The better educated Swede however, had very broad intellectual interests. He was well acquainted with the better

254

works of American authors and read the min the original. As soon as an American book came off the press and met with any success in America, it was translated into Swedish and found a ready market.

Some American authors have been accepted in Sweden almost as if they were Swedes, and Swedish conditions were read into their works. The remarkable productivity of American literature since World War I in some ways reacted unfavorably upon Swedish literature. The competition of American works with native Swedish fiction sometimes placed Swedish authors at a disadvantage on the book market. It was sometimes felt that nothing really exciting happened in Sweden. In great America, on the other hand, interesting social, economic and political problems presented themselves, many of which had existed in America for more than a century.

The American movie was a very strong factor in the rapid Americanization of Sweden prior to World War II. Though Sweden had a fairly profitable movie industry of its own which outlined a sensible program based upon its own resources and sought to stick close to the Swedish soil, the Swedish movie public preferred the Hollywood product. The movies taught American mannerisms and slang expressions. Unfortunately there was little discrimination between good and bad American influences, which was the more unfortunate as the Swede was less superficial than the American, and American jokes and puns lost their finesse in Swedish.

After World War I, however, America had a cultural influence, which, indiscriminately accepted, played havoc with a deep-rooted native Swedish culture. American Negro jazz band leaders were feted as if they were kings. Young girls tried to develop "it" and later "oomph," painted their lips and nails, waved their hair, and for good measure bleached it. The young Swedish man dressed in American clothes, sang "Sonny Boy" and later "Hallo, Mr. Shean." Swedes danced the "Big Apple" and went mad over "The

Lambeth Walk," and this type of "Americanization" has continued unabated after World War II.

One evening the Concert Hall in Stockholm might be the scene of a concert by Kreisler or Stokowski and the next the setting for the impressive ceremony of the Nobel prize awards, and the next, a Negro jazz band would try to lift the roof of the same building. Outside the building thousands of Swedish jazz enthusiasts would gather to secure the autograph of a king of jazz. While one awaited the appearance of the Negro band leader, words like "week-end," "shopping days," "baby," "O.K.," "best seller," "all right," "camping" and numbers of other American terms would be heard, with a quaint Swedish inflection.

The tourists from America also played their part in Americanizing Sweden. They and the returning emigrants introduced the cocktail hour and promoted a greater use of fruit and vegetables. The change in the Swedish diet was almost revolutionary. The government encouraged this change by exempting numerous fruits and vegetables from customs duties. Though tomatoes, lettuce, artichokes, avocado pears, melons, Brussels sprouts, and numerous other vegetables and fruits, all of which were rare in 1920, decorated the Swedish dinner table, the Swedes had not discarded all their old customs. The Board of Health was especially critical of the Thursday Dinner, which as far back as man can remember consisted of pork and pea soup with pancakes and lingonberries for dessert. The Swedes insisted upon eating this almost indigestible mess for Thursday Dinner, and intimated that if the Board of Health sought to legislate Thursday Dinner out of existence, Sweden would witness a violent revolution. They wanted to eat and act as much as possible like Americans, but on Thursday they wanted to be Swedish.

Modern American political campaign methods were introduced. Party propaganda was issued by the ton and campaign orators barked from automobiles with loud speakers. During the last fifty years in Sweden a new man and a new society were built upon the concept of the dignity of man.

It was essentially inspired by America, which had provided a fertile ground during the nineteenth century for the ideals of the Enlightment. It might be said that America was the heir of Europe's great cultural heritage, and in the twentieth century it proceeded to share its riches with those who had endowed it. This does not consist of clothes, mannerism, foods, dances, or slang expressions; it is a way of life dedicated to humanity.

But it would be foolish to assume that American influences have been the only ones transforming Swedish life. French influences continued to be strong in both painting and sculpture, except that the Swedish artist tried to express something Swedish in his art. The old school of painters, Zorn, Larsson, and Liljefors, had no followers who attained to their international fame. But the art of sculpture reached a new height. Two sculptors in particular became well known, namely, Carl Milles and Carl Eld. The two were quite different in their interpretations, Milles, being the bolder of the two, was not at once appreciated in Sweden. This great artist emigrated to the United States where his art attracted wide acclaim.

Romanticism in architecture, the efforts to blend foreign, especially Italian design, and old Swedish design, as expressed in old Swedish forts and castles, into a unified whole with little thought of the practical reached its peak in Ragnar Östberg's Stockholm City Hall, which was completed in 1923. American influences were particularly noticeable in the skyscrapers erected in Stockholm on Kungsgatan. Ivar Tengbom succeeded in adapting a neo-antique style with its severity and simplicity to modern requirements in the construction of the Stockholm Concert Hall. But his designs marked only a transition period toward a new style of architecture in which Sweden assumed leadership in the world, namely, the modernistic or functionalistic architecture. This design became popular in Sweden after 1930, and American architects were not slow in recognizing the virtues of the developments in Sweden.

The developments in art industry and art handicraft were very interesting after 1920. The former were noticed especially at the Exhibition of Decorative Art in Paris in 1925. Since that time, Sweden has more and more concentrated upon the production of wares of beauty and quality at a cost which would not be prohibitive. Art industry and art handicraft expressed a rejuvenation inspired by new ideas. Orrefors glass blowers and engravers attained international fame. Hand iron, copper, and pewter work witnessed a renaissance. Pottery too expressed the new age in combining beauty and usefulness. Though these arts were based upon old Swedish traditions and skills, they had a universal appeal. The influences of architectural changes and the functionalistic style should naturally be felt even to a higher degree in the construction of furniture. Here utility, comfort, and feeling found even fuller expression in meeting the new conditions of living. The taste which combined beauty and simplicity was no doubt influenced by the success of the Swedish Home Sloyd Association in fostering a folk art in spite of modern trends. This old art, best expressed in the textile handicraft, did not reject that which was new, but efforts were made to adopt new styles in an old art which were in accord with modern taste.

Selma Lagerlöf's writings have undoubtedly not been without influence upon Swedish art. In her declining years, she spent most of her days in her beloved province of Värmland, living a simple life more reminiscent of what had been than of what was. No Swedish author equaled her fame. She was aware of America and always interested in its people, but America seemed indeed far removed from the aging writer's home in rural Värmland. Her own influence upon contemporary writers was unquestionably great, and many Swedish authors after 1920 did express a warmth of nationalism, a love for Sweden and its nature, which made it more difficult for the American to understand them.

But a new figure rose on the scene, namely, Pär Lagerkvist, who bravely faced the present and changing times. He reflected a pessimism over the great international problems after World War I. With almost a Strindbergian realism, he more than any other writer in Sweden portrays the significant changes in Sweden and the problems of the age which has followed two World Wars. The interests of Lagerkvist are essentially such that he could be understood and appreciated by any one who has lived through the last two decades. He was not a spokesman for the proletariat in the strictest sense. There were many others in Sweden who represented the working class much better than Lagerkvist. The best one of these was perhaps Wilhelm Moberg who has successfully utilized the emigrant theme in his novels. Moberg is a great artist with a deep sympathy for humanity.

Turning from literature to science, it might be observed that Sweden like the rest of Europe, placed a greater stress upon theory than upon experimental science. America had far greater financial resources, and it was natural that our scientists should turn to applied science. The impact of experimentation in American laboratories was great upon Sweden. It was not mere accident which caused Sweden also to turn her attention to applied science. Hans von Euler-Chelpin won international recognition through his experiments which led to the production of pure cultures of enzymes and fermenting enzymes which impel digestion, respiration, movement, and secretion. The Svedberg devoted his time to the production of colloid solutions. Both men have been awarded the Nobel Prize. Hardly less famous have been the contributions of Manne Siegbahn in X-Ray spectroscopy and refraction. Carl Kling discovered a means of providing immunity from chicken pox, and his method of treating scarlet fever with convalescent serum and theories on sleeping sickness have made him well known.

In political economy a group of men led by Gustav Cassel provided this study with a practical aim, the foundations for the economic policies of Sweden. The influence of those and other scholars upon Sweden since 1919 has been considerable. Besides Cassel, who is best known for his studies on money and exchange, such names as Eli Heckscher, Gösta Bagge, Bertil Ohlin, Ernst Wigforss, and Gunnar Myrdal should be included. All of the above men have attained international recognition.

Prior to 1914 America had provided an incentive for important economic, social, and political changes largely in order to combat emigration. Humanism, however, was a universal force, and in the form of socialism, it found a more fertile soil in Sweden than in America. The patterns of Western thought and the universality of historical forces during the twentieth century encouraged similar evolutions of social democracies in all of the Scandinavian countries. To what extent the Swedes displayed courage and originality in finding a "middle way" between capitalism and socialism is difficult to ascertain.

The tendency would be for a historian to overestimate the influence of such a popular leader as Prime Minister Per Albin Hansson in reducing friction, bitterness, and partisanship among the people as he sought social reforms. At his death in 1946 he had served as prime minister almost without interruption since 1932 and had won the deep affection of the people as no other political figure because he had identified himself with the interests of the people rather than with a political party. He had also become a symbol of the triumph of democracy, an errand boy who had become a prime minister and an intimate friend of an aging monarch. Genial Ernst Wigforss, who had ably administered Sweden's finances in spite of criticisms, resigned in 1949, after serving almost continuously since 1932.

Though opposition to additional social reforms increased upon Hansson's death, significant changes were inaugurated in 1946 and elaborated upon until the death of King Gustav V. These have been adequately described in *Social Sweden,* published by the Board of Social Welfare in 1952. The reforms were related to almost every aspect of life, such as social insurance schemes, welfare, and health service, delinquency, housing, education, employment, workers' protection, and employees' welfare. Though there have been no anti-trust laws in Sweden since World War II, cartels became subject to public scrutiny. The shortage of hard currencies and the need for a strong national defense strengthened opposition to social reforms, though the government did not view the general standards of nutrition, and of housing as satisfactory. In 1946 hospital treatment was provided free of charge in connection with the introduction of compulsory sickness insurance. In the same year a basic rate of social security was established for all pensioners regardless of their previous incomes. In 1950 Sweden spent 2,621,824,000 crowns for social services of which 863,874,000 crowns represented the cost of social security.

An expanding program of social reform was viewed by many as essential in checking the growth of Communism. The Communists had gained strength in the elections of 1942 and 1944 and suffered a serious setback in 1948. The program of social legislation outlined in 1946 might have been partly responsible for the weakened positions of the Communists. But it is not sound to minimize the strength of Swedish nationalism and fears of the emergence of a stronger Russia after 1945. In 1951 Sweden proceeded to further strengthen the national defense which had called for greater and greater sacrifices. Sweden did not wish to become the battleground between the East and the West, and it literally "dug" itself in to be prepared for any eventuality.

On October 29, 1950, Gustav V died, closing the longest reign of any monarch in Sweden's history. The King had succeeded in adjusting himself to democratic changes without surrendering a deep sense of duty, which made him something more than a symbol. Although fate has somewhat tarnished the memory of the aged monarch, it can not depreciate the real accomplishments of his long and eventful reign. His obsession for peace was shared by his people, and it was therefore hardly surprising that the new King, Gustav VI Adolf, should have dedicated himself and his people to a traditional foreign policy of peace and mediation.

Index

tions with Woodrow Wilson, 120; and League of Nations, 123, 197-198, 202-205, 206; prime minister, 129-131; cabinet of, 130; popularity of, 130; socialization, 130-131; Åland Islands, 131; forms second cabinet, 132; seeks cooperation of Liberals, 131, 132; recognition of Russia, 132; minister of foreign affairs, 132; attitude to National Federation of Trade Unions, 140; resigns in 1923, 144; death of, 146, 150, 154, 205, 206; attitude toward Sandler, 168

Brazil: 205
Bremer, Fredrika: 240
Brest-Litovsk: 115
Briand, Aristide: 10, 205
Bright, John: 6
Brunnsvik: 34-35, 252
Brussels: 204
Bucharest: 86
Budapest: 149
Buenos Aires: 101-102, 110
Bureau of Forestry: 62

Carnegie Institute of Technology: 254
Cartels: 59-60, 190
Cassel, Gustav: 149, 259
Cedergren, Henrik Tore: 60
Central Bank of Mortgage Associations: 246
Central Europe: 112
Central Organization of Swedish Workers: 29
Central Powers: 90, 92, 99-100
Chamberlain, Neville: 205
Chevalier: 240
Chicago: 243, 247
China: 205
Christianity: 20-21
Christian Student Movement: 250
Church: 248, 250
Churchill, Winston: 90
Civil Service: 148-149, 154
Civil War: 240, 241, 242
Clason, Isak Gustaf: 5
Clemenceau, Georges: 10, 199
Clothes: 74
Cobden, Richard: 6
Cold War: 238
Collaborating Educational Association: 252
Collective agreements: origin, 12, 24-25, 29; development of, 141, 191
Columbia Emigrant Company: 243
Combe: 240
Commission on Industrial Democracy: 152-153
Commission on Socialization of Industry: 153, 183
Communism: 34
Communistic party: strength of 146; schism in, 149-150; mentioned, 194

Communists: 142, 164, 220, 235, 236, 261
Concert Hall (Stockholm); 256, 257
Conservation of forests: 61-62
Conservative party: leaders of, 78, 79, 154-155; strength of, 79-80, 91, 111; pro-German, 86-87; on suffrage reform, 116-117; mentioned, 111, 165, 215
Conservatives: record of, 7, 9-10, 13; attitude toward Socialists, 10-11; strength of, 13-14; on national defense, 13-17 passim; on League of Nations, 196, 197, 202; mentioned, 19, 102, 111, 220
Consumers' Cooperative Association: 64
Consumers' Cooperative Society: 34
Contraband: 94-97 passim
Controlled currency: 162
Cooperatives: farmers, 178-179; housing, 188-189; consumers,' 189-192
Cooperative societies: 64
Copenhagen: 80, 82, 84, 98
Corporation Law: of 1895, 57; of 1905, 64
Council of the League of Nations: 198-206 passim
Court of Arbitration: 154
Covenant of the League of Nations: 203
"Cow Deal": 171, 177
Credit Fund Corporation: creation of, 133-134; mentioned, 155, 183
Crown parks: 61
Cunard Line: 243
Customs of people: 74
Czar of Russia: 84, 85
Czechoslovakia: 160, 207

Dairy farming: development of, 42-46; creameries, 44; cooperatives, 45-46; importance of, 171, 178-179; mentioned, 53
Dalarna: 74
Dalén, Gustav: 63
Danish political parties: 89
Danzig: 212
Dardanelles: 89
Dawes plan: 144
Dayton case: 247
Debs, Eugene: 247
De Geer, Jr., Louis: 78, 132
Delaware: 185
Denmark: trade with, 52, 98, 207; relations with, 84-85, 89, 216, 218; fears of, 112; inflation in, 135; vulnerability of, 217-218, 219; invasion of, 228; during World War II, 229, 230, 231, 234, 235, 236, 237, 238; mentioned, 37, 101, 211
Demilitarization: 218
Depressions: of 1921-22, 157; of 1929-33, 161-182, 187
Dewey, John: 252
Dickens, Charles: 240
Disarmament Conference: 208
Dutch defenses: 231

267

269

Unemployment: 132, 135, 136-139, 153, 161, 170-175 *passim*
Unemployment Commission: 137-139, 142-144
Union Pacific: 242, 243
United Canning Corporation: 59
United Knitting Mills: 59
United Nations: 236
United States: trade with, 42, 52, 62, 77, 91, 92, 94-95, 99-100, 101, 102, 127, 133, 144, 160, 174; depression in, 133, 161; and League of Nations, 196, 197; relations with Finland, 219, 220; causes of emigration to, 239-248; Civil War of, 240, 241, 242; "Eldorado," 241; influences of, 249-257 *passim;* mentioned, 233, 237
Ukraine: 211
Unrest: 109, 110, 114, 117, 119, 127, 151, 203, 222, 239 *(See* Labor)
Utility service: 184-185

Vandervelde, Emile: 10, 120
Vänern Lake: 52
Varberg: 87
Vargön: 158
Värmland: 51, 258
Vännersborg: 52
Vasa: 113
Västerås: 52
Vennerström, Ivar: 110
Verdandi: 34, 69
Versailles: Treaty of, 147, 196, 197, 208, 211
Vesterbotten: 74, 172
Vesternorrland: 172
Vienna: 149

Wages: 158, 173, 246-247
Wahlman, L. I.: 5
Wallenberg: 79, 192
Wargön: 58

War Housing Commission: 126
Warsaw: 149
War Trade Commission: 103-104, 125-126
Waterway transportation: 56
Wenström, Jonas: 60
Western Powers: 221
White Ribbon (W.C.T.U.): 68
Wieselgren, Peter: 68
Wigforss, Ernst: 149, 151-152, 260
Wilson, Woodrow: 91, 107, 120, 121, 200
Winqvist, Sven: 63
Wisconsin: 242
Wohlin, Nils: 155, 245
Women's Christian Temperance Society: 68
Woodpulp industry: 58-59
Workers' Building Association: 73
Workers' Educational Association: 34-35, 252
Workers' Subsistence Homestead Fund: 180
World Court: 206
World Housing Congress: 73
World War I: outbreak of, 18, 19, 49, 50, 53, 80-81; Sweden's neutrality policy in, 85-88; economic chaos of, 125; mentioned, 162, 174, 176, 178, 182, 188, 189, 190, 194, 195, 202, 218, 219, 229, 237, 247, 249, 251, 252, 253, 255, 259
World War II: outbreak of, 212-213, 215; mentioned, 179, 180, 249, 252, 253, 258, 261
Wright, Fanny: 240

Y.M.C.A.: 250
Y.W.C.A.: 250

Zimmerwalden Berne Commission: 121
Zorn, Anders: 5, 257

Date Due

MAR 2 1 2006			